EFFECTIVE GROUP COACHING

Tried and Tested Tools and Resources for Optimum Group Coaching Skills

EFFECTIVE GROUP COACHING

Tried and Tested Tools and Resources for Optimum Group Coaching Skills

Jennifer J. Britton

John Wiley & Sons Canada, Ltd.

Library and Archives Canada Cataloguing in Publication Data

Britton, Jennifer J.
    Effective group coaching : tried and tested tools and
resources for optimum group coaching results / Jennifer J. Britton.

Includes bibliographical references and index.
ISBN 978-0-470-73854-2

    1. Executive coaching.   2. Employees—Coaching of.   I. Title.

HD30.4.B75 2010   658.4'07124   C2009-906211-9

Production Credits
Cover design: Joanna Vieira
Interior text design: Natalia Burobina
Typesetter: Thomson Digital
Printer: Friesens Printing Ltd.

John Wiley & Sons Canada, Ltd.
6045 Freemont Blvd.
Mississauga, Ontario
L5R 4J3

Printed in the United States of America

10 9 8 7 6 5

This book is dedicated to coaches and group facilitators around the world who are committed to refining their craft.

Also, to the teams and groups globally which I've had the privilege of working, and learning, with.

And, of course, to Matthew and Andray, Mom and Dad, without whose support this book would not have been possible.

CONTENTS

List of Figures and Tables

Acknowledgments

Just as group coaching is not all about the coach and is created by the experience and wisdom of the group, there are a number of people I would like to thank who have made this book possible.

First, I would like to thank the group coaches who took the time to share their insights and work in the realm of group coaching. I would like to thank: Mary Allen, Ginger Cockerham, Maureen Clarke, Ann Deaton, Suzee Eibling, Eva Gregory, Deena Kolbert, Jill MacFadyen, Heidi Michaels, Lynda Monk, Marlo Nikkila, and Rita Weiss.

I would also like to thank the Alumni Community of the Group Coaching Essentials™ program. Since I launched the program in January 2006, I have been fortunate to have been able to work with hundreds of talented coaches from around the world. Your questions and comments, as well as your work with your clients, have shaped much of what is written in this book. More importantly, your work continues to ripple out with your clients and their communities.

Thanks also to the team at John Wiley in Toronto who have made this process so smooth. I would like especially to thank Don Loney, my editor, as well as the marketing team. It's no surprise that a Muskoka connection was found.

I also want to thank my right hand and eyes, Andray, and our son Matthew. Andray and Matthew, along with my parents Margaret and Grant, have been there to review drafts, support me and each other, while I have closed the door numerous times to head off to facilitate a group coaching program or to write this book. Thank you for your support and understanding.

Professionally, I have been blessed to interface with so many wonderful practitioners from across the training, education, humanitarian, and coaching fields for the last twenty plus years. In particular, I want to thank my team coaching partner Sharon Miller, Gail McGuire a great collaborator here in Toronto, and my former colleagues at UNDP/UNV, VSO, and YCI. Together we have created great work. Whether our conversations and work together happened in board-rooms, on planes, in the jungle, on a beach, or by phone, thank you for sharing your wisdom and the journey with me, while enabling me to continually learn and grow.

Jennifer J. Britton
Toronto, September 2009

Introduction

Over the last few years, economic realities and client requests have propelled group coaching to become one of the most quickly evolving areas of the coaching profession. Moving out of its early adopter days, group coaching is starting to become recognized as a subdiscipline of coaching by coaches and clients, organizations, and individuals alike.

For years, there has been little written about the experience and foundation of group coaching. This book serves to finally put into the hands of coaches and group practitioners core information about what group coaching is, core skills, and best practices, as well as practical how-tos for designing, marketing, and launching your own group coaching programs.

This book provides a foundation and practical perspective on group coaching—what it is and how it differs from one-on-one coaching and training, ready-to-use tips and resources for coaches/practitioners in the development, implementation, and marketing of their own group coaching programs. Highlighted in this book are case studies from coaches who are undertaking this work with widely diverse groups around diverse topics.

Effective Group Coaching takes a practical, resource-rich look at group coaching—one of the fastest-growing parts of the coaching profession. Organizations, community groups, and individuals are discovering that group coaching is an exciting and sustainable model and process for learning and growth.

Written for coaches (both internal and external), HR professionals, trainers, and facilitators wanting to expand their work into this area, this book provides tested tips and tools. New and seasoned coaches will find *Effective Group Coaching* a practical road map and go-to guide when **designing, implementing,** and **marketing** their own group coaching programs.

Groups have been my passion since the late 1980s when I first started as an outdoor experiential educator and leader. My work with groups blossomed over the years to include work in the realms of facilitation, training, and performance improvement. As a global manager and director working in the international development sector, it was usually up to me to develop my teams and groups. Since 1988, I have run group programs in over sixteen countries and touched others virtually in many more.

I entered into the coaching profession as a professional coach in 2003, surprised to find that a coaching approach with groups was not widely pervasive. In fact, as I moved through my coaching certification in 2005, I could not even count my group coaching hours towards certification. In wanting to follow my passion—groups—and also to leverage my own skills and expertise in the areas of small group process and facilitation, I have been one of the pioneers in taking this work forward. Since 2004, having supported hundreds of coaches who were eager to launch their own group coaching work through the Group Coaching Essentials™ program, group coaching is now becoming mainstream.

As more and more coaches are adding their voices to what group coaching is and how it impacts the world, I have invited a number of coaches to add their voice throughout this book. I am pleased to be joined by other thought leaders and pioneers in the realm of group coaching, such as Ginger Cockerham, MCC; Suzee Eibling, PCC; Mary Allen, MCC; and Eva Gregory, MCC, as well as several other stellar practitioners who are breaking ground across a number of industries and issues: Deena Kolbert, CPCC, ORSCC; Maureen Clarke, CPCC; Lynda Monk, CPCC; Jill MacFadyen, ACC; Victoria FittsMilgrim, CPCC; Ann Deaton, PhD, PCC; Marlo Nikkila; and Rita Weiss.

As you read through this book you will notice that I often use a number of terms interchangeably, including participant and client, as well as coach and facilitator. It will no doubt become obvious to you that group coaching has strong roots in the realm of training and facilitation, as well as small group process.

I encourage you to engage fully with this book—mark it up, undertake the exercises, and create some accountability for yourself as you read through it.

OUR ROAD MAP

Throughout the book are various "In the Spotlight" and "Voices from the Field" sections, which spotlight real-life group coaching experiences and the voices of coaches undertaking this work. These will highlight practical strategies around what works and what you need as a coach to make successful group coaching programs happen. Group coaching programs range from in person work to virtual phone-based programs, programs for the public, to programs run for small business owners, community groups, and managers.

The early chapters of the book set the context for group coaching. Chapter 1 will provide you with foundational information, such as What is group coaching? How is it defined? How does it differ from one-on-one coaching, therapy, workshops, facilitation? How is it the same? This chapter also includes a discussion on the Continuum of Group Process to illustrate the similarities and differences between different disciplines.

Coaching does not take place in a vacuum, and increasingly individual and corporate clients and sponsors are asking "Why is this work important? What impact does it really have?" Chapter 2 looks at the "Business, and Learning Case, for Group Coaching."

Core principles of adult education, learning styles, experiential education, and group process form the foundation for work within the group coaching realm. Chapter 3 looks at "The Foundations of Group Coaching: The Essentials of Adult Learning." This chapter will provide new insights, or a refresher, on these core topics.

Coaches, and other practitioners, are eager to not have to reinvent the wheel. Chapter 4 looks at "Core Skills and Best Practices for Group Coaching." Throughout this chapter we will also hear from coaches across the industry with some of their best practices for group coaching.

The next set of chapters provides you with practical exercises, tools, and templates to help you design, market, and implement your own group coaching program.

Many coaches have great ideas for their programs but don't know how to move from vision to actual program. Chapter 5 looks at "Designing Your Own Program," and inclues several core tools for design work, including the Group Coaching Design Matrix™.

With group coaching work taking place in person, by phone, and by web, Chapter 6 explores "Powerful Delivery Options" including virtual delivery in both phone-based and web-based environments. This chapter includes a short self-assessment for you to check your readiness for virtual work.

Chapter 7 covers "Essential Elements for Your Own Group Coaching Program" including core items you will want to add to your toolkit, questions for group coaching and other resources. The chapter also includes lessons learned from group coaches in the field.

Chapter 8 covers the essential topic of "Marketing Your Group Coaching Program." Without clients on the phone or in front of you, the most important ingredient for group coaching is missing. This chapter covers seven core areas of marketing including foundational marketing principles, claiming your niche, developing a powerful marketing message and creating a marketing strategy and plan. Specific considerations for marketing corporate group coaching is also included in this chapter.

Chapter 9 covers "Preparing for the Program—Systems and Logistics." This chapter covers core business and program systems that will streamline your work, facilitating the entire program cycle—from design to marketing, registration, implementation, and evaluation. The chapter also covers core logistical tips and includes a group coaching checklist.

Coaches are often eager to learn from the past and avoid possible pitfalls in group coaching work. Chapter 10 covers "Implementation Tips and Pitfalls" to avoid in your group coaching work. Challenges faced by group coaches and suggestions from the field are also included.

This book would not be complete without the inclusion of group coaching exercises. The appendix includes a mini-toolbox of exercises for coaches and other practitioners to adapt for their own group coaching work.

For those interested in undertaking this work with a partner, or co-facilitator, you can email Jennifer at info@potentialsrealized.com for a bonus chapter on Co-Facilitation.

This book is a starting point for a very diverse field. Add your voice to the diverse tapestry of group coaches around the world—visit the **Group Coaching Ins and Outs blog** at http://groupcoaching.blogspot.com.

CHAPTER 1

WHAT IS GROUP COACHING?

A leader is best
When people barely know he exists,
Not so good when people obey and acclaim him
Worse when they despise him,
But of a good leader, who talks little
When his work is done, his aim fulfilled
They will all say "We did it ourselves"
— Lao Tse

THE CONTEXT

The time is now! The coaching industry generates approximately $1.5 billion (all dollar amounts are in U.S. dollars unless otherwise noted) annually[1] with group coaching quickly gaining ground. The economic events that began in 2008 continue to make group coaching a pronounced growth area for clients.

Group coaching is still a young profession as can be seen in the ICF Global Coaching Survey (2009)[2] estimated that there are approximately 30,000 active coaches. A majority of coaches has been operating for fewer than ten years.

When asked about their coaching specialties, 58.1 percent indicated that their specialty involved leadership, 57.8 percent indicated executive coaching, and 53.6 percent indicated business or organizational issues.

In 2007, $139.39 billion was spent by U.S. organizations on employee learning and development. Two-thirds or $83.62 billion was spent on the internal learning function, including staff salaries, and internal development costs. One-third, or $50.77 billion, was spent on workshops, vendors, and external events.[3]

Throughout this chapter we will explore:

1. Is group coaching for you?
2. The diversity of group coaching—models for group coaching
3. What group coaching can look like—virtual/in person and corporate/public
4. Why group coaching is even more important today
5. Continuum of group processes: coaching, training, facilitation, and retreats
6. What is the role of the group coach?

You will meet and hear from other group coaches undertaking this work with their clients while reading through this book.

WHAT IS GROUP COACHING?

Fusing together principles, skills, and practices from the realm of group development, coaching, and facilitation, group coaching can be defined as follows:

> Group coaching—a small-group process throughout which there is the application of coaching principles for the purposes of personal or professional development, the achievement of goals, or greater self-awareness, along thematic or non-thematic lines.
> —Jennifer Britton, MES, CPT, CPCC, Potentials Realized

Ginger Cockerham, MCC (creator of the "Power of Groups"), defines group coaching as:

> a facilitated group process that is led by a professional coach and formed with the intention of maximizing the combined energy, experience, and wisdom of individuals who chose to join in order to achieve organizational objectives and/or individual goals.

Grounded in coaching processes and skills, group coaching utilizes core coaching skills and competencies, while adapting skills and approaches from facilitation and training.

The International Coach Federation (ICF) defines coaching as "partnering with clients in a thought-provoking and creative process that inspires them to maximize their personal and professional potential."

The ICF continues, "Coaching honors the client as the expert in his/her life and work, and believes that every client is creative, resourceful, and whole.

"Standing on this foundation, the coach's responsibility is to:

- Discover, clarify, and align with what the client wants to achieve;
- Encourage client self-discovery;
- Elicit client-generated solutions and strategies; and
- Hold the client responsible and accountable."

Source: www.coachfederation.org

Over the past two decades I've worn an array of hats—manager, facilitator, trainer, coach and performance improvement specialist—as I have engaged with groups throughout the learning process. Over the last six years, in fusing coaching with my other approaches, I have seen even greater impact in our work together. Supporting hundreds of coaches in acquiring group coaching skills has led me to identify core skills and approaches which make great group coaches.

I believe that *great* group coaches bring to their profession solid group facilitation skills, as well as mastery of core coaching skills and approaches. They create a solid and intimate connection with their groups, and listen for what the participants want is important to them, so that the group's agenda is respected. Great group coaches adopt their style and approach based on the different needs, creating the space for clients to learn from each other and share experiences is paramount in the group coaching process.

Most significantly, group coaches distinguish themselves from other group facilitators with their strong focus on having the client identify and take action on their goals. A key priority for group coaches is to hold the space for clients *to be accountable* for taking steps in achieving their goals and *integrating their learning* to their "real life" and work. It is this focus on making the learning and results stick that drew me to coaching years ago, and continues to be a primary focus and driver in my work.

As we will see later in this chapter, group coaching exists along a continuum of group processes, including training (workshops, retreats), facilitation, and other group processes. Coaches will find that they sit on different places along the continuum, heavily influenced by what the client wants. Some programs will be more *pure* group coaching than others. The continuum is offered as a foundational principle, which we will continue to revisit throughout the book.

THE DIVERSITY OF GROUP COACHING—IN PERSON, VIRTUAL, CORPORATE, AND PUBLIC

In her interview for this book, Suzee Eibling, the coordinator of the Coach U Group Coaching SIG, commented on the tremendous diversity that exists within the coaching profession around what's offered to both individuals and group coaching. Throughout the book you will hear directly from a dozen coaches about the group coaching programs they offer, as well as their insights on what makes this work successful and rewarding. The sections "In the Spotlight" include spotlights and comments from group coaches undertaking this work.

Group coaching is occurring in corporations, small businesses, government programs, and with the general public, either as intact groups or groups of strangers coming together. Gaining significant ground in North America, group coaching is also taking root across Europe and Australasia.

Regardless of the themes groups are coached around, at its simplest distinction, programs may be in person or virtual. Chapter 6 of this book provides you with more information on the considerations for group coaching programs in virtual environments.

What Does Group Coaching Look Like?

As you may have guessed, group coaching can take a number of forms. Group coaching is becoming just as diverse as clients' needs and preferences are.

Throughout this book, we are going to explore a number of case studies—programs that take place in person and those that take place virtually (by phone or web). We will also explore the work of coaches and programs that are delivered in organizational settings, as well as those marketed publicly to individuals who then form a group.

In-Person Programs

In-person group coaching programs may include:

- A one-hour drop-in session with different participants each week, where clients are coached on specific themes or topics;
- A six-hour program delivered over the course of several weeks or months in smaller modules (i.e., one-hour sessions) to the same participants;
- An evening group coaching program; or
- A one- to five-day intensive group coaching program.

From Experience: In-Person Female Entrepreneur Group Coaching

One of my favorite group coaching programs that I both developed and delivered was a series of group coaching programs for small business owners. As part of a nine-month government-funded program for new female entrepreneurs, I was invited to launch the first two weeks of the program several years ago. For ten consecutive business days I met the women for a three-hour group coaching session.

I was asked by the program coordinator to launch this intensive nine-month program by coaching the group and setting a positive learning foundation. We had thirty hours to create and move through a very powerful business development program using a group coaching approach. Over the span of those two weeks, the women and I explored topics such as strengths, values, the wheel of life, work-life, and time management, as well as core business areas such as business vision and planning. Having been given *carte blanche* from the program coordinator, I was able to really bring in a wide variety of approaches and coaching tools. We had small group discussions, large group discussions, assessments, and visualizations, and we kept journals. Each afternoon, I designed the next session from where we had left off in the morning with the questions and priorities. The group's feedback at the end of the session as well as the check-ins the next morning iteratively pointed us to the next topic.

This experience allowed me to truly clarify the difference between using a training and coaching approach. It also allowed me to experiment with many of the core coaching tools in a small group environment. Looking back almost four years later, more than 90 percent of these women are still self-employed, a much higher statistic than the norm.

Practically, the experience of working with two separate groups of female entrepreneurs allowed me to adapt much of the material that I was using as a business faculty member and lecturer for the group coaching context. This experience also created the foundation for the 90 Day BizSuccess Group Coaching™ program that I now offer quarterly to business owners globally, in a virtual format.

So, what are other coaches doing in person?

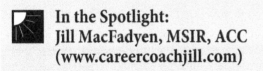 ## In the Spotlight:
Jill MacFadyen, MSIR, ACC
(www.careercoachjill.com)

Jill MacFadyen, a career coach, writes the following about her group coaching programs in the nonprofit sector:

I offer an in person two-day group coaching program on how to get a new job. It covers dealing with transition issues; identifying values; visioning the future; writing a resume; job search techniques; writing cover letters; networking; interviewing; and salary negotiation. It is very interactive and energetic. It runs from 9:00 to 4:30 over a two-day time span. Ideally, there would be a week in between the two sessions.

I also offer a two-hour in person coaching program on any of the topics mentioned above.

JB: Who are your participants/clients? What do they value the most from your programs?

JM: My clients have been local nonprofit agencies. Participants are those looking for a new position. Frequently, they are people who have been laid off. On a personal level, participants have mentioned that they feel empowered and energized afterwards.

JB: What have been the successes of this program?

JM: Clients develop job search skills. We practice in the session and this increases self-confidence. Some who have been in a rut have learned techniques to re-energize their search.

Virtual Programs

In addition to in-person programs, many coaches develop group coaching programs which are delivered virtually—by phone and/or web to clients around the world. Virtual programs might include:

- A one-off group call;
- A monthly group call held with the same participants each month (1 to $1^1/_2$ hours per session);
- A six-week program delivered weekly by phone (one hour) to a group of eight participants around a common theme;
- A twelve-week program which meets every other week with assigned work in between; or
- A ninety-day program, delivered as both group calls and email support;
- A blended program of two group calls per month, and one individual coaching call between sessions.

From Experience—Needing to Virtualize

Almost a year into my starting my business I gave birth to my son. I quickly realized that I did not want to continue traveling to deliver programs to teams and groups either locally or around the world. At the same time, I needed to keep revenue coming in to support my growing family. This was enough to push me to look at how I could take my in person offerings virtual, which at the time, revolved around work-life issues, leadership, training issues, and business development issues. The trial-and-error process I undertook during that first intensive year of converting all of my offerings to a virtual format has informed a lot of this book.

As you will see throughout this book, group coaching can be a very powerful vehicle for connecting clients around the world. As a former global manager myself, there is nothing more exciting than having participants from five or six different countries and time zones all on the same group coaching call. The diversity of perspectives, insights, and "ahas!" are greater than we could ever create in an in person environment with the same effort.

 ### In the Spotlight: Victoria FittsMilgrim, CPCC (www.truelifecoach.net)

Sovereignty Circles is a group coaching program which I offer over a six-month period. It includes group calls twice a month, and a private thirty-minute coaching call once a month. For a full description, please visit *www. truelifecoach.net/sovcircles.htm*.

JB: Who are your participants/clients? What do they value the most from your programs?

VFM: My clients so far for group coaching have all been women looking for tools to increase self-awareness, self-care, and living as the Sovereign in charge of their own lives. I believe they value:

- The coaching tools I provide to unveil who they are to themselves more fully;
- The connection with others—to see themselves in the mirror;
- The clarity about obstacles they generate internally and how to overcome them.

JB: What have been your successes with group coaching?

VFM: With the Sovereignty Circles, I feel my success comes from creating a safe and loving space of acceptance to try new modes of *being* and *doing*. I have seen my clients grow and become more confident in this container to moving into authentic action towards their goals. My success comes when I facilitate a place to grow, learn, and take action in alignment with their true selves.

JB: What's the one tip you'd like to share with other coaches as your golden nugget (i.e., your most important lesson)?

VFM: Designing as many ways as possible for the group to interact, listen to each other, and connect even outside the scheduled calls (Yahoo! group, buddy system that rotates), all fosters more trust and openness among participants. This, in turn, makes the calls more lively and open, as people feel safe to be transparent. They can remove their masks.

Public/Corporate Programs

Another distinction I will make throughout the book is that groups may come together in corporate realms, or a group may consist of individual members who are initially strangers to each other. These groups I call public groups.

Corporate group coaching programs are increasingly becoming very popular. Lower in cost than traditional one-on-one coaching, group coaching programs get more employees involved and have the potential for greater impact. As we will see in Chapter 2, a group coaching approach may also build internal capacity and be an important tool in shaping and changing corporate culture.

Typically, corporate group coaching programs will bring together employees from different parts of an organization. Providing employees with the opportunity to share experiences and learn together, the new collective wisdom created by this cross-functional, multi-disciplinary group has the potential to effect significant change within organizations and industries.

Corporate Group Coaching

 **In the Spotlight:
Rita Weiss of Pinnacle Consulting**

I currently offer three group coaching programs for business leaders, managers, and business professionals:

1. Thriving in Times of Uncertainty and Change
2. What's Your Next Step? Creating Your Road Map to Success
3. Leadership and Culture: Achieving Results through Inclusive Leadership

I offer three-month and six-month programs that can either be conducted in person or virtually (by phone). In general, my clients choose to start with the three-month program, and about 50 percent continue for a second three-month program. Currently, my group coaching clients have all requested in-person meetings, which I find is generally preferred with corporate clients.

Participants are senior leaders in corporate, government, and academic/educational organizations. I'm currently coaching the senior leadership team at a major government agency, senior administrators at a private college, and leaders and high potential managers at several corporations.

My clients tell me that what they value most are:

- The opportunity to think strategically about issues and challenges and develop long-term plans and strategies;
- Receiving confidential and objective feedback;
- Sharing ideas with and learning from colleagues; and
- Identifying new approaches to achieving their goals and building better relationships.

Successes:

1. I provided a three-month group coaching program for the senior leadership team of a major public company. The team started out fiercely noncollaborative, with entrenched silos and little respect among the VP leaders. As a result of group coaching, the team now appreciates the value of working collaboratively, and they actively work together to resolve issues and achieve individual, team, and organizational objectives.
2. A six-month group coaching program at a global pharmaceutical company resulted in improved cross-cultural communication and interaction, better relationships with colleagues and customers, and promotions for several executives in the coaching program.
3. I provided a three-month, 360 feedback plus group coaching program for the high-potential leaders of a financial services company that resulted in significantly increased leadership skills, improved management of staff, and a clear succession plan for the company.

4. A six-month group coaching program for the administrative leaders (Deans and Assistant Deans) of a private university resulted in a more balanced focus on both the academic and business requirements of leading a successful academic institution.

Other corporate case studies can be found in Chapter 2 under the heading "Business Case for Group Coaching."

Public Programs

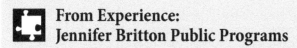 **From Experience:**
Jennifer Britton Public Programs

A number of coaches, like myself, will also design a program and market it for the public domain. In these instances, the inspiration for a new program may come from a direct request from one or more individual clients, requests from past group program participants, or from noticing trends or unfilled gaps in the marketplace.

Over the past six years, I've offered a range of programs for the general public in a variety of formats. These programs have included:

The BizSuccess Series: Building on my own work expertise as a former business faculty member who worked with small businesses and startups, I wanted to continue providing high-value programs for my small business and entrepreneurial clients. The 90 Day BizSuccess™ program for business owners was launched in 2006. In 2007, I also added quarterly business retreats held virtually for business owners. The BizSuccess Virtual Retreat is a focused retreat for business owners who are looking to plan and take action on their business. Held over the span of one to two sessions with a follow-up group call, the BizSuccess Virtual Retreat continues to get rave reviews from business owners.

In addition to continuing to offer these programs myself, I also licence these programs to other coaches who wish to offer it to their clients.

Your Balanced Life™: Offered initially as a five-week session in 2004, over the years this program has become a three-month session, meeting twice a month. Several years ago I also adapted it for a one-day intensive format, which is delivered by phone. This program is called Your Balanced Life Virtual Retreat and has been offered on a quarterly basis.

The inspiration for this program came from my own passion concerning work-life issues as I transitioned into my role as business owner from former global manager. I ran this program quite frequently throughout the period of 2004–2007. I also hosted a blog on the same topic (http://yourbalancedlife.blogspot.com).

I now licence this program to other coaches who wish to deliver the material to their clients as a virtual retreat and/or 90-day program.

Get Organized Virtual Retreat™: Partnering with professional organizer and TV host Hellen Buttigieg, the Get Organized Virtual Retreat is designed for individuals who want to take action around, and gain insights on, getting organized. Delivered over one day or two evenings, the program has provided participants with the opportunity to delve into organizing tips, explore their preferences and most importantly, take steps to getting organized in a supportive group environment.

In Chapter 6, you will also read about the highly successful work of three coaches who deliver their work by phone—Heidi Michaels and her virtual vision board program, as well as coaches Eva Gregory and Mary Allen.

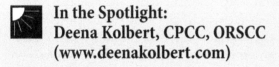

In the Spotlight:
Deena Kolbert, CPCC, ORSCC
(www.deenakolbert.com)

Coach Deena Kolbert offers four different group coaching programs across the public and organizational domains. All of her programs are virtual and vary in length from one and one-half hours to two hours, usually with four to six participants. For people in groups that do a lot of professional traveling, she uses a minimum of six people to form the group. Some groups are international, but the language is English. Each group determines the number of times per month that they meet, usually one or two times.

1. Taking Charge of Money Issues: For people seeking to better understand their relationship with money while working towards creating financial well-being—personal, family, institutional, and for some, a broader movement.

These monthly call-in group sessions help them clarify issues, build strong foundations, and look at their feelings and actions in their journey towards change. The experiences are designed to strengthen participants' ability to make sound financial decisions and not feel alone as they explore their behaviors and boundaries or lack thereof. I offer an environment that is structured, supportive, open, and warm. There is time devoted specifically to each client to be heard through reporting back, strategizing actions, and asking for, and receiving, specific support from group members.

My clients are executive leaders who work internationally. While their skills are highly developed professionally, on a personal basis, they have not taken good care of themselves. On a financial basis, they feel they are not showing true leadership in all that they can be.

Skills Used: This co-active group coaching includes experiential exercises, creativity, ORSC (Organization and Relationship Systems Coaching) skills, techniques, and inquiries (assignments) that help each participant identify their financial goals and learn how they can move through the process of acquiring them. In so doing, the participants take responsibility for their decisions, learn to acknowledge their gains, and empower themselves to continue on the journey they have chosen for themselves.

Successes: The financial group improved on many levels. The key learning was the intensity of the work. Some of the issues are very complex and need time and are consciously being worked on. The list is long because much work was accomplished on foundational issues such as communication, accountability, responsibility, values diversity, negotiation, and alignment on choice. Much time was spent on defining, claiming, and knowing the conditions of trust. They all were able to articulate their definition of a rich, fulfilled financial life. Successes include paying several years of back taxes; meeting with family members over financial matters; moving forward on lawsuits; writing wills; combining financial accounts; knowing how and where money is spent; budgeting and making comparisons between proposed and actual spending; living within their budget; and saving money.

Challenges: The leadership skills within this group of women was amazing and they traveled much of the time. Doing follow-up assignments and inquiries between sessions was quite challenging, so little took place between the coaching sessions. Much was learned by doing specific exercises during our times together, but individual actions were hard to come by. Emotionally, they needed time to assimilate the information and then, maybe, little steps were accomplished. This was a self-formed group that found that the financial security aspects had taken over its initial intent, which was to be an emotional support group. They needed healing time to emotionally get back together, which has been happening.

2. *The Wisdom of Knowing Ourselves:* Provides an opportunity for people to explore and reflect deeply within and with others, as well as to connect in a social and spiritual context that gives them renewed inspiration and a source of confidence, hope, and fulfillment. I direct the focus and intentionality on their journey forward using their deep sacred wisdom. Thus, the sage in us all is brought forth and can be filtered throughout participants' communities and the greater world.

This is a group of strong female leaders, racially diverse, from different professional fields. They want to deepen their knowledge and move to the next level of achievement with more confidence, empowerment, and ease. They want to know that they know and own their own wisdom with confidence within. We work from a philosophical, scientific, body/mind/spirit, and cultural perspective. We also work from a historical, economic, wellness, and social aspect. As women leaders, we are also noticing a "shadow" self— the impostor, coming from people who feel they are unable to internalize a sense of themselves as competent and talented.

Skills Used: I use the co-active coaching model with relationship, group, and team exercises—experiential exercises, creativity, hands-on, exploration of archetypes, meditation, ORSC skills and techniques that help one identify with their personal visions for change and to deepen their knowing.

Successes: The foundation for this group is based on calling forth participants' wisdom from their experiences. The group is relatively new.

Challenges: The standard challenges of building trust and spaciousness for deep work. Each person is responsible for an "opening/closing" ritual/meditation that brings the group together to do the work at hand. Finding leadership at the beginning holds its challenges unless someone jumps in, which is not the case in this group.

3. *Taking Charge of Your Health:* Participants become empowered to take charge of their health care. They "design new alliances"—with themselves, doctor(s), disease, and relationships (family, friends, colleagues). Suggested segments are not limited and include *You Are Not Alone; You Have the Right to Know; You Have the Right to Choose Your Own Treatment(s); Realigning Your Relationships; and Living the Life That You Want.* A warm, open, and supportive environment is very necessary to draw on each other's strengths and gain courage to move forward.

This group is mixed gender, people who have ongoing health issues. They want to learn to incorporate their disease into their whole lives in a conscious, direct, and natural way.

Skills Used: Sharing, using each other as resources and support is fundamental to this group. Within this group context of learning, there is an energy field established for inner knowing (intuition) about one's health that is invaluable. The group support allows a feeling of not being alone. I use the co-active coaching model with relationship, group, and team exercises, experiential exercises, creativity, hands-on, meditation, ORSC skills and techniques that help one identify with their personal visions for wholeness and well-being.

Successes: Building a spacious, trusting, open environment has been accomplished. The group is new.

Challenges: Allowing feelings to be expressed without clients' flooding (literally and figuratively), because they haven't had an opportunity to be seen or heard. Overcoming fears is a huge challenge, as is not trusting themselves to know what is right for them.

4. Perspectives: As coach, host, and producer of several local radio programs, current events discussions included experiences with a variety of elected officials, policy makers, and advocates who all participated in exercises bearing upon a wide array of issues. The goal of the workshops was to open new perspectives by broadening participants' currently-held positions.

This senior group was open to new members from week-to-week so that many different people were present over the course of time. Many were active in their communities and members of both genders attended.

Skills Used: Sharing, using deep democracy and getting all voices, opinions and perspectives heard; using ORSC and group coaching skills, debate techniques, and learning to listen to others' views; and inviting outside guests to speak on a topic for one-half hour and then using ORSC skills, integrate the listening and nuggets of learning.

Successes: This group had new members every session, so designing an alliance each time was new for older members and served as a successful lesson to use at the beginning of each session. There was a lot of buzz about the sessions, which allowed many more people to attend.

Challenges: New members came every week for months, so the nature of the work shifted to accommodate its members. Every week we worked on different topics and issues, rather than digging deeper into one theme.

WHO CREATES THE THEMES?

I often get asked, "*Do you provide the themes of the group coaching sessions or do the clients?*" Over the years, I've tried several approaches and I often say, "It depends." What has worked well for me, and what my clients find to be very useful, is to have a theme defined in terms of what is bringing them together. For example, people know that they are signing up for a group coaching program about work-life issues, leadership, business development, or parenting. If you are marketing your group coaching program to the general public, it will be very difficult to market and implement it if there is no common theme. I'm not saying it is impossible, but from experience I have found that it is extremely challenging. Within a program theme (i.e., work-life, business growth) I will also set broad themes for every session. A broad theme might be values or vision or strengths.

There are always a number of things I want to do to make sure I understand my clients' agenda(s). First, before the start of each and every program, I always meet with each individual member of a group coaching program. I like to connect with each participant, to find out *what are their major issues/questions/ pains* related to the anchoring group coaching topic (i.e., work-life or business growth). I also like to ask them *what are topics they would like really addressed* during the program? You will find more detail about this approach in Chapter 5: Designing Your Group Coaching Program under the heading "Knowing Your Client."

In our first group session, I present the themes that emerged for the group based on my pre-calls, as well as other issues that I have seen as having been very useful for other groups to work on. This is an opportunity to start designing the process with the group and I inquire if there are any changes, additions, or deletions we want to make as a group.

The way we approach exercises will be influenced by our client. For example, when working with values, there are a myriad of ways we can approach this topic. We could undertake values clarification work; we could provide a values checklist for clients to complete; or we could undertake demonstration coaching at the front of the room with a client while other clients look on. The demo coaching method gives the group an idea of what values are, and models an approach so they will be able to identify their own values.

A values checklist is a more directed approach. Clients can individually rank their own values. Next, you may wish to pair them up with another member to discuss a series of questions. For example, *What values are most important to you? How are these values reflected in your work? How are they not? How are values reflected in your decisions?* Provide each pair with questions. Don't hesitate to provide your learners with opportunities to develop coaching skills and approaches such as powerful questions. This approach to values could wrap up with each pair reporting to the larger group and some facilitated large group discussion.

Getting to know your clients is an important ingredient for success with this work.

DIFFERENT MODELS FOR GROUP COACHING

This book explores and provides a number of different models and structures for group coaching through the provision of spotlighted case studies of coaches undertaking this work in the world.

As we will see, time and again, the model and approach for group coaching is shaped by what the client wants and needs, as well as your own coaching preferences. Coaches may adopt a pure group coaching model (with little or no content), or one where there is a heavier emphasis on learning and coaching at the same time. Later in this chapter I will discuss the "Continuum of Group Processes," along which most group coaches place themselves.

Coaches may also coach groups differently depending on the topic areas, agendas, etc. In general, there are two different focus areas for group coaching—coaching a group as a set of individuals versus coaching a group as if it were a system. The former may be very appropriate when groups of strangers come together for a program; the latter may be more effective if the group is part of a larger entity or system—for example, a community group. In this instance, more focus would be put on developing the group process, and coaching the group towards its' vision, values, etc. This is in contrast to a group coaching approach for a group of ten separate business owners where the focus would be more on strengthening the individual capacity of each business owner, rather than the capacity of the group itself.

In addition to a group focus, for years I have also explored and implemented a **hybrid approach** which I consider to be a mix of group calls and individual one-on-one sessions. During the 90 Day BizSuccess Group Coaching™ program, I found that group calls alone were not maximizing the traction for individual business owners. Over the past two years, I have added a monthly laser coaching call (20 minutes) in addition to the two group calls per month along with regular e-BizTips being delivered to participants' inboxes.

Mary Allen of www.BeyondSixFiguresforCoaching.com identifies three main models for coaching:

1. **A pure group coaching model:** In this instance, a small group of individuals hire a coach and each person gets a certain amount of one-on-one coaching time during a session. In this instance, participants can listen to each other being coached and can participate in the process.
2. **Hybrid:** Some teaching/lesson focus with an agenda and coaching orientation. This approach is interactive. This approach pulls dialogue from the group and also includes teaching.
3. **Open Coaching Forum:** As part of ongoing programs, there may be four calls per month. The first three have a lesson focus. The fourth monthly call could be a guest expert call or open coaching forum (OCF). During the OCF, the coach will show up, but there will be no formal agenda with the agenda being pulled from the group. The coach will take an inventory at the front end to determine the theme. For example, time management may show up as the theme for the session as the participants check in.

The "Continuum of Group Processes" will further illustrate the range of activities that may fall under group coaching.

THE CONTINUUM OF GROUP PROCESSES

I often speak about the fact that group coaching occurs along a continuum of group processes. Throughout this book you are going to meet a dozen coaches who have shared their real life group coaching experiences. As you read them, you will see the great diversity that exists amongst their work. In fact, this is due in part to the different approaches these coaches bring to this work, as well as the clients they serve.

Group coaching is created by a foundational weave of facilitation, training, and coaching. There exists a continuum of small group processes, which includes, but is not limited to group coaching, facilitation, and training sessions (workshops and retreats).

Figure 1.1: The Continuum of Group Processes

Group Coaching   Facilitation   Training

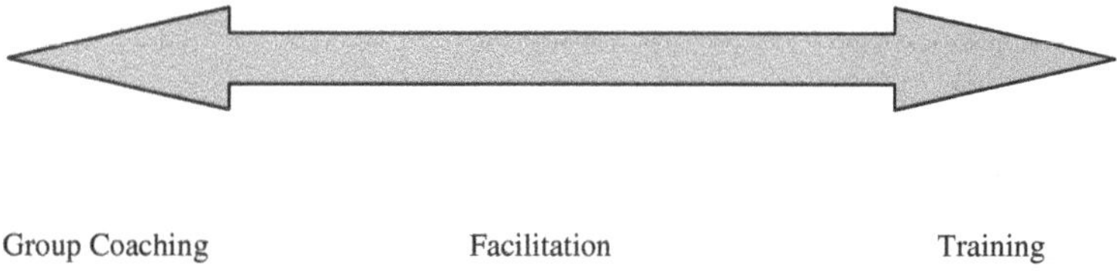

The programs that are highlighted in this book, along with the work that you undertake, will fit somewhere along this continuum. Depending on your clients, their needs, and preferences, each program you design will look and feel different. Some programs may be more purely group coaching, others may weave in stronger elements of facilitation and training. The mix, as we will see, is determined by the client.

Let's take a look at each of these areas along the continuum.

Training

Let's start by looking at the far right end of the continuum where I have placed training. This might include workshops, e-learning, and/or retreats. In its purest form, traditional training has focused on providing a learning experience where a participant acquires new knowledge, skills, and abilities. These are known as the KSAs (knowledge, skills, and abilities). A common definition for training is as follows:

> *Training: the acquisition of knowledge, skills, and abilities*
> *to improve performance on one's current job.*
> – Alan M. Saks, Robert R. Haccoun[7]

Traditional training environments have typically been in the face-to-face realm—often called workshops or seminars, and if more intensive, perhaps retreats. In recent years, teleseminars (training delivered by phone) and webinars (training delivered using a web-based platform) have become mainstream training approaches.

Common characteristics of training programs, in its purest (but not always participatory) form, are:

- High levels of content that the trainer or instructor wants to get across;
- More instructor led than participant discovery;
- Set objectives you wish to get across to the participant;
- Objectives set by trainer and/or organization who is the expert;
- Agenda pre-created/set by the trainer or facilitator;
- Focus primarily on learning in the classroom and not as much on how to apply the learning in real life/work; and
- Little follow-up back to the work/personal environment.

These descriptions are, of course, related to pure training. As an experiential educator who has used participatory training approaches for years, I am generalizing here to make an important distinction between training and coaching.

Facilitation

In the middle part of the spectrum we have facilitation. The word facilitation comes from the Latin word *facilis* which means to make easy.[8]

John Heron describes a facilitator as "a person who has the role of helping participants to learn in an experiential group."[9] In this definition, facilitation is not just about the KSAs, but it is about a group process.

Spinks and Clements[10] provide this alternative definition of facilitators and indicate that "facilitators are essentially *enablers* or *encouragers* of learning who seek to achieve this by focusing on the *experiences and activity of the learner*." In this definition, learners take center stage.

Process facilitators typically elicit information from a group, providing a framework and process whereby groups create their own content. This is also an important part of group coaching in which the group coach creates the framework for participants to explore and learn. Facilitators, especially third-party facilitators, are not there as experts, they are there to guide the flow.

Ingrid Bens[11] states that "basic facilitation skills such as active listening, paraphrasing, and feedback are at the center of today's leadership skills/competencies," which she includes under training, mentoring, coaching, and team building initiatives.

Bens identifies the following as core skills for facilitators[12]:

- Listens actively
- Supports
- Probes
- Clarifies
- Offers ideas
- Includes others
- Summarizes
- Harmonizes
- Manages conflict

The International Association of Facilitators (IAF) includes the following as core competencies for facilitators:

- Create collaborative client relationships
- Plan appropriate group processes
- Create and sustain a participatory environment
- Guide group to appropriate and useful outcomes
- Build and maintain professional knowledge
- Model positive professional attitudes

As Rothwell notes,[13] specifically, facilitators will focus on four main areas or stages:

1. **Prepare for the facilitated sessions:** Including establishing an agenda, preparing questions, and gathering background information about the issues facing the group.
2. **Open the facilitated session:** Manage introductions, clarify ground rules, and review agenda.
3. **Manage the group interaction during the facilitated session:** Including posing questions, noting responses and surface issues, identifying possible solutions, securing agreement, identifying action plans, and evaluating.
4. **Conclude the facilitated session:** Focus the group on follow-up and responsibilities, evaluate, identify any issues to be carried forward to future meetings.

Core tools that facilitators may use include the nominal group technique; brainstorming; visioning; root cause analysis (fishbone diagram or cause and effect charting); and force field analysis.

As you will note, there are a number of common practices and skills used by facilitators and coaches. Some of the differences between these two disciplines are merely from differing approaches. As coaches move to work with groups, the integration and adaptation of many of these core facilitation skills and competencies are critical.

Group Coaching

On the far left end of the spectrum, I have placed group coaching. Returning back to our definition earlier in the chapter group coaching has a foundation in core coaching competencies skills and approaches.

Sometimes when the term "group coaching" is used, coaches have been met with raised eyebrows. It is similar to what coaches have experienced when using the term "coaching" in different marketplaces. Over time the terms "coaching" and "group coaching" are being more widely understood. Coaches new to group coaching often ask "What do I call my work?" What I label my program (workshop, facilitation, coaching) is probably not as important as stating what **approach** I will use—i.e., using a group coaching approach. With certain client groups I continue to get raised eyebrows if I say I'm holding a group coaching session. People may actually understand the term better from an intellectual level if I say I'm holding a one-day session or a one-day workshop using a group coaching approach, which will include small group discussions, reflective exercises, action planning, and setting accountabilities and commitments. The label you use for your work is likely to depend on your client, their language, and where you position yourself along the group process continuum.

One of the biggest distinctions with group coaching is that the agenda comes from your group. The group itself will drive the process and strongly determine and/or influence the direction, pace, and themes you discuss. The group will also inform and influence the exercises you include in your work. Group coaches will lead from their toolbox of coaching skills and exercises.

Within group coaching, the agenda is primarily the client's agenda and "client" might be a group of four or eight or twelve. The ICF has taken a stand on what they consider to be group coaching for credentialing purposes as a group of fifteen or less. If you look at the marketplace, there are many programs being called group coaching that are really teleseminars, which are simply one-way passages of information and tools so you can move forward into your work. In a pure group coaching approach, there is going to be minimal content, less talking from the coach, more experiential discovery for the client, and a heavy use of core coaching skills and competencies, such as powerful questions.

Group coaching is different from one-on-one coaching, because in a group or team setting the coach will need to be more directive and take charge. It is a very fine balance, one that I call a *tension*, between holding the space for the client's agenda and being directive. We'll continue exploring this tension throughout the book.

Coach Deena Kolbert summarizes this tension well by stating, "The group ultimately provides the agenda, even though you may have created the outer structure to bring them into the group process."

The feedback from clients over the years indicates that they need a *theme* to come together around—whether it is money, balance, leadership, or business development. Without that common anchor, it was very frustrating for the participants and they wanted more direction and focus. As a facilitator, it was very challenging as you can only do so much work on your feet with the group. This has led me to believe strongly that you really need to have a structure. So, with group coaching, there is the delicate balance of a client's agenda as well as direction from the coach.

Flexibility comes in at the start of every session, where I begin the call with a check-in. I ask participants what the issues are that they want to be looking at in the day's session as it relates to the topic. Clients' comments provide us with a menu of where we can go or their collective agenda. This provides the flexibility to have the client's agenda included.

It also means that as the facilitator, I'm really going to be using my coaching skills to look at what direction should we be going. Unlike the one-on-one context, you may have four, six, or eight different agendas present. A key question to consider is: What's going to give the greatest benefit and greatest impact to the majority of the clients in that session?

Many readers will notice that I interchange the wording of facilitator and coach throughout the book. Group coaches do require strong facilitation skills. There is the whole group dynamic that needs to be monitored and addressed in addition to the client's agenda.

This book is one of the first books about group coaching, and as this sub-discipline of our profession continues to evolve, I am hopeful that our research base and models of what constitute group coaching become even more crystal clear. We will continue to benefit from the cross-fertilization and insights from facilitators and trainers, who, like me, decided years ago to also acquire professional coaching skills. Likewise coaches will also continue to acquire new skills in facilitation or other learning modules.

Where do you stand along the continuum?

Group Size

How large are group coaching groups? An important distinction was made several years ago around what size of group was acceptable by the ICF to be considered for credentialing. They identify a maximum group coaching size as **fifteen.** Coaches interviewed for the case studies ranged from group sizes of three upwards to twelve or more.

The 2008 Group Executive Coaching Survey from the Air Institute indicated that group size was important. "Forty-eight percent coach groups between two and six coaches and 48 percent between seven and twelve. The optimal size of group coaching seems to drop-off dramatically after twelve coachees *(clients),* where it becomes more difficult to differentiate between coaching and facilitation. The study also found that seven, as a group size, was optimal."[4]

Anecdotally, there is a trend towards increased group size as group coaching experience and further confidence are acquired. At the same, I would also posit that "Small Is Beautiful" (just like economist E.F. Schumacher wrote in 1973). Some of my favorite group coaching programs are groups of four to eight members.

Session Length—Individual Sessions and Program Length

In terms of how long sessions run, the Air Survey found that 47 percent of coaches interviewed held sessions for one to three hours, and 15 percent held sessions for one day.[5] Coach Deena Kolbert notes that she remains flexible, considering what the group wants in terms of length and frequency. There was a general consensus from coaches such as Suzee Eibling, PCC, and Mary Allen, MCC, among others, that 90 minutes or an hour and a half is the maximum threshold for virtual calls.

In terms of the length of the assignment or engagement, the Air Survey states, "Over a third of group executive coaching takes place over three to six months, with only 7 percent exceeding one year." Specifically, 33 percent of the coaches surveyed undertook their group executive coaching work over three to six months, 10 percent over a six- to twelve-month period. Five percent of respondents said that the length of the assignment varied.[6] Great variances were found with the coaches interviewed for this book.

WHAT ARE THE DIFFERENCES AND SIMILARITIES BETWEEN WORKSHOPS AND GROUP COACHING?

As we have seen, there is often a fuzzy dividing line between workshops, retreats, and group coaching. Components of all three can be present in a program and labeled with any of these three titles. The title used often depends on your audience and what label is most important to them.

Some of the similarities between the approaches are:

- workshops, retreats, and group coaching programs all can be offered in an intensive half-day, one-day, or longer format; and
- all draw on group facilitation, skills, and often experiential principles.

It is possible to bring a group coaching approach to workshops or retreats. Alternatively, we can also have a *pure* group coaching program where the agenda and exercises are created in the moment at the start of a session, just like a one-on-one session, the only difference being the different numbers.

Differences (often dependent on facilitation style approaches) include:

- Workshops usually focus on the transfer of knowledge, skills and abilities (KSAs) versus group coaching, which focuses on having the clients self-discover knowledge.

- Workshops often have a greater emphasis on the agenda of the facilitator versus group coaching's agenda being set by the participants.
- A key distinction between workshops and group coaching rests on the principle of *being unattached to a specific outcome*. In workshops, trainers are measured on the outcome metrics which are typically set by the organization. In coaching, the outcome and its measurement comes from the client.
- The paramount importance in confidentiality is group coaching work.

WHAT IS THE DIFFERENCE BETWEEN GROUP COACHING AND GROUP THERAPY?

The ICF Global Coaching Study indicates that a key differentiator for the industry is that coaching is seen as an "action plan" rather than as an exploratory process. When asked why they selected coaching instead of alternatives such as therapy or counseling, some focus group participants indicated that coaching offered them an "action plan" rather than an opportunity to explore their "issues."[14]

Table 1.1: Comparison Chart of Group Processes

Characteristic	Group Coaching	Team Facilitation	Therapy Group	Training/ Workshop
Size	6–12	5–20	4–10	Any size
Decision to participate	Participants opt in	Participants are enrolled	Participants opt in or are enrolled	Participants are enrolled or opt in
Source of members	Same company different companies Community	Same company or organization	Community, self-referral professional referral	Community, company (same/ different), individuals
Accountability	Personal and group	Team	Personal	Personal and/or organization
Group agenda	Group creates or helps create agenda	Facilitator sets the agenda	Therapist sets the agenda	By organization
Goals	Individual and group	Team	Individual	Individual, Team, Organizational

Leader	Coach	Facilitator (may or may not be a coach)	Mental health professional	Trainer (may or may not be coach)
Connection	Personal or professional goals or interest, business goal	Business goals, professional goals	Personal health or development goals	Goals (personal/professional)
Examples	Entrepreneurs Sales professionals Executives Career transitioners Leaders Emerging leaders	Sales teams Project teams Nonprofit boards Leadership teams	Divorcees Individuals with addictions Cancer survivors Caregivers	Middle managers Business owners Professionals Soft Skills training Cross Cultural effectiveness

Source: Ann Deaton, Phd, PCC, and Gay Lynn Carpenter, ACC, 2009. Adapted with permission.

Coaching deals with the present in a person's life, focusing on possibilities and potentials, rather than unearthing issues from the past. Group therapy has tended to focus on fixing problems by encouraging clients to revisit their past life issues in order to move forward. By contrast, group coaching starts from the completeness of a client, their resourcefulness, and is structured such that the focus is towards who the person is **being** or **becoming**.

For more information about the contrast between coaching and therapy you may want to refer to documents that have been created by the ICF (www.coach federation.org).

One of the coaches interviewed for this book, Ann Deaton, PhD, PCC, a clinical psychologist and group coach, provided the following table which summarizes the differences between therapy group, team facilitation, and group coaching. I have also added a fourth category of training /workshops to round out the distinction.

WHAT IS THE ROLE OF THE GROUP COACH?

In addition to the responsibilities of the coach outlined by the ICF at the start of the chapter, what else is the role of a group coach?

From the Field:
Views on the Role of Group Coaches

Here is how coaches who are undertaking group coaching describe their role:

A group coach is more than a facilitator—she/he becomes the coach for both the group and the individuals. A group coach creates an environment of confidentiality and trust where group members are open to being coached. Learning and champion for interaction starts from a place of acceptance and values.

—Ginger Cockerham, MCC

I see myself as creating the space where groups can take over. Inevitably, a corporate setting leads you to some information about trends and next steps. My work as a group coach in the corporate context is taking me more into the organizational development field.

—Rita Weiss

To hold the space really big with love and rigor for clients' learning and growth— at the same time know it may not happen on a call or at a site. Changes behind the scene are at deeper, hidden levels. Consistent focus on intentions.

—Victoria FittsMilgrim, CPCC

I see myself as a facilitator and connector. I am very much using the same skills with group coaching—asking powerful questions, etc.

—Heidi Michaels, CPCC

I believe in the art of group coaching—create that heart space where people can share things that they couldn't share otherwise. Confidential Space. Always learn as a coach from the experience.

—Suzee Eibling, PCC

My role is to provide clients with the tools and to create a space to inspire each other.

—Jill MacFadyen, ACC

Create a safe space for people to explore, while creating direction, flexibility, and support.

—Marlo Nikkila

CHAPTER REVIEW

Reflect on the following questions. I suggest you make notes and return to them as you progress through the book.

- ☐ What is your vision for group coaching?
- ☐ What types of programs do you want to deliver?
- ☐ Where do you sit along the continuum of group processes?
- ☐ What do you see as your role as a group coach?
- ☐ What's your biggest question about group coaching?
- ☐ What's been relevant about this chapter for your own development of group coaching work?

CHAPTER 2

MAKING IT STICK—THE BUSINESS (AND LEARNING) CASE FOR GROUP COACHING

As I train more and more coaches who are creating their own groups in businesses and organizations, I recognize that group coaching has reached the tipping point. Previously it has been an uphill task to enroll companies and organizations in the idea of adopting group coaching
—Ginger Cockerham, MCC

Economic conditions are increasingly making group coaching a popular, and essential, modality for personal, professional, and staff development. This chapter explores the business and learning cases for group coaching. We will look at group coaching benefits from the perspective of both organizational and individual clients who join group coaching, as well as from the perspective of coaches. It also provides real-life case studies from coaches around the world who are undertaking this work.

THE CONTEXT

Recent years have seen some great changes in the realm of talent management, learning, and development.

The economic events of 2008–2009 have led to a softening of funds earmarked for learning and development across most industries. At the same time, economic pressures have led to the adoption of newer learning approaches such as m-learning (mobile learning), and further expansion of e-learning, and other virtual learning modalities.

Regardless of the economic conditions, Ginger Cockerham notes that *Fast Company* has indicated that 64 percent of companies with coaching programs expect to increase them in the next five years, despite the economic situation.[1] Cockerham indicates that a number of these companies are looking to expand the impact of coaching more widely within their organizations through the introduction of team and group coaching.

Whether you are a coach who works with corporate groups, nonprofit organizations, or groups of individuals who come together, group coaching is gaining in both popularity and prevalence. This chapter will look at the impact of group coaching from four different perspectives:

1. The business case for coaching—the impact of coaching organizationally
2. The learning case for coaching—the impact on learning of group coaching
3. The benefits of coaching as identified by clients
4. The benefits and impact of group coaching as identified by coaches.

We will explore the myriad benefits to a group coaching model for clients, organizations, and coaches in this chapter.

Some of the core reasons group coaching is gaining popularity include:

- Leveraging of time and resources (for clients and coaches)
- Economies of scale (more impact with less time and money)
- Effecting change
- Harnessing the collective wisdom of a group
- Scalability
- Making it stick

Leveraging of Time and Resources

Clients and coaches alike indicate that group coaching is a more effective way to leverage people's time and resources. Typically at a lower price point per capita, group coaching is increasingly being seen as a way for an organization to bring coaching to more of their workforce. Group coaching is a very popular option for individuals who may be paying out of their own pocket, given the lower price point.

Economies of Scale and Effecting Change

Group coaching works well from an economy of scale perspective—more impact with less time and money. As a result of their experience in a group coaching program, participants across departments within organizations may share common language, insights, and baselines. This can have a tremendous impact on effecting change in an organization. We will hear from two coaches, Maureen Clarke and Rita Weiss, about their perspectives on how group coaching effects change within organizations.

Harnessing the Collective Wisdom of Groups

As we will hear from Ginger Cockerham, MCC, one of the greatest impacts of group coaching is the opportunity to harvest the collective wisdom of the group. For organizations who recognize that today's complex challenges cannot be solved using traditional approaches, group coaching approaches can be leveraged to harness more of the collective wisdom of groups, leading to more innovative, sustainable solutions.

Scalability

Many group coaching programs have the opportunity to be scalable, or the potential to roll out to two, four, fifteen, or more clients with a similar framework. This potential for scalability can be a strength for innovative program design.

> As the industry continues to grow and evolve, movement beyond the one-on-one executive coaching model typically offered at the highest levels of organizations to a more collaborative group and team model can provide an effective and scalable solution for expansion.
>
> —Cockerham and Mitsch[2]

Making It Stick!

I've titled this chapter "Making It Stick" for a good reason. Making it stick was what originally drew me to coaching years ago.

Throughout my former career as a global manager with the UN and other development agencies, I had the opportunity to run some very high-impact retreat and training programs globally. Coming from the performance improvement field myself, and having led corporate and individual retreat programs around the world for fifteen years, I was looking for a more effective way to get the learning to stick for my staff and participants. I was originally drawn to coaching as a modality to make the results of my programs stick. I realized quite quickly as Stolovich states, **"Training alone produces 10-30 percent of desired performance."**[3]

Each retreat I would see the creation of terrific learning and great positivity; however, six months later, some, but not all, action steps were realized.

Back in 2002, I was drawn to a presentation at the American Society for Training and Development (ASTD) International conference by a coach who talked about work-life balance. As someone who was working eighty to one hundred hours a week, and traveling to anywhere from three to five countries every two weeks, I really needed balance. I was intrigued by the slightly different approach the coach was taking from my own participatory facilitation approach and, hence, the seeds were sown for where I am today. A little more than a year later, I signed up for my first coach training program with the Coaches Training Institute. It was a powerful experience, even though the model was still a one-on-one model in those days. Looking at what I could bring back to my group clients, I realized at that point I would need to adapt what I was learning as a coach for the group content. Almost immediately, adding a coaching approach to my retreat work started having leverage.

We will explore this topic of "making it stick" more fully under the heading "Learning Case for Group Coaching" below.

 ## In the Spotlight:
Reach and Relevance—Ginger Cockerham, MCC
(www.coachginger.com)

Ginger Cockerham, MCC, has been leading group coaching groups within companies and organizations since 1997. At that time, she launched two pilot groups at North West Mutual. That number eventually expanded to ten groups. The program still continues, now led by internal coaches.

Cockerham indicates that one of the greatest benefits of group coaching is the **reach and relevance** it provides. Here is what she says about the benefits of group coaching:

- Group coaching provides benefits from a reach and economic point of view. When you hire a professional coach to work with groups it is more affordable and you can enroll more people in the coaching initiative.
- Group coaching promotes full group engagement. Everyone is so involved. Companies don't question the ROI. They see the return and results when they track internally the production, retention, and initiative successes individuals in the groups make.
- Group coaching teaches skills on moving an unformed group to a formed group, which facilitates full group engagement.
- Group coaching serves both the company and the coaches. More global companies are effectively putting together virtual groups for both environmental and economic reasons.
- As a coach, it's a great model, and it is more lucrative per hour. Group coaching gives more time to focus on other things and still have your work be financially viable.

Cockerham notes that group coaching provides the following benefits to individuals:

- Support from the coach and other members of the group;
- Increased motivation for forward movement;
- Bigger vision for what is possible;
- Collegial relationships with like-minded people who have the same purpose/goal, etc.;
- Personal development enabled in a safe, confidential environment;
- Professional development skills and tools;
- Improved health and well-being.

The benefits to the organization include the fostering of long-term sustainable change, happier and healthier employees, cost efficiencies, and more integrated thinking and connections across the organization.

BUSINESS CASE FOR COACHING

ROI for Coaching in General

Studying the ROI (return on investment) of coaching is continuing to evolve. Early studies such as the 2001 study in *The Manchester Review* found that coaching investments averaged 5.71 times the initial investment. *The Manchester Review* study[4] posits:

- Coaching translates into doing.
- Doing translates into impacting the business.
- This impact can be quantified and maximized.

The recent ICF Global Coaching Client Survey[5] states:

> The ROI for companies can be significant: The vast majority (86%) of those able to provide figures to calculate company ROI indicated that their company had at least made their investment back. The ROI for companies is quite a bit higher, with a median return of 7 times the initial investment. In fact, almost one-fifth, 19%, indicated an ROI of at least 50 times (5,000%) the initial investment, and a further 28% saw an ROI of 10 to 49 times the investment.
>
> The median personal ROI indicates that those who seek a financial gain can expect a return in the range of 3.44 times their investment.

The ROI for group coaching initiatives is still in its infancy stage and much more attention needs to be paid to this topic. The intent of this chapter is to plant the seeds for coaches and other HR and OD (organization development) professionals, to encourage them to start to quantify and measure the impact of their own group coaching initiatives.

The Manchester Review study,[6] noted that executive coaching interventions had the following business impacts:

- Productivity (53%)
- Quality (48%)
- Organizational strength (48%)
- Customer service (39%)
- Reduced complaints (34%)
- Own retention (32%)

As well, the study[7] cited intangible business impacts from one-on-one executive coaching in:

- Improved relationships with reports (77%)
- Improved relationships with stakeholders (71%)
- Improved teamwork (67%)

- Improved relationship: peers (63%)
- Improved job satisfaction (61%)
- Reduced conflict (52%)

BUSINESS BENEFITS FOR GROUP COACHING

This chapter explores a number of business benefits for group coaching that have been identified through conversations with clients, as well as coaches undertaking their own group coaching work. Several of the business benefits identified include:

- Time
- Money: cost effectiveness
- Scalability and reach within the organization
- Effecting change more widely
- Cross-functional fertilization
- Culture change, and
- Enhanced retention.

Effecting Change within Companies

Saul Carliner[8] notes that Dana and James Robinson advise, "Managers and executives are more likely to value the efforts (of training and HPI professionals) and that these efforts are most likely to effect change, if they are directly tied to a business need."[9]

Coach Maureen Clarke states, "Coaching is a necessary component to any change initiative, and in today's business world, the only constant is change itself. Coaching provides sustainability to individuals and organizations and is one of the principal leverage tools that businesses have for developing their people."

Coach Rita Weiss echoes the sentiment by saying, "Group coaching helps to create a culture within an organization and creates a core group of people who can effect change."

> The most common business case for group coaching is the fact that, in companies and organizations today, major business decisions are reached through cross-functional teams. This requires the ability

to work collaboratively, to communicate effectively with diverse colleagues, and influence successfully. Group coaching programs enhance all of these skills.

The bottom line impact I've seen is qualitative rather than quantitative. Group coaching increases retention of key leaders, improves commitment to the organization, accelerates the achievement of goals and objectives, and increases the chances of success of business initiatives.

The business issues I've been hired to address include improving collaboration across functions, enhancing cross-cultural interaction, integrating two corporate cultures, and developing global leaders.

—Rita Weiss (www.pinnacleconsultingservices.com)

 ## In the Spotlight:
Deena Kolbert, CPCC, ORSCC
(www.deenakolbert.com)

Deena Kolbert has delivered group coaching programs to small- to mid-size businesses. She notes that the business case for her work with these organizations has been grounded in the following results:

- Enhanced productivity and positivity through better collaboration, communication, listening skills, and clarity about each other's perspectives, combined with the participants' commitment to team members, have led to a move towards more constructive actions.
- Administratively, developed better management reporting systems, timely billing, monthly budget review, and an increased marketing effort.
- HR's bottom line has decreased expenses due to fewer people leaving and replacement is less costly. Team spirit and collaboration have increased efficiency.
- The bottom line is moving upward, paying down debt, and not borrowing more. While the impact is large, the pace of return is still not aligned with expectations, especially in a downward market. Overall, group coaching has kept morale higher during this economic downturn, as these small businesses open up to new perspectives and opportunities, including attention to quality of life.

In nonprofit organizations, Kolbert noticed the following:

1. Produced more efficient fund and board development, systems and processes for organizational and staff management, succession planning, and expanded marketing for fundraising events.
2. Bottom lines increased and affected organizations' functionality and perception of themselves and their abilities.

 ## In the Spotlight: Maureen Clarke, MA, CPCC, ACC (www.blueprintgroup.ca)

Maureen Clarke is a certified coach from British Columbia who developed an eight-week group coaching program around "wellness" for a global pharmaceutical organization. The program was delivered using a phone-based approach focused on work-life issues.

Passionate about adding rigor and measurement to our coaching work, Clarke decided to use this as a case study[10] for measurement.

Maureen looked at the question "How are the intangible benefits of wellness programs measured in order to ensure that plan members and organizations are receiving bottom-line benefit?"

Before the program, participants answered survey questions about their perception of work-life balance, levels of engagement, and management behavior in upholding organizational principles of work-life balance.

Here are the results after eight weeks of participation.

Pre-program:

Thirty-eight percent of participants agreed that they had considered looking for a position elsewhere in order to address work-life balance challenges.

Post-program results:

- 84% felt their productivity had increased.
- 86% agreed that they had developed concrete strategies to balance work and personal lives.
- There was an increase of 25% of participants who felt they had the opportunity during the last two months to perform their jobs without work-life conflict.

- Impact on stress indicators:
  - 28% increase in healthy habits;
  - 22% decrease in overall stress; and
  - 14% increase in psychological well-being.

Clarke notes that the changes identified with group coaching clients translate to an average annual savings of $6,000 per employee. This amount was calculated using the Johnson and Johnson formula that determines a saving of more than $4 for every $1 spent on work-family programs.

RESULTS FOR COACHES

Group coaching solves the great conundrum—there are more people who want coaching and can't afford it, and coaches want to help more people but can't afford to lower their fees too much. Group coaching offers the perfect balance. It's less expensive for clients, yet three to four times more profitable to coaches, since they are leveraging their time among fifteen to twenty (or more) people. Coaches make more money per coaching hour, and the clients get coaching support. It's a win-win.
—Mary Allen, CPCC, MCC

Coaches interviewed consistently indicated that group coaching is a terrific model for leverage. The model allows you to leverage your time and resources while being in service to a client base that is often short of resources—time and money.

Here's what the coaches said:

Group coaching provides an added service that people are interested in (short term, less expensive, topic focused). This is a great way to leverage your time, because you can work with more people with the same amount of time, while making more money. Group coaching programs can be duplicated, which allows for more ease in implementing over and over again. Products can be created out of the group coaching programs to reach even more people. Overall, by offering group coaching, you can increase your services, the number of people you serve, and your income with little extra effort.
—Marlo Nikkila

Group coaching allows you to leverage your time. From a business perspective, it is a fabulous business model—it allows you to serve people while serving yourself.

—Rita Weiss

Group coaching is a much better way to leverage my time.

—Ann Deaton, PhD, PCC

EFFECTING CHANGE

As we saw earlier, one of the benefits of group coaching is the potential to effect change within the client base. For years, I have called this the ripple effect. Group coaching has the potential to impact more people in a shorter amount of time than one-on-one coaching. It is no surprise that my business logo is the water drop, to represent the ripple effect of the work I undertake with groups.

Many coaches are also drawn to group coaching work in order to have an impact either globally (around the world) or to effect change more quickly.

Ginger Cockerham noted, "Thomas Leonard remarked years ago that coaching would go around the world and change the way people interact and communicate forever. As group coaching becomes an integral part of companies, organizations, and people worldwide, his vision is coming true."

Question: How are your programs affecting change within organizations? Communities? Businesses?

THE LEARNING CASE FOR COACHING

Studies on coaching report an ROI of five to seven times the initial investment. Coaching is often customized to address individual needs, with week-to-week support, and opportunities to integrate learning into real-life work experiences. This sustains any leadership and life training programs, in contrast to other training models where learning is often forgotten upon leaving the training room.
—Maureen Clarke

There are at least five main learning cases for group coaching:

1. It offers more impact at a lower cost.
2. Facilitates culture change.

3. Makes it stick.
4. Reinforces learning and enhances the transfer of learning.
5. Builds internal capacity and knowledge.

1. More Impact, Lower Cost

Typically, a group coaching program can reach more members of an organization at a lower cost than traditional one-on-one executive or personal coaching. It is common for group coaching programs to involve employees at mid-management levels and lower.

2. Facilitates Culture Change

As previously discussed, group coaching provides opportunities for culture change, or as Rita Weiss states, "Group coaching helps to leverage the power of a group to effect change." Given that change initiatives often have a poor track record for sustainability,[11] group coaching is a modality that can support groups over a longer period of time as they move through the change process.

3. Makes It Stick

Grounded in the principles of reflection and action, group coaching encourages clients to take ongoing action and create public accountability about their commitments. It is suggested by coaches that the act of publicly declaring a commitment enhances the likelihood of follow-through.

In particular, coaching paired with training seems to really "make it stick," as F. Turner[12] writes: "A study featured in *Public Personnel Management Journal* reports that managers that underwent a managerial training program showed an increased productivity of 22.4%. However, a second group was provided coaching following the training process and their productivity increased by 88%."

4. Reinforces Training Initiatives

With learning transfer rates ranging from 10 to 30 percent,[13] group coaching is starting to be seen as a way to reinforce training initiatives while continuing the dialogue from the "classroom." Over the past few years, I have followed up corporate training programs with regular group coaching calls.

It is important to recognize that learning needs to be reinforced. Vidakovik[14] states that people retain:

- 20% of what they *hear*;
- 30% of what they *see*;
- 50% of what they *hear and see*;
- 70% of what they *see, hear, and say* (e.g., discuss, explain to others); and
- 90% of what they *see, hear, say, and do.*

Group coaching allows the client to see the material, hear it, speak about it and take action, or do it. Group coaches will often connect with participants for several months following a training session through scheduled group coaching sessions. It is in this post-training phase where participants translate their action plans into reality with their own work as well as with their teams. The public accountability also seems to "up the ante" leading to reported change.

5. Builds Internal Capacity and Knowledge

Tapping into the collective wisdom of an organizational or industry group can build capacity internally, creating a stronger culture and environment. Group members will share common frameworks and have the opportunity to focus in on, and discuss, core business issues.

 From the Field:
Coaches were asked, What do you see as some of the learning benefits of this work?

Here is how they replied:

Coach Rita Weiss states, "Group coaching accelerates learning as more leaders can participate in a group coaching leadership development program. Group coaching also creates a core of leaders who share values, focus, vision, and commitment, and provides them with a language to communicate new ways of interacting and new leadership skills."

Ann Deaton's experience has been that "clients are able to implement action and report back to group. Ongoing accountability is created in the same community after the group ends, as others have a level of intimate knowledge and an investment in their success and check in with them as well as sharing resources, making referrals, etc."

Ginger Cockerham, MCC, states: "I think of coaching objectives—teaching and instructing are not the purpose of group coaching from my perspective. I think of the coaching objectives—that each member of the group grows both personally and professionally, that they are able to achieve things that they have not achieved on their own, and that they have more tools and resources to navigate successfully as a person, parent, professional, etc."

Maureen Clarke, CPCC, notes that group coaching provides the following learning benefits:

- Creates a supportive community post group coaching for sustainability
- Fosters richness of learning in this type of environment
- Requires a facilitator that can be in the moment and be free from "learning objectives" *per se*
- Teaches participants while modeling the skills, that if you stay in the process, the results will come and the learning will have depth

Mary Allen, MCC indicates: Learning is enhanced because there is so much opportunity to tap into multiple perspectives of various participants. We all have the tendency to see things through "our" one limited perspective and within a group—as each person is coached, and shares from their own experience—learning expands exponentially.

Deena Kolbert writes that group coaching has helped with the following:

- There is fluidity and flexibility to groups that allow for all kinds of learning, openings, and perspectives.
- Group development flows through a variety of methodologies, all of which are compatible for that group nothing is fixed.
- There is an understanding within the group dynamic to experience new/unknown interventions based on their own resourcefulness and creativity.
- Group dynamics provide a wisdom that wouldn't happen by being coached alone. Once the participants hear that wisdom, it rings true with their values.

- People who are fearful of working on themselves sense that group process offers stability and safety. The group process allows them to hear others' perspectives. It can offer a feeling of normality. They can observe how others behave, think, and take actions in ways that they may not have thought about.

THE GROUP CASE FOR COACHING—WHAT IT IS LIKE FOR THE CLIENT?

When asked what group coaching is like for her clients, group coach Ann Deaton stated, "They learn from each other and see themselves in one another. They also see things in one another they didn't even know they had to learn."

In the Spotlight:
Ann Deaton, PCC, PhD, DaVinci Resources
(www.DaVinciResources.com)

Ann Deaton runs a number of group coaching programs, which are outlined below.

Program 1: Executive Dialogue—NAWBO (National Association of Women Business Owners)

These sessions are held in person, monthly, two hours per session, and are about nine months long. There is a *Fierce Conversations* structure to the session, a focus person who shares a challenge/opportunity in their business that they would like to have input on which they share with the group virtually ahead of time. The coach facilitator provides the frame with a theme that has emerged about the focus issue as captured in a quote (e.g., spread self too thin, mixture of fear and excitement about taking risks). Questions are provided to enable each member to apply to their own business. At the end of the session, each person shares a takeaway and the focus person offers a commitment about what actions they will take. They will then share how it turned out at the start of the next session.

Most likely, they will have another NAWBO meeting in between group coaching sessions, which contributes to the development of bonds among the group members.

Program 2: Nonprofit Leaders

These programs are held in person, every two weeks, two and one-half hours per session, and are three months long *or* held once a month and are six months long.

Deaton found that meeting every two weeks was better—this provided continuity and structure to focus on themselves. It's difficult for these leaders to pull themselves away from work and to put their own development first. It is common to hear, "Thought that I couldn't come, too many demands" but after the session they indicate that they feel more "focused and productive." Sessions allow these leaders to feel relief and joy, as well as get perspective, add tools for being more effective, and learn some coaching skills to use with their staff.

The structure of these groups includes a weekly focus topic with a brief 20–30 minute introduction to an issue, and experiential exercises, conversations, and coaching, e.g., topics have included powerful "no," requests, and promises.

Deaton has also held sessions that help nonprofit leaders learn coaching skills by coaching one another on challenges. The leaders are provided with coaching questions and some coaching frames. They receive feedback on their coaching from the coach facilitator and one another.

Program 3: Executive Fast Track: Virginia Commonwealth University Graduate Degree Master's in Information Systems

This program is held in person, monthly, one and one-half hours per session, and is fourteen months long. The program also involves a 360 leadership tool—The Leadership Circle—at the beginning and the end, with individual debriefs both times by the group coach, in the context of a Master's program with a focused leadership component.

The program is now in its fourth year, but in the second year of the program they introduced group coaching and 360. There are five coaches each with groups of five to seven people. The graduate program is two days executive fast track, two weekends per month; coaching occurs once per month in a group. At the beginning and the end of the program, the Leadership Circle is used to help clients to initially create their individual development plan, and at the end to evaluate changes.

Deaton provides the following comments on the benefits of the group experience for clients:

- Clients see others with the same challenges, see themselves in others, and see others respond to coaching on those challenges.
- Clients have the opportunity to gain self-awareness through the coaching conversations that take place, as well as the "truths" they share with one another about what they observe.
- Clients invest in one another's success and hold each other accountable for taking action.
- Clients often learn some basic coaching skills, and certainly a coaching attitude (ask instead of tell, being curious instead of judging) that they take back to their own teams and also into their daily lives.
- Clients' relationships often endure after the structured group experience ends.

GROUP COACHING BENEFITS

Coaches often find it difficult to explain or discuss the benefits of group coaching. It is hoped that this chapter will provide readers with a better understanding of what coaching can do for an organizational group or an individual who wants to join a group.

In addition to what was mentioned earlier in this chapter, coaches have identified the following benefits:

Deena Kolbert, CPCC, ORSCC
In addition to what has been discussed earlier in this chapter, some of the benefits Kolbert has seen with group coaching clients in the business sector include:

- A company remained open, planned new marketing strategies, and one year later is paying off debt with a workable budget and a monthly billing system in place;
- Groups within a small company have less resistance in their workplace, ideas are considered openly at regularly held staff meetings, problems are discussed openly before they become "bottom line" negative problems;

- Group goals and objectives are checked every other month to maintain focus, with adjustments made as needed; and
- On April 15, taxes in the U.S. were due and all U.S. members of the financial security group filed returns, for the first time, on time, with one person paying several years of back taxes.

Mary Allen, MCC

Allen works, in general, with groups of individuals and found the following benefits from group coaching. People:

- Found greater freedom for authentic expression;
- Realized their goals—from losing weight, getting out of debt, getting organized, experiencing greater inner peace, business building, etc.;
- Created community with like-minded individuals;
- Formed long-term friendships;
- Became more accountable; and
- Became inspired as they saw others realize their goals.

CHAPTER REVIEW

What would you indicate as the business and learning case for your coaching efforts? What are the cases for undertaking this work with clients for you:

- ☐ From your perspective as a coach?
- ☐ As a business case?
- ☐ As a learning case?
- ☐ In terms of impact?

CHAPTER 3

THE FOUNDATION OF GROUP COACHING—THE ESSENTIALS OF ADULT LEARNING

In addition to core competencies in coaching, successful group coaches need to acquire a solid understanding of adult education and group development principles and processes. Most group coaching occurs against the backdrop of adult education and small group process. For many coaches, these principles may require an introduction or a refresher.

This chapter will provide core information on four key areas that create the foundation for our work as group coaches:

1. Core principles of adult education
2. Experiential education
3. Small group process
4. Learning styles

In lead-up to this chapter, take a moment to reflect on your experience as an adult learner as well as your experience in small groups. What has been your experience? What has worked? What has not?

CORE PRINCIPLES OF ADULT EDUCATION

A majority of coaches will be undertaking their work with adults. An understanding of core adult education principles can enhance the impact of your program and ensure that participant and/or client needs are being met.

This section reviews core principles of adult education, such as:

- Leverage the life experience and expertise of the group;
- Create a safe and confidential learning environment;
- Create opportunities for client ownership and co-create the agenda and exercises;
- Make sure the approach and focus of the program are clear;
- Create opportunities for clients to discover knowledge;
- Establish coach and participant/client expectations at the start of the program; and
- Make It Stick!—Link the learning to real life.

LEVERAGE THE LIFE EXPERIENCE AND EXPERTISE OF THE GROUP

A key consideration when working with adults is to leverage the knowledge base of your clients. Collectively, your clients will bring a wealth of life experience and expertise. Wherever possible, draw on this life experience and expertise. Coaches are neither considered to be experts nor "jacks of all trades." Create opportunities for sharing the life experience and expertise of the group.

One of the key benefits of group coaching identified by coaches and clients alike is the powerful experience of sharing experiences between peers. Provide sufficient time for sharing between the group members. Group coaching's strength is not just about the relationship between the coach and each member of the group, but the interconnected web between all group members, including the coach.

Wherever possible, design activities that link themes or concepts to clients' life experience. Practically, this may include:

- Asking participants for "stories" they can share:
- Asking "What has been your experience with this topic?"
- Asking "What's your greatest learning from this experience?"

Create a Safe and Confidential Learning Environment

Creating safety and maintaining confidentiality are paramount in enabling a powerful learning environment, especially with group coaching. Experienced group coaches such as Ginger Cockerham, MCC, and Suzee Eibling, PCC, both stress the importance of creating a safe and confidential group experience.

To create safety and confidentiality, you will want to:

- **Set ground rules or ways of working** during your first session with each group. Please refer to Chapter 4 for a brief discussion and common ground rules you will want to bring into your programs.
- **Talk about confidentiality**, or have the group define confidentiality for themselves. Typically I define it for my groups as "what is said in the room stays in the room." Confidentiality is a core consideration for group coaching programs as people will be sharing very personal information. This is particularly important for group programs where groups are intact, within organizational settings, or within small communities (geographic, industry, and/or virtual). It may be necessary to revisit, or remind participants, about this principle throughout the program. For more information, refer to the **ICF Code of Ethics** at www.coachfederation.org.
- **Provide participants with the opportunity to get to know each other**. Spend time allowing each person to introduce who they are and what they want out of the program.

Have the Participants Take Ownership

One of the four areas of the ICF Core Competencies includes "Co-create the relationship."

A foundational principle in coaching is that we co-create, or co-design, the coaching relationship with the client. This includes the topics they want coaching around, the approach, and even the exercises. In setting expectations for the program, it will be important to explicitly state your expectations of client involvement and their key role in creating the agenda, as well as what the group coaching experience will be like.

As discussed in Chapter 1, coaches may place themselves along the continuum of learning approaches by taking a *pure* group coaching approach where the agenda is completely created by the group. Other groups may be seeking more direction from the coach and will be expecting the coach to provide structure and direction through session-by-session topics and/or themes that they can then add on to.

One of the best practices I use in the design of the coaching relationship is to hold a short (15 minute) pre-call discussion with each participant to find out more about their expectations, what they want to derive from the program, and anything else that is useful about their needs and preferences (for example, their learning style).

Make Sure That the Approach and Focus of the Program Are Clear

Spend time at the start of the program discussing the structure it will take, what participants can expect, and what the overall focus of the program will be. Depending on where you sit along the Group Program Continuum, open a dialogue on what participants want to get out of the program. In group coaching, it is likely that individuals will find their own additional impact of the program as they hear others speak. You will want to set aside time at the start of a program to discuss their expectations and focus. Throughout the program, you will also want to create checkpoints whereby clients can check on their own individual goals. Ideally, this will be done on a weekly (or session-by-session) basis.

In Chapter 4, which covers best practices for group coaching, a core best practice for group coaching includes spending time at the start of a program discussing:

- Ground rules for Ways of Working for the group;
- Expectations of the coach and clients; and
- Goals—individual and/or collective (depending on the type of group and their focus).

Create Opportunities for Participants to "Discover" Knowledge

Group coaching is heavily grounded in an experiential approach. Lecture-based teaching or excessive use of tools such as PowerPoint do not lend themselves well to the core approach of group coaching.

A central tenet of adult learning is that adults learn best when they are provided with the opportunity to discover knowledge and insights for themselves. Coaching rests on this premise of discovery for self, with the client having the expertise and answers. Likewise, group coaching also needs to create ample opportunities for clients to discover their own knowledge.

Experiential education provides an additional approach to creating opportunities to "discover" knowledge. This topic is discussed later in this chapter.

Establish Coach and Participant Expectations at the Start of the Program

- Spend time during the initial session or initial half hour finding out what your clients' expectations are.
- Create an environment where participants have ownership of the process—they can decide how they want to work together.
- Spend time working with the group to establish ground rules on how the group wants to work together. As a facilitator you may want to get the ball rolling by suggesting some, or you may want to ask the group to create their own list of ground rules for "ways of working together."

Make It Stick!—Link the Learning to Real Life

Many group programs fall short of providing the space for participants to create frameworks or structures in which they can take the learning from programs back into their everyday life. The strength of group coaching is in creating opportunities to have the **learning stick**!

Provide space in your program for exercises such as action planning, setting commitments, creating structures, and identifying accountability steps. Remember to also check in on the steps people have undertaken and the goals they have accomplished.

Questions to Consider—Adult Learning Principles

Looking at the adult learning principles, how can you incorporate these into your group coaching work?

_____

_____

_____

_____

What approaches will work best for you?

_____

_____

_____

_____

Based on these principles, what will your ideal program/look like?

_____

_____

_____

_____

Are there any pitfalls you want to take note of?

_____

_____

_____

_____

EXPERIENTIAL EDUCATION

> *Experiential education is a philosophy and methodology in which educators purposefully engage with learners in direct experience and reflection in order to increase knowledge, develop skills, and clarify values.*
> —Association for Experiential Education

Joplin[1] states that there are number of core characteristics which define education as experiential:

1. Student based rather than teacher based.
2. Personal not impersonal nature—how is the topic related to you as a learner?
3. Process and product orientation—the journey is more important than something being right.
4. Evaluation for internal and external reasons.
5. Holistic understanding and component analysis.
6. Organized around experience.
7. Perception based rather than theory based.
8. Individual based rather than group based—"the emphasis is, however, on the individual's relationship and role within the group, and that person's awareness of the group functioning and his part in it."

As you will note, coaching grows from these same core characteristics.

Key components of an experiential education cycle[2] include:

- Experience—What?
- Reflection—So what?
- Application—Now what?

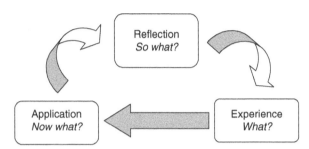

Coaching programs that take into consideration, or integrate, these three stages—experience, reflection, and application—throughout the overall program will find enhanced results for their clients.

Let's take a brief look at each stage of the experiential cycle.

Experience—What?

The first stage of the model is to provide participants with an experience. In training, this may be an initiative exercise or a creative problem-solving exercise or even a self-assessment. In coaching, very simply, participants may be asked to consider a real-life experience they are moving through—for example, career transition, a new relationship, new management experiences. For learning to occur, individuals need to participate in an experience—the **what** or "What did you experience?"

Reflection—So What?

A core component of experiential education involves a reflective process called a "debrief" during which participants are encouraged to consider a series of questions. In order to engage in learning, the participant needs to have the opportunity to reflect on what happened. This is also known as the **so what** or, as facilitator might ask, "So what did you experience?" Group coaching programs should provide clients with ample time to reflect on what they are experiencing.

Application—Now What?

To complete the learning cycle, an individual must apply their learning—the **now what** or "Now what can you do with this learning?" Coaches are probably well versed already in asking this question. This is where learning is brought back to the real world of life and work. It is during this part of the cycle that group coaching can provide huge benefits and opportunities for strengthening the link and transferability to the workplace.

All models of experiential education come back to the concepts of **experience, reflection,** and **application**. Throughout the course of many learning experiences participants only have the opportunity to *experience* and are not given the opportunity to *reflect* or debrief the experience. The reflection stage asks questions such as "So what happened?" or "What does this mean to me?"

Many learning experiences do not take the process that one step further in providing the experience for learners to apply what they have learned, or "Now what do I do with this information? How do I apply it within the context of my life?" Without closing this loop, learning is inhibited.

The **Now What** is what drew me into coaching years ago, having worked with thousands of professionals in leading leadership development programs, training, and retreats. So many times the learning got left behind even with an experiential approach, as there was often little follow-up to real life and work. Coaching has the potential to provide the link back to real life and work, with many group coaching programs focusing on this important transfer point. In addition, many group coaching programs will be held over weeks or months, following participants back to the workplace and checking in on their accountabilities, as well as their new learning and insights.

The Importance of Debrief

Providing space for **debrief** or discussion after an exercise is critical in both experiential education models and group coaching. Debrief can take just as long to complete as an actual activity itself. In group coaching, we hold that the discussion and sharing among the group is just as important as the exercise itself.

As you look at the following, you will notice how intimately connected experiential education is with coaching.

Borrowing from an experiential education process, some questions you may want to consider adding or adapting to provide deeper insights into the exercises you complete with your clients are:

What?

- What did you do?
- What did you observe or think about during the exercise?
- What feelings did you have during the exercise?

So What?

- So what did you learn or have reinforced?
- What are the implications of this exercise for you?
- How does this exercise relate to your "real world"?

Now What?

- How do you want to do things differently in the future?
- How can you extend the learning you had?
- What steps can you take to apply what you've learned?

GROUP PROCESS

Group coaching takes place against the backdrop of small group process. Think back to your own experiences as a group member. What did you notice in terms of how the group progressed? What was memorable? What rough spots did you encounter?

Bruce Tuckman's work has had tremendous influence on the way we look at small group processes. One of his theories, Tuckman's Stages, was published in 1965.[3] His theory proposed that *all* groups go through a series of stages in group formation or dynamics. These stages include **forming, storming, norming, and performing**. Later, in 1977, he added a fifth stage, **adjourning**, which is aligned with the important component of closure.

Whether you are leading a virtual or in person program, it is important to keep in mind that your groups may be moving through their own group process, in their own way, and in their own time. At each stage there will be particular issues which surface that will require different styles of facilitation. The typical stages of group development may be more pronounced during intensive programs— for example, throughout a weekend group coaching retreat or during a one-year group coaching program.

It is also important to note that not all groups will go through the process in a linear fashion and may vacillate between stages.

As a group coach, it is important to notice what the general needs are in terms of safety, conflict, and interdependence, and what adjustments you will want to make to your own style. Remember that, of course, all of this is still against the backdrop of your core coaching style and approaches.

The following chart outlines some of the key characteristics you will find at each stage of group development, and what you can do as a group coach facilitator to support the needs of the group at that stage:

Table 3.1: Stages of Group Development

Stage	Group Characteristics	What to Look for/ What You Might See	Facilitation Approaches
Forming	Polite Concerns and apprehensions can be high — i.e., What will I get out of the program? Who are the others in the group? Will this be worth my investment in terms of time and money?	Quieter group than usual Very polite Quieter members may need a prompt to participate	Group is dependent on facilitator/coach Facilitator should take the lead and will need to provide structure and direction Work with group to set themes, pace, Ways of Working Set a positive, safe tone Discuss confidentiality Create opportunities for the group to: get to know each other; identify their agendas; and set Ways of Working
Storming	Noisy Conflict Individuals within the group are finding their own role and establishing their own identity within it Do I stay or go? can be a common question if members do not feel comfortable Fight/flight	People talking over one another Raised eyebrows Overt conflict Passive, aggressive behavior Those uncomfortable with conflict may shut down or withdraw	Direction around process from coach is critical to keep the group flowing Conflict is common as the group discovers how they can work together Skills to use: active listening, clarify comments, curiosity create open dialogue; May need to address "problem" individuals outside of session Focus on issues that arise through the process as people learn to work together

Norming	Cohesion	Group is very comfortable sharing and communicating their experiences	Focus on process and providing resources and structure as requested
	The group is comfortable with each other		Group process is usually smooth at this stage, but group may need assistance in helping to come to decisions/actions within the time frame.
	Group wants to talk and share experiences with each other		Provide activities that help to build the group and practice working effectively together
			Questions to consider asking:
			What do you need to know?
			What's going to take you to the next step?
			What's the next stage(s)?
Performing	Interdependence of group	Lots of sharing, dialogue	Focus on problem solving and decision making
	The group is now performing and is effective in dyads, small groups, and the larger group.	Accountabilities are followed through	Provide activities for participants to interact with and reflect on information
	The group will have reached its peak in terms of sharing openly and working effectively (for example, asking questions, providing support to others).	Interdependence within the group	Facilitate debriefing and reflection (i.e., What did you learn? What did you observe? How was that significant?)
			Facilitate transfer to real life —
			• How can the lessons learned be applied to the real world?
			• What would you do differently?
			• How will you apply this?

(Continued)

Table 3.1 (*Continued*)

Stage	Group Characteristics	What to Look for/ What You Might See	Facilitation Approaches
Adjourning	Closure Group is focusing on closure, transfer of the learning to their own context, saying "good-bye" to other participants. Wind-down.	Sadness Celebration Withdrawal of members who may be uncomfortable dealing with end of the process Sense of achievement/accomplishment	Activities to bring closure to the program and transition participants back to workplace or real life Walk through the learning journey you have taken together Summarize key themes you have explored and main learning points which have surfaced Focus on closure and transfer to the work/life context Create post-program linkages —community newsletters, virtual groups, collaborative spaces, and/or a virtual community Celebration!

BEST PRACTICE—CREATING A SAFE SPACE

Creating a safe space for your group program, be it a group coaching session, a workshop, or retreat, is paramount in creating a positive learning environment.

What are the core components of creating a **safe space**?

First, **confidentiality**. Confidentiality is extremely important in any group coaching program, and even more so when a group consists of colleagues who work together or participants all live in the same community. Often, personal information is divulged within a group coaching session that might not be shared in a regular group environment. As part of creating "Ways of Working" with each of my groups at the start of the program, I include confidentiality as part of our ground rules, and ask the group to define what confidentiality means for them.

Group programs can provide the opportunity for participants to **stretch** and explore areas of their life or work that they might not go to otherwise. As a facilitator, it is important to recognize that each person's "stretch" points are going to look very different. What may appear easy for one person can be a huge stretch outside another person's comfort zone. Getting to know your participants, their needs, and their comfort zones prior to the program, or at the beginning of a program, will enable you to support them most effectively. Ask yourself if you are checking in with members individually or as a group throughout a program (particularly if the program is long or involving multi-sessions).

A third way is to ensure that I am **transparent with the process.** Wherever possible, I like to co-design programs with participants' needs in mind, based on pre-session meetings (needs assessments). When contracted as an external facilitator, I spend time discussing with the sponsor their expectations for my role, as well as my philosophy of being an external "neutral" third party, with no other agenda than that for the success of the group.

How else do you create a "safe" space for your participants? What do you do to ensure they can stretch, explore, and learn the most?

LEARNING STYLES

How do adults learn? Research shows that an average of 60–72 percent of adults are visual learners, 12–18 percent are primarily auditory learners, and 18–30 percent are kinesthetic/tactile[4].

As learners, we each learn in different ways. Individuals will have a dominant learning style, either *visual, auditory*, or *kinesthetic* (by touch). In addition to a dominant learning style, we will often have a preferred mix, or combination, of different learning styles.

Visual Learners

Approximately 60 percent of adult learners have a preference for visual learning. This means that they really like flip charts and things they can see. A visual learner prefers colorful material filled with charts, diagrams, and pictures to support the presentation. In a virtual or phone-based environment, visual learners can be left behind if you don't build in enough visual support. This might include booklets or module notes sent out prior to a call, or adding a web component (i.e., via WebEx or GoToMeeting) where they can view an accompanying PowerPoint presentation.

Visual learners are supported in the learning process by sight. They benefit from lots of graphics including color charts, diagrams, and pictures to support the presentation. Needing stimulation and input visually, they may find phone-based programs challenging to participate in and learn from, particularly if there are no visual cues provided. Visual learners may have a preference for webinars to get the visual cues, if this is an option.

Provide Support for Visual Learners

How do you enable participants to access the visual side of things in your group programs? Whether it is a workshop, retreat, or group coaching program, here are some suggestions for supporting the visual learners in your programs:

1. Provide a participant's notebook or other handout, where participants can see and follow along what you are discussing. This is particularly important for phone-based programs.

Participants' notebooks and handouts can serve additional purposes, including:

- capturing the main learning points for people to take forward; and
- a marketing tool—include your contact details, bio, and any other information on upcoming programs that may be applicable to the group.

A takeaway might be:

- a blank journal;
- a workbook created in Word;
- an electronic workbook distributed on USB/CD;
- links to online worksheets; or
- a blank postcard on which participants write down their own action steps and/or commitments to take back to the office. This can also be a great indirect marketing tool.

What other takeaways could you provide for your groups?

2. For in-person programs: Provide small discussion groups with a piece of flip-chart paper so they can capture the key points they have discussed.

These can be shared with the larger group and then posted on the walls for future reference.

3. One of my favorite closure activities is the "Gallery Walk." During this exercise, each participant is given several minutes to walk around the room where the program is being held and look at all of the flipcharts that have been created during the workshop. I often set up this activity by asking participants to come up with a list of their top three learning or action items. More information about this exercise can be found in the Appendix: Exercises for Group Coaching.

4. Another tip I usually introduce to participants is the importance of writing things down. Physiologically, our brain gets imprinted as we move through the simple act of writing. Writing things down becomes a reference for the future, helps to keep people focused, and also supports the brain learning function.

5. Use PowerPoint sparingly! Avoid the *Death by PowerPoint* phenomena and use flipcharts, photos, and other props to make things memorable. The focus in group coaching is primarily on discussion and self-discovery, rather than content and lecture.

When developing exercises, consider how participants can create "visual output" such as collages, drawings, and vision boards, rather than just verbal discussion.

What other methods do you use to support visual learners in your programs? What ideas will you incorporate into your next program?

Auditory Learners

In today's virtual classrooms, auditory learners are very comfortable. An auditory learner learns best by listening or hearing. They learn best by listening to presentations and explanations, and being in dialogue with others. Auditory learners may really benefit or gravitate to phone-based/virtual programs. If you are working by phone or web, keep in mind the length of calls, interactivity, and other checkpoints to ensure and measure engagement.

Provide Support for Auditory Learners

Ideas for supporting the needs of auditory learners throughout your program include:

- Provide participants with ample opportunity to discuss their ideas and hear from others in small and large groups, as well as pairs and triads.
- Consider building in a buddy or peer system where participants connect between calls to brainstorm, discuss their learning, and/or progress on their accountabilities.
- If it is a distance or virtual program, be sure to include audio of some, or all, of the materials rather than only written materials.
- Look to develop podcasts—short 15-minute audiobites—as part of, or support to, your learners between sessions.
- Arrange for group follow-up calls to keep the momentum going.

Kinesthetic Learners

Kinesthetic learners learn more by doing. This may involve writing, drawing, collaging, or physically getting involved in exercises. Kinesthetic learners love action and activity. These learners thrive on trying things out and discovering for themselves.

Get learners with a kinesthetic preference involved, and create opportunities to discover their learning. Simple exercises can be built into group coaching programs such as mind mapping to meet the needs of kinesthetic learners.

Provide Support for Kinesthetic Learners

Kinesthetic learners learn by doing. Fortunately, much coaching work is grounded in a kinesthetic approach where it is about discovery and doing. Some things you can do to address the needs of kinesthetic learners include:

- Adopt a body-centered approach or use geography in coaching.
- Get participants actively engaged and "hands-on" in the exercises. For example, rather than simply talking about their professional or personal vision, have participants create a collage or vision board.
- Encourage clients to draw, use clay, and even sculpture.
- Bring human sculpture into your exercises.

As a group coach you need to be sensitive to the different learning styles your group members have. It is important to tailor your activities and delivery methods to meet the needs of diverse learning styles, as you will likely have a cross-section of styles in any given group.

Discuss with your group, as part of the first session or as part or their registration process, what you should know about their learning style as the facilitator of the program.

Your Style and Preferences as a Coach

What is your preferred learning style? Think about it for a moment—how do you best learn?

Do an online learning assessment yourself. Type "Online Free Learning Style Assessment" into your Internet browser. As you reflect on your style, ask yourself:

- What is your style?
- What are you biased towards?
- What do you need to keep in mind to meet the needs of other learning styles?

Key principle: Tap into and allow participants to use as many different approaches and senses as possible when it comes to programs.

Being aware of your preferred learning style can uncover some of the biases you may hold as a facilitator. For example, if you are an auditory learner your program may be very full of great audio content, but you may not have enough written materials, posters, or flip charts to support the needs of visual learners.

Likewise, if you have a predominance towards kinesthetic learning, you may bring a bias towards learning through doing, without providing sufficient "direction" for visual learners or auditory learners.

SELF-REFLECTION

What style(s) are you? (visual, kinesthetic, auditory)

_____

_____

_____

_____

_____

What are the characteristics of your style?

_____

_____

_____

_____

_____

What implications does this have for your learning?

_____

_____

_____

_____

_____

What implications does this have for your coaching?

_____

_____

_____

_____

_____

What implications does this have for your group programs?

_____

_____

_____

_____

_____

As you reflect on the groups you are working with ask yourself:

- What are the learning styles present in my group?
- What do I need to pay attention to?
- How will I need to adapt my style to meet their needs?
- How will I adapt my exercises to meet their needs?

OTHER INFLUENCERS

A final education influencer to my work as a group coach has been the work, and writing, of Paulo Freire. I was first introduced to the work of Freire as a graduate student.

Paulo Freire is a well-known critical educator. In 1973, he wrote the *Pedagogy of the Oppressed*, which was followed by *Pedagogy of Hope* in 1993. A main premise of Freire's work is that social change is the goal of teaching adults.

As Patricia Cranton[5] indicates, some of Freire's main premises are:

> The educator is also a learner, listening to and understanding the needs and culture of the individual.
>
> Learners participate actively in the learning process, through dialogue with their teacher, who is a co-learner with them.
>
> Educator and learners are mutually responsible for the teaching and learning process.[6]

As we saw in Chapter 2 on the business and learning case, through its attention to harvesting collective wisdom and having the potential to impact greater numbers, group coaching can be a vehicle for social change. Similar to Freire's premise, our role as coach often involves an active role of co-learner.

CHAPTER REVIEW

- ☐ Review adult learning principles and the related questions.
- ☐ Consider how you can integrate an experiential approach into your group coaching work.
- ☐ Reflect on the questions around learning styles.

CHAPTER 4

CORE SKILLS AND BEST PRACTICES OF GROUP COACHING

Competence as a group coach comes from the belief, value, and passion of coaching. It takes a lot of courage to stand in front of a group or audience and coach on the spot. That confidence comes from the belief in, and trusting, the coaching process.
—Ginger Cockerham, MCC

This chapter continues to explore the foundation of group coaching and answers the following significant questions:

- How is group coaching the same as, and different from, individual coaching?
- What core skills are required for group coaching?
- What are best practices of group coaching?

HOW IS GROUP COACHING SIMILAR TO ONE-ON-ONE COACHING?

There are many similarities between group coaching and one-on-one coaching. A majority of core coaching skills, tools, and approaches can be adapted for the group coaching environment. Group coaching is grounded in the eleven core competencies that have been identified by The International Coaching Federation.

The International Coach Federation identifies the following Eleven Competencies for the Coaching Profession

A. SETTING THE FOUNDATION
1. MEETING ETHICAL GUIDELINES AND PROFESSIONAL STANDARDS
2. ESTABLISHING THE COACHING AGREEMENT

B. CO-CREATING THE RELATIONSHIP
3. ESTABLISHING TRUST AND INTIMACY WITH THE CLIENT
4. COACHING PRESENCE

C. COMMUNICATING EFFECTIVELY
5. ACTIVE LISTENING
6. POWERFUL QUESTIONING
7. DIRECT COMMUNICATION

D. FACILITATING LEARNING AND RESULTS
8. CREATING AWARENESS
9. DESIGNING ACTIONS
10. PLANNING AND GOAL SETTING
11. MANAGING PROGRESS AND ACCOUNTABILITY
www.coachfederation.org

Specifically, some key similarities between one-on-one and group coaching include:

1. **Holding the client's agenda.** Holding the client's agenda is a core principle of any coaching engagement. The coaching relationship rests on allowing the client to set the agenda, tone, and focus of the work. The same holds true with group coaching. In a group coaching context, we want to create programs which are based on the needs of your participants. More discussion about this topic can be found in Chapter 5 with the Group Coaching Client Assessment™. What is it that your clients want to take away from the session? How are you ensuring that their agenda, and not yours, is driving the session?

2. **Maintaining flexibility** or "dancing in the moment" with what the group needs. Dancing in the moment is a popular coach-ism, meaning be flexible with what shows up with your client base. In a group coaching context this may practically mean being flexible with **where** and **how** clients want to spend time during the session, or what topics are covered.

3. **Being unattached to the specific outcome.** A key distinction between workshops and group coaching rests on the principle of being unattached

to a specific outcome. In the group coaching context, outcomes should be identified at the start of a program by the clients. Should participants choose to explore one area with a different rhythm and timing than yours, assess the program's impact from the participant's angle. Ask them "What's been the impact of this session for you?" or "What's been your biggest learning or takeaway?" What you as the coach define as success or failure may be very different than what your participants feel that they actually take away from the program.

The Principle of Confidentiality

Confidentiality is a core principle for all group coaching work. At its most basic level it may be defined as "What's said within the group, stays with the group." Upholding this principle and taking time to discuss this at the start of a program is critical.

Core Coaching Skills that Remain the Same

There are several foundational core coaching skills that remain the same whether you are working with individuals or groups. These include the skills of:

Listening—Listening is a core skill in any coaching model. Many models of coaching include a deeper approach to listening, such as the Three Levels of Listening of the Co-Active model which include:

- Level 1—Listening to self
- Level 2—Listening to the client
- Level 3—Environmental listening (Noticing what is happening in the environment around you—dogs barking, the energy of the call, even your phone connection being dropped.)

Effective group coaches will also listen to what is being said as well as what is *not* being said in coaching sessions with the group.

What is not being said in your group coaching sessions?

Leverage powerful questions—Questions form the backbone of any individual coaching session. Likewise, questions will continue to drive a group coaching engagement. Specifics on creating powerful questions can be found in the

Appendix—Exercises for Group Coaching, as well as **Twenty Plus Great Group Questions for Your Next Program** in Chapter 7.

What are your top 10 powerful questions?

Leverage-Curiosity—Curiosity is a key approach for coaches. Rather than coming with the answers as a consultant would, a coach comes from a place of curiosity to help the client uncover what they already know. What makes your client tick? What are they really interested in? Coming from a place of curiosity rather than already *knowing* the answer allows group members to feel that they have been heard.

How are you coming from a place of curiosity with your clients?

Everybody gets to be right—Each participant will come to the program with varying life experiences, perspectives, and insights. The principle of "everybody gets to be right" enables you and the group to fully appreciate, and leverage, the diversity of all participants.

Expand clients' awareness and support them in taking action—Create opportunities for participants to deepen their learning and insights, as well as take action forward. Insights without action will not lead to change, nor will action uninformed by insights lead to professional or personal growth.

Create opportunities for participants to deepen their learning and insights, as well as take action forward.

How do your group coaching exercises support both awareness and action?

Using inquiry, challenges, requests—Core coaching skills of inquiry, challenges, and requests (as defined in the Appendix) continue to play a key role in helping clients take action on their new learning. Most coaching models are based on the premise of "Deepen the Learning and Forward the Action." Thus inquiry, challenges, and requests support group coaching clients to deepen their insights and take action in between sessions.

What exercises, inquiries, requests, or challenges are you leaving with your clients this week? How do you check in on this?

Create opportunities for accountability—Remember that coaching really does happen between sessions when clients start to integrate their learning into their life and/or work. Wherever possible, have each group member identify what they are going to take action on, and be accountable for, before the next session.

What steps are you taking to create accountability in the calls?

Create opportunities for collaboration and conversation

As Mary Allan states: "In group coaching, you have the wisdom of the group to tap into. It is not just about what you are offering. It is about the shared experience in which people can really relate to each other. Also, in group coaching, I like to set up structures for participants to interact with each other in between the calls, including smaller masterminds (two to five people) and online forums. Yahoo Groups is the one I've used the most."

What structure can you add to your next program to ensure that group members are continuing the dialogue?

Sharing the skill of bottom-lining

Given the importance of hearing all group members during a single group coaching session, it is important to share with your clients the skill of bottom-lining or zooming into the essence of a story. Clients can often get carried away by their story, to the detriment of hearing from other group members. Share with your coaching groups the coaching skill of bottom-lining. You may even wish to come up with a gesture to represent this so all group members can take ownership for flagging when bottom-lining needs to happen.

From Experience: Jennifer

One example of where I have used the skill of bottom-lining quite successfully was with a Women Entrepreneurs group. During our first session together, it was very apparent that there were several very verbose members of the group, who had the potential to dominate the conversation to the detriment of the overall group.

As a proactive measure, I introduced the concept of bottom-lining to the group in the first hour. To introduce it I stated, "An important part of our work together in the group coaching context is to ensure that everyone's voice is heard. Part of your success as a business owner will entail succinct, clear communication with your clients and customers. In service of these two ideas I'd like to share with you a coaching skill called bottom-lining. In communication, when we "bottom line," we want to get to the core, or essence, of what we are trying to say. We want to hone into the main message rather than provide a long story. As a cue that you might need to bottom line your comments, rather than interrupt I will flag you with a gesture."

With that I demonstrated the gesture—starting with my hand held above my shoulder, palms open, which I closed as I brought my hand down to my hips so that my fingertips were touching. I then asked if this was a skill and gesture everyone would adopt during our time together. They agreed.

This gesture and skill became a very powerful tool during our work together. Whenever a group member started going into a long-winded story, the gesture came out. As group members became more comfortable and confident with each other, they gestured each other, taking responsibility for their own group learning process.

Questions to Consider—Core Coaching Skills

Ask yourself the following:

- *What other core skills do I bring which will be useful to the group coaching environment?*
- *What skills am I already good at?*
- *Which skills will I want to enhance?*

Also consider . . .

- *What other similarities do I see between group coaching and one-on-one coaching?*
- *What other differences do I see between group coaching and one-on-one coaching?*
- *What is the difference between group coaching and one-on-one coaching?*

WHAT FURTHER TOOLS AND SKILLS ARE NEEDED FOR GROUP COACHING?

While the fundamental coaching skills used with individuals can serve as a strong foundation for group coaching, there are several additional tools you will want to consider adding to your toolbox:

- An understanding of group process
- An understanding of adult education principles

- An understanding of experiential education
- Group facilitation skills and experience

Chapter 3 provided you with a basic overview of group process, adult education principles, and experiential education.

In terms of gaining group facilitation skills and experience, ask yourself: What skills do I need to acquire?

Ginger Cockerham, MCC, also writes on the skills and tools for group coaching, which continues to expand our appreciation of core skills and approaches to group coaching.

Essential Practice: Creating Ground Rules

Building in time at the start of your next group program (workshop, retreat, or group coaching program) for the group to create some ground rules, ways of working, or terms of engagement creates a safe and even playing field for all group members.

Spending time at the start of any new group coaching program to create a list of group ground rules or Ways of Working is a critical component. Write these down and refer back to them throughout a program. I typically set aside 5 to 10 minutes with each group I am working with to create a "Group Charter" or set of ground rules that we will all follow for the time we are working together. It is very similar to designing the alliance in an individual one-on-one coaching session and is part of establishing the coaching agreement. In the group context, it facilitates the design of a group alliance. I undertake a ground rule/Ways of Working exercise with groups that are just forming, as well as intact teams that may be joining me for a half-day program or longer.

I like to have the group come up with their own ways of working—how they will be together. Many times groups come up with their entire list themselves, other groups may need a little prompting. Some of the ground rules I will propose for the group to consider include:

- Start and end on time;
- Confidentiality (What is discussed in the room, stays in the room.);
- Respect for others' experiences, differences, and perspectives;
- Come fully prepared for the call—review the material, know your own focus/agenda;
- Focus during the call—turn off email, Blackberrys, etc.;
- Everyone gets to share; and
- Agreeing to participate or play fully during the course of the program.

Some of these guidelines/Ways of Working may seem very basic, but people are people, and groups are groups. I will post the Group Charter/ground rules/Ways of Working in the venue setting so we can refer back to them as we move forward with the program. Sometimes we need to refer back to them even six weeks into a multi-week program.

You can also facilitate this process in a virtual environment during phone-based programs—suggested changes can be found in Chapter 7. In these instances you may wish to post and/or circulate them among group members by e-mail or on your virtual notice board.

 ## Thoughts from the Field: Core Coaching Skills and Practices

Coaches interviewed for the book were asked *"What are some of the core coaching skills you use?"* As you read through these, note the skills in which you are currently strong, and also those skills and practices that you need to develop further.

Rita Weiss:

- Setting ground rules
- Setting clearly defined goals for each participant—what? by when?
- Identifying with crystal clarity what success will look like for each participant
- Active listening
- Ensuring that the group takes responsibility for achieving success as individuals and as a group (or as a team if it is an intact team)
- A focused, yet flexible, agenda
- Competency assessments and debriefs as part of the coaching program
- Setting up small groups to work together within the larger group, and
- Managing and facilitating the learning and development process within the group context.

Mary Allen, MCC:

- Holding the big group agenda to maximize value
- Acknowledging

- Drawing the wisdom from the group
- Creating a safe space
- Being fully present with the group
- Asking powerful thought-provoking questions and inquiries
- Synthesizing what participants are saying
- Debriefing
- Locking in the learning, and
- Accountability.

Heidi Michaels, CPCC:
I use powerful questions, active listening, Level 1, 2, 3 listening, my intuition, some balance, fulfillment, and process coaching too.

Jill MacFadyen, ACC:
The key ones are my life coaching skills, which allow me to help attendees with shifts in perspective and to recognize that they have been heard. Additionally, my understanding of the job search process is key.

Maureen Clarke, ACC:
Usually, all the core coaching competencies from the ICF (outlined earlier in this chapter), as well as the core competencies for the International Association of Facilitators (refer to Chapter 1).

Additionally, I would say that as a facilitator of group coaching, these skills are applied on a broad scale with the group—sort of a marriage between coaching and facilitating

Marlo Nikkila:

- Listening skills
- Being able to create and provide visual and audio resources through notes, recordings, and photos
- Membership site
- Good at creating and implementing exercises—before call/during call
- Redirecting and pulling the group back on track
- Honoring, and
- Allowing the time and space for people to interact and to build a safe space so that they can share and meet with participants before the program.

Ann Deaton, PhD:

- Listening, trusting my intuition about connections, asking questions instead of telling
- Trusting my intuition
- Asking questions instead of telling
- The importance of the coach being transparent
- Telling the truth to your client. Comfortable saying to the group, not sure where we could go. Sensing that there may be two or three ways we could go. Where do you want to go? Letting the group set the course for what's important.
- Vulnerability/depends on the level
- Going around the room and identifying takeaways make sessions more action oriented. Asking clients at the end of a session: What resonated with you today? What will you do?
- Skills in coaching
- Letting go.

Victoria FittsMilgrim, PCC, CPCC:
Listening, intuition, dancing in the moment, metaphors, spaciousness, vulnerability (willingness to be transparent, imperfect), and humor/lightness.

Lynda Monk, CPCC:

- Deep listening skills to really hear what is mattering to clients/participants
- Powerful questions—to deepen the learning and forward the action on behalf of clients
- Understanding of group dynamics and the development of a group
- Training and facilitation skills—sharing information, teaching—all done through a coach approach in the group coaching program
- Curriculum development skills—to write the program in the first place, including any tools and support materials.

Deena Kolbert, CPCC, ORSCC:
For all groups:

- ORSC (Organization and Relationship Systems Coaching)
- Design an alliance (DPA, DCA) in the beginning
- Ask group how individuals can interact and/or collectively help each other participate to achieve actionable goals

- Towards the end of a session, ask what worked well
- What's the group as a whole taking away and what is the individual taking away from this session?
- What next?
- Work collaboratively on the agenda for the next group session.

Eva Gregory, CPCC:

- Holding the group agenda—maximizing value
- Creating a safe space
- Being fully present with the group
- Asking powerful thought-provoking questions and inquiries
- Synthesizing what participants are saying
- Speaking to participants individually versus general broadcast
- Being authentic
- Locking in the learning
- Being unconventional
- Using humor/entertaining—keeping it light
- Drawing from the wisdom of the group
- Laser coaching
- Using stories, case studies, or metaphors.

BEST PRACTICES OF GROUP COACHING

A Best Practice asserts that there is a method, process, activity, incentive, or reward that is more effective at delivering a particular outcome . . .
—Wikipedia

Regardless of whether you are developing a group coaching program for a corporation or the public, in person or virtually, there are some core best practices to consider. These core best practices will be expanded upon throughout the book, providing you with specific tips and tools. As you continue to refine your own group program ideas, consider how you can integrate these best practices into your program.

1. Less Is More

One of the most important best practices for group coaching is the principle of "Less Is More." It is very common for many coaches try to squeeze in too much content in a group coaching program. As we saw in earlier chapters, a key differentiator between training and group coaching is that group coaching is more about self-discovery, rather than learning concrete skills or pieces of information.

In your programs, ensure that you allow enough time for participants to engage with, and explore, the exercises and topics you have included.

2. All Participants Learn in Different Ways

As we discussed in Chapter 3, learning styles play a key role in client engagement and participation.

Remember that some learners are visual (learn by seeing), some auditory (learn by listening), and others kinesthetic (learn by doing or by touch and activity). In any group you work with, you may have differing representations of these learning styles. Activities you include in your program should meet a range of learning styles. Create your activities accordingly. You will also want to refer to Appendix: Exercises for Group Coaching.

3. Assign Work between Sessions

Coaching really happens between sessions is a common adage of the coaching profession. Real change happens outside of the coaching conversation, when clients are able to start applying, and taking action on, the new insights they have gained. Just as coaches assign requests, challenges, and inquiries for individual clients between sessions, assign your group coaching clients work between sessions.

4. Meet with Participants Prior to the Group Coaching Program

Meet with the participants before the program begins to find out what their needs truly are. In the training world, we call this "needs assessment." In individual coaching work this is the discovery session. In group coaching, finding out what the group clients' needs are can be undertaken in a number of ways, including:

- Short 10–20 minute telephone conversations when the participant registers, or at a date closer to the program start

- Via questionnaire
- Via a web-based survey program

Choose a format that melds with your own philosophy and approach, and also reflects the needs of the clients you serve. For a busy professional, a short web-based survey may be more appropriate than a longer telephone discussion. For corporate groups, spending 15–30 minutes at the start of a session may fulfill this role more effectively. Specific suggestions on what questions you may want to ask during these meetings can be found in Chapter 5: Knowing Your Client.

5. Collaborate with a Partner

Bring co-activity and collaboration into your leadership, and explore opportunities to partner with others. Undertaking this work with a co-facilitator can add extra depth and richness for yourself and clients. A bonus chapter, which includes tips and more information on co-facilitation is available for download at http://www.groupcoachingessentials.com.

6. Allow Yourself Space when Launching a Program

Many coaches who work with groups have multiple programs on the go at any one time—some by phone, others in person. Ensure that you provide yourself with enough breathing room to fully market, develop, and launch a new program. Ask yourself: What's my priority? What's the rush?

7. Leverage Your Content

Give thought as to how your programs can be developed into other programs and services. Leverage your content and what you have already created in a smart marketing approach. For example, how can an in person group coaching program be developed into a teleseminar series? How can part of the content be developed into an e-book?

Throughout this book I will refer to a modular approach to developing programs and services, which will allow you to create different services/programs/products with similar material. We'll also return to a discussion about leveraging your content in Chapter 8 on marketing.

8. Align Your Programs with Your Passions

The development of a solid group coaching program takes many hours. Traditional instructional design estimates that it takes fifteen to forty hours of preparation to deliver one hour of instruction (Carliner, 2003). Group coaching design and preparation time is probably closer to the bottom end of the spectrum, and is assisted by your passions.

As you consider developing your own group coaching work, ask yourself the following questions:

- Are you truly passionate about your program topic?
- How many times do you think you will run a program? Once, quarterly, monthly, etc.?
- How can your program topic be further developed into other programs and services?

9. Marketing Success

Marketing is the focus of Chapter 8. Many great coaches are not successful in this work because they cannot form the groups needed. Getting voices on the line, or participants in the room, is as important as designing a powerful program. Chapter 8 will provide you with ideas and tips for marketing your program—within and to companies, as well as to individuals in the public.

Some key tips for marketing success include:

- Be persistent—it can sometimes take up to seven approaches before a potential customer will want to buy.
- Ensure that your marketing message matches the clients you are serving.
- Clients who have already satisfactorily experienced your services or product are more likely to buy than those who "don't yet know you."
- Word-of-mouth marketing is always one of the best ways to get the word out about your program.

10. Remain Flexible with Timing

Timing will most likely change as you move through programs. After undertaking a pilot program, you may realize that the content you have and ideas you wish to cover are better suited for a six-week program rather than a one-month program, or that each call should be extended by an additional fifteen minutes. Remain flexible with timing.

11. Ensure That You Evaluate

The power of feedback and a testimonial should never be overlooked. What are your participants saying about the program? About your material? Your approach? About whether their needs were met? This information is critical for marketing and future program development. Specific evaluation techniques and approaches will be covered in Chapter 7: Essential Elements.

12. Follow Up as a Value Add

You can provide your participants with a follow-up conference call after your program (perhaps two, four, or six weeks later), as an added value piece at no cost. The focus of this call can be both for celebration and accountability. The follow-up call is also another important way to get feedback about the longer-term impact of your program on people's lives and work.

Learning, and the transfer of learning, does not happen overnight; so, by meeting with groups at a later date, you will be able to more effectively measure the real impact of the coaching. This also then becomes an important marketing and program development piece.

What Research Shows

In early 2009, Air Consulting published their *Group Executive Coaching Survey*.[1] This survey, conducted between August and October 2008, surveyed over 170 respondents across Europe, North America, and Asia Pacific, representing forty countries in total. The survey identified a number of key critical factors for making group coaching engagements in the executive realm successful. The top four critical success factors identified were:

- Coaches' ability to build trust and rapport (23%)
- Process of defining goals (22%)
- Ensuring clear rules (12%)
- Willingness for people to be coached (12%)

Additional critical success factors identified by this study included:

The Coach	The Process	The Client
Coaches' ability to build trust and rapport (23%)	Specific goals	Willingness to be coached
Coach experience	Rules of engagement	Commitment with respect to time and meaningful participation
Coaches' ability to manage group dynamics	Management buy in	Be open to sharing thoughts and feelings
Being successfully briefed on the project by management		
Letting the group do the work		

Source: Air Consulting

 ## Thoughts from the Field: Selected Best Practices from Other Practitioners

Here's how group coaches responded to the question **"What are your best practices for group coaching?"**

Ginger Cockerham, MCC:
That once a group becomes a formed group, they accept ownership of the group and co-create the group's agenda and share the very best of their business acumen, their personal wisdom, and insights, the group becomes a powerful and transformative environment. The best practice is not to be the teacher or instructor in group coaching, but to be their coach.

Mary Allen, MCC:
At the end of the call, asking "What is the gem (learning), you're taking from the call?" This helps to anchor the learning from the group.

Eva Gregory, CPCC:

1. Creating a highly interactive class with lots of acknowledgement of the individuals in the program and the wisdom within the group.

2. Ensuring a safe space within which to play and experiment.
3. Never making anyone wrong.
4. Always tying whatever you are coaching an individual on, back to the group and the learning at large.

Ann Deaton, PhD:
An attractive, consistent space that is not in the workspace of any of the participants, unless this is designed in to the group.

Lynda Monk, CPCC:

- Pre-course one-on-one calls and a follow-up call with the group;
- During the follow-up call to explore what worked and what didn't;
- Invite a testimonial from group members;
- Creating emotional safety and trust is critical—co-creating the agenda, confidentiality, working with the wisdom and experience of the participants—is all part of creating this emotional safety;
- Most important is confidentiality. When I send out materials, I get the informed consent from group members to share their e-mail addresses with others.

Heidi Michaels, CPCC:
I always make sure everyone is introduced. I always ask them to introduce themselves and what brought them here. It creates harmony right away. Also, it's important to follow up on "homework" during a series. I also send a card in the mail to each participant, thanking them for coming.

Maureen Clarke, ACC:
The "skill of facilitator" is a best practice for me in group coaching. Coaches should bring:

1. Serious skill in coaching which they can acquire through a certified coaching program;
2. Skill in facilitation; and
3. Practical experience—certification with feedback.

All of the skills required as a one-to-one coach are needed for group coaching. Additionally, I would say other best practices include:

- Using a workbook as a guide for practical application of new skills learned between the coaching calls;

- Time between calls for reflection and application;
- Meet your group where they are at and be flexible with that;
- Understand and apply the principles of adult education and action learning throughout the group coaching process.

Deena Kolbert, CPCC, ORSCC:
Solid preparation, agenda building, creativity, structures, and then being open and fluid to toss it all out the window when something else shows up that the system is asking for.

Jill MacFadyen, ACC:
Jennifer Britton told me to over-prepare. Most recently, one whole aspect of my presentation was knocked out by misinformation given to me by the hiring company. Thankfully, I had alternate material to fill in the gap.

Marlo Nikkila:

- Build relationships individually and as a group—send out cards
- I provide one-on-one coaching calls if participants express interest
- Unlimited e-mail support during the program

Victoria FittsMilgrim, PCC, CPCC:
Create an outline for each call that has a balance of individual sharing and some kind of new learning to keep everyone engaged.

Rita Weiss:
Letting the group members set the agenda, and keeping the agenda flexible.

GROUP COACHING SELF-ASSESSMENT

As we've seen in the first three chapters, there are many considerations and factors in becoming a **great** group coach.

Take the pulse of where you are right now in terms of the skills and resources you have for group coaching by completing the Group Coaching Self-Assessment below.

Table 4.1: Group Coaching Self-Assessment

On the scale of 1-10 rate yourself on the following with 1 being very low/no skills, 10 being expert/strongly agree.	1	2	3	4	5	6	7	8	9	10	n/a
I am comfortable with these core coaching skills: Asking powerful questions											
Active listening at different levels											
Designing goals											
Creating accountability structures—i.e., an action plan											
Self-management											
Holding the client's agenda											
Creating assignments — challenges, inquiries, etc.											
Facilitation Skills											
I have experience with small group facilitation											
Group Process											
I am aware of the stages groups go through											
I am aware of what challenges may emerge around group process											
I know how to deal with participants											
I know how to create a safe and confidential learning environment											
I know how to foster trust with, and within, the group											
Program Design (Designing with the client in mind)											

(Continued)

Table 4.1 (*Continued*)

	1	2	3	4	5	6	7	8	9	10	n/a
I am clear on what my clients want											
I know the issues and challenges my clients face											
I have a clear understanding of the topics my clients want group coaching around											
I know what my clients preferences are in terms of: Program delivery Pricing Venue (virtual or other)											
When programs are offered (dates and times)											
I have a strategy to learn about my client's agenda so I know what themes they want coaching around											
Marketing											
I know what my strengths are in terms of marketing											
I have developed a marketing strategy for my group coaching program											
I have a marketing plan in place for my group coaching program											
I can clearly define my target market											
I can clearly define what programs I have to offer											
I can clearly state the benefits of my program											
I can clearly describe my program											
My program description is easily understood by others											

I can clearly state what people can expect from my program										
I can clearly state the features of the program — what my program includes										
Getting the Word Out										
I have a list of prospects to market to										
I have a list of sources I can market to online										
I know how I can market my program offline (to the local area)										
I have a network of others who can spread the word about my program (online or individuals)										
Material Design										
I know what to include in a participant workbook										
I know what the essentials of PowerPoint design are										
I know what the essentials of flipcharting are										
I have a virtual discussion board for my group										
I have a virtual location where materials can be found and downloaded										
Program Delivery										
I am aware of typical pitfalls that might arise with program delivery										
I know what bridgeline services to use										
I have at least one bridgeline available for my calls										

(Continued)

Table 4.1 (*Continued*)

	1	2	3	4	5	6	7	8	9	10	n/a
I know what questions to ask to evaluate											
I have a basic toolkit of supplies for in person programs											
I have a good set of resources at my disposal (books, training, etc.)											
I have a number of venues which could be possible locations											
Group Program Systems											
I have a registration system in place											
I have a process to track attendance											
I have a cancellation policy											
I have a refund policy in place											
I have the necessary insurance in place											
I can record calls											
I have a virtual discussion board/chat room/blog for participants											
I can deliver my forms in a PDF format											
I have a system to accept payments by mail											
I have a system to accept payments online											
I have a system to accept payments by phone											
I have an invoice system in place											
I have the necessary insurance in place											

Take a look at your ratings in these main categories:

- Group Coaching Skills
- Group Process
- Program Design
- Materials Design
- Marketing
- Material Design
- Program Delivery
- Group Program Systems

The areas which are my strengths include:

_____

_____

_____

_____

The areas which I need to brush up on include:

_____

_____

_____

_____

Specific things I want to put in place are:

_____

_____

_____

_____

_____

As a result of this assessment, I am going to undertake the following steps:

_____

_____

_____

_____

CHAPTER REVIEW

☐   What are the core skills you want to make sure you bring into your
    group coaching work?
☐   Which skills do you need to brush up on?
☐   What are the best practices you want to make sure you integrate into
    your work?

CHAPTER 5

DESIGNING YOUR OWN GROUP COACHING PROGRAM

One of the first steps to designing your group coaching program is to **Know Your Client**. Whether you are a coach working with public groups or organizational groups, internally or externally, it is imperative to start your design, implementation, and marketing approaches from the perspective of your client.

Each of you will be approaching your design work from different perspectives. In general, there are three main possibilities:

1. You have been **engaged by an intact group** to customize a group coaching program for them.
2. You are **engaged by an organization** (internally or externally) to roll out a group coaching program for them.
3. You are **designing a program around certain themes** (i.e., leadership, work-life balance, organizational) that you **will market to the general public**.

Regardless of which category you fall under, the critical first step is getting to know your client. Historically, in training, we have called this needs assessment.

Exercises and tools in this chapter will focus on the design phase of group coaching. Depending on where you sit along the group program continuum covered in Chapter 1, your attention to this chapter may vary.

This chapter focuses on:

1. **Knowing your client:** Holding to your client's agenda is a foundational principle for coaching. One of the core principles in group coaching is knowing who your program is for. This is key to setting the foundation for your program, including your content, questions, delivery, venue, and timing. The Group Coaching Client Assessment™ template will be provided in this section.
2. **Tools for design:** The second part of this chapter will introduce a number of design tools to support you in developing your own program. These include:
   - Getting your topics: MindMaps and index cards;
   - The Group Coaching Design Matrix™; and
   - The modular approach to program development.
3. **Additional design considerations:**
   - Creating a powerful vision for your work;
   - How much do I include? Consider the 80/20 rule;
   - The accordion approach to design;
   - What's the essence I want to create?
   - What are my client's needs and preferences?
   - How much time will this take?
   - The three "Rs" to program development: reduce, reuse, and recycle; and
   - Generational differences.

PART 1: KNOWING YOUR CLIENT

As we saw in Chapter 3, two of the core differences between a training and group coaching approach are the amount of direction the group coach takes with the participants and who really drives the agenda, or what is covered, during the program. We also explored how group coaching will have less of a focus on content delivery and more on discussion and discovery.

Readers who are coaches will know how integral it is in coaching to hold the client's agenda. The agenda will include the topics, issues, and priorities a client has identified. Holding this focus on the client (or participant)—their agenda and needs—is a key distinction between coaching and training, even if you are the most participatory or experiential of trainers.

How Well Do You Know What Your Participants Want, Need, and Prefer?

A best practice we discussed in Chapter 4 was to connect with participants before the start of a program to learn more about them and their needs. In the world of training we call the process of knowing your client *needs assessment*, which is typically recommended to take 10–15 percent or more of the overall project time.[1] You may choose to complete your "Knowing Your Client" work through one-on-one discussions with individual group members, via web-based surveys such as Survey Monkey, or through other forms of formal and informal research.

Some simple questions you may want to ask in the pre-call discussion include:

1. What has led you to enroll in this program?
2. What would you like to get out of this program?
3. What are your primary needs regarding (insert topic name)?
4. What should I know about how you learn best?

The more you know about your client or participant, the more effective your program design, implementation, and marketing will be.

THE IMPORTANCE OF KNOWING YOUR CLIENT

Clients are the focus and starting point for any group coaching process.

Knowing your client as well as you can will help you exponentially in terms of:

- Creating and delivering meaningful programs;
- Addressing the themes and topics that are of greatest importance and priority for clients;
- Marketing your services most appropriately (using the best method, placement, and wording);
- Offering programs at the most convenient time;
- Offering programs in the most convenient format; and
- Providing meaningful resources for client needs.

A few years ago I created the Group Coaching Client Assessment™. This quick template helps coaches clarify who their clients are, and what their clients want.

It prompts coaches to start thinking more deeply and holistically about their clients, their needs, and their preferences.

Here are some questions to consider regarding your group coaching clients:

- What are the key goals your clients have?
- What are the key challenges they are facing?
- What is their availability? During the week/weekend/or across the year?
- What are their preferences regarding undertaking sessions—face-to-face, phone- or web-based work?
- What are their spending patterns? When do they have money available, or not? (This can be important when setting dates for their programs.)
- What is their disposable income? (This will have an impact on pricing.)
- What do they read, view, or listen to?
- What websites/newspapers/radio stations do they listen to?

The responses to these questions will influence everything from your program pricing to the date and time of offering, the themes or content being included, as well as program length and delivery mode.

The following questions and Group Coaching Client Assessment™ template are intended to support you in getting clear on who you serve. This information will be useful for marketing, program/product development, and communication purposes.

Take some time to consider the following questions. Space is provided on the following page for you to take notes:

- Who will be attracted to your products/services?
- Who do you want to attract to your products/services?
- What are their needs?
- What are the issues and challenges that are relevant to them?
- What does this client group look like?
  - Age
  - Socioeconomic status
  - Level of education
  - Geographic location
  - Employment/professional status
  - Associations they may belong to, and
  - Spending patterns.
- When do these people have income to make a purchase?

- When would be most convenient for them to access your program? What is their availability (days of the week, time of the day)?
- How can you reach this group? Which of these vehicles will you use to spread the word about your programs:
  - Media (print);
  - Word of mouth;
  - Internet;
  - Social media;
  - Publications; and
  - Professional associations.
- Who else serves this group? Who are your competitors? Who can you partner with?

If there are several distinct groups of clients you will be working with in separate group coaching programs, complete additional Knowing Your Client—Group Coaching Client Assessment™ sheets.

Not all questions will be relevant for every reader. For example, coaches or HR professionals undertaking their work internally may not necessarily need to think about the external marketing of the program, but they will need to consider this from an internal marketing standpoint. Adapt these questions based on your role, work, and function.

Table 5.1: Client Profile—Group Coaching Client Assessment™

Overall description of client:

Client's needs	
Client's main goals	
Client's main issues (of interest)	
Client's main challenges	
Age range	
Gender	
Socioeconomic status	
Geographic location	
Employment/professional status	
Spending patterns	
Associations/organizations they belong to	

(*Continued*)

Availability (days of week, times of day, seasonal differences)	
Preferred delivery format: How programs are offered (virtual/in person; length)	
Marketing approaches: Consider what are their preferences for:	
Newspapers they read	
Internet sites	
Blogs they read	
Publications they read	
Radio stations they listen to	
Experts/authors they follow	
Venues that would reflect their preferences	
Other	

As you complete your own Knowing Your Client templates, also consider the following and take note of these:

1. What are your clients' most important needs? What is their pain?
2. What are the challenges they face?
3. What are their preferences in terms of delivery:
    - phone/in person
    - dates and times
    - seasons/time of year
4. Pricing
5. Collaborators/partners for this initiative
6. Other

What is your next step in getting to know your group coaching clients?

PART 2: DESIGN

> *Whatever you can do, or dream you can...begin it.*
> *Boldness has genius, power, and magic in it.*
> —Goethe

As we have seen, group coaching can take a number of forms—virtually by phone or web, in person with groups in organizations, as well as groups of individuals coming together from the general public. Your program will be shaped by factors including your clients' needs and preferences, the themes or topics you cover, as well as your style and preferences.

This section focuses on designing your group coaching program. There are a number of tools you can use in developing your program, including:

1.   MindMaps
2.   Index cards, and
3.   Templates.

These different tools are illustrated in this chapter to provide you with the opportunity to select, adapt, and apply as you move through the design and development of your group coaching program.

DESIGN TOOL 1: MIND MAPPING

Mind Mapping is a powerful right-brained brainstorming tool. Often attributed to Tony Buzan, it is a brainstorming approach that stimulates non-linear thinking, and can be applied to developing any type of group programs.

Here's how it works:

Take out a piece of blank paper. In the middle of the page draw a circle. In the middle of the circle, write down the name of one of the topics you have for your program. For each new idea that comes into your mind about that topic, draw a line extending outwards from the circle—like a ray of the sun—and label it with this topic name. Continue with this process and write down whatever comes to mind—do not self-censor!

You may have new lines extending out related to themes/topic, exercise ideas, marketing, venue, cost. Refer to Figure 5.1 below for a sample MindMap.

Further subdivide each one of the lines and capture specific ideas or sub topics. A subtopic might be marketing ideas—for example, e-zines, professional associations, speaking events, blogging, podcasts, etc.

How to Build onto This Tool

Another design suggestion may be to pull out your MindMaps every few days or weeks and see what new ideas and concepts you can add on. You may also wish to create new versions of your MindMaps and file them so that you can see your progression.

Figure 5.1: Sample MindMap

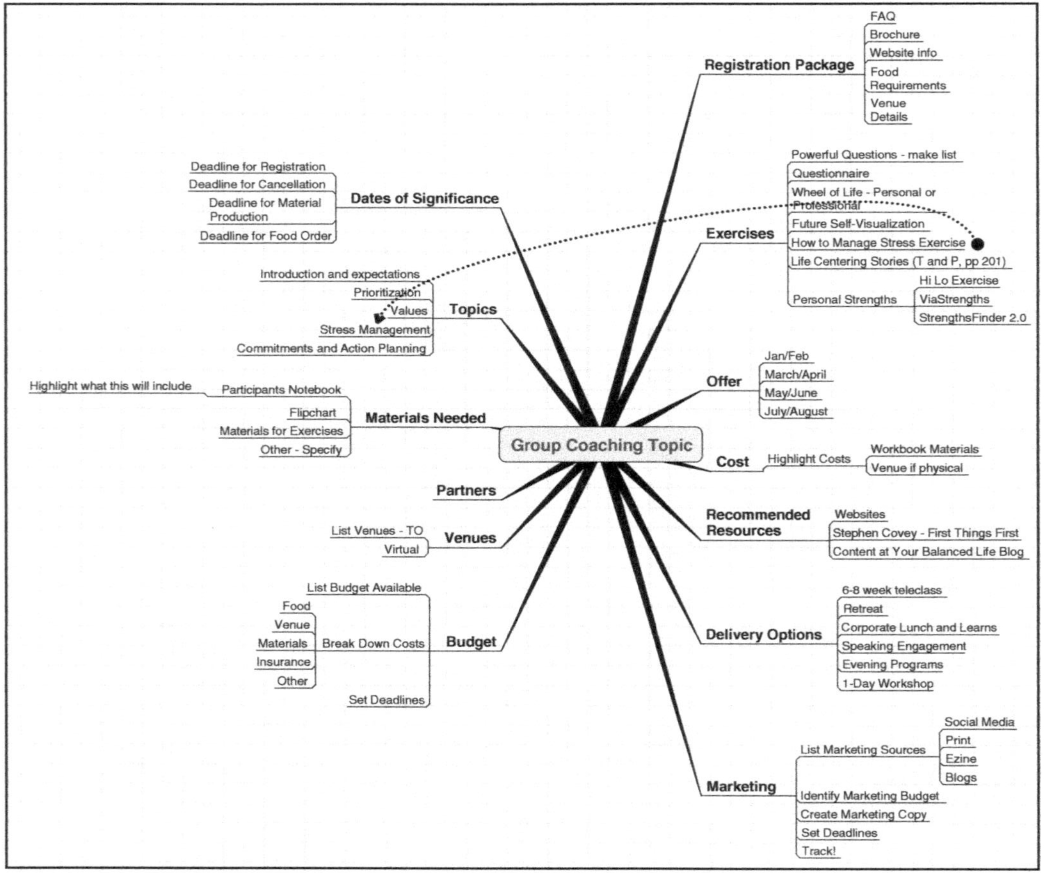

Exercise:

Take 5–10 minutes and MindMap one of your program or theme ideas. Follow the process outlined in this chapter.

After five minutes, look at what you have created. Ask yourself the following questions:

- What is emerging?
- What are the themes that are emerging?
- What exercises have you identified?
- What is clear to you?
- What is your next step?

Return to your MindMap and for the next few minutes add the following:

- What are the main topics I am addressing?
- What exercises do I want to use?
- What format do I want to offer the course in—in person or by phone?
- What will the program look like? (course length, timing, structure)
- How many participants do I want to have in the program?
- When do you want to launch the program?
- When do you need to market the program?
- Who will my participants be? Add your thoughts around:
  - Where are they located?
  - Who are they?
  - Where can you find them (i.e., Do they belong to a certain industry? Professional association?)
  - What is their demographic profile?
  - What are their needs?
  - How do they learn best?

Spend further time building onto this skeleton. Over time you may want to create separate MindMaps for each subtopic.

For those who prefer to work with a computer, there are some excellent Mind-Map tools available such as www.MindJet.com, as well as several open source applications.

MindMapping is a terrific approach for program design as well as business development and even one-on-one client work.

Questions to Consider

How can you use MindMaps with your work?

DESIGN TOOL 2: INDEX CARDS

Blank index cards can also be used as a brainstorming and program development tool.

Get out a set of blank index cards—preferably a set of fifty or more. Use one blank index card to capture one specific idea about the programs you hope to create. Take 15–20 minutes and brainstorm, writing down **one thought per card**.

Here are some questions to get you started:

- What topics do I have in mind?
- What is my program called?
- What ways can I deliver my program (in person, teleclass, or retreat)?
- What are the main topics I want to cover?
- What exercises do I already have?
- What exercises do I need to find or create?
- Who is my target audience?
- What are the main issues of interest to my target audience?
- How much will I charge for the program?
- When will I run the program?
- What venues are available to host my program?
- How will I market the program?

After your brainstorm, you will have a large stack of cards which you can now lay out on a large surface (a table or the floor). Looking at all of the cards, what themes are emerging? What connections can you create? How can these be broken down into different sections? You can sort the cards in a wide variety of ways. Use this as a starting point to develop your program. For the purposes of program development, as a starting point, you may want to **sort out the cards** according to topics and exercises.

You may either choose to develop your program simply from the index cards, or you may want to put this information into a Group Coaching Design Matrix™. You will find a copy of this matrix later in this chapter.

THE MODULAR APPROACH TO PROGRAM DEVELOPMENT

As a result of your Mind Mapping or work with index cards, it is likely that you will have enough ideas for not just one, but several, programs and products. Keep all of these ideas, and ask yourself, What type of program do I want to develop?

As mentioned in Chapter 1, group coaching programs can take a number of forms—a one-hour session, a six-week program, or a ninety-day program or longer. The choice is yours, and will often be shaped by the preferences of your clients.

One way to design your own content and material is to look at developing your materials using a modular approach. This modular approach to program development will allow you to develop shorter modules of different topics. Each shorter topic can then be mixed and matched according to what type of program you wish to run and what your client is asking for.

Metaphorically speaking, I like to use the concept of building blocks to describe and bring to light the modular approach. Imagine that the modular approach starts with shorter blocks or sections (for example, 30–90 minutes in length) with each of these representing a different building block. I might have a module (or block) on values, a separate module on strengths, or a module on priorities. I might also have a module on style—for example, leadership style, communication style, conflict style, or other. Depending on the specific needs of the client group, I can quickly combine different modules (my building blocks) to create an entirely different program (or building).

I always want to keep in mind that I am starting from the client's agenda. Therefore, a modular approach will be adapted specifically for the needs of that group. You will likely find that even if you run the "same" or similar program consecutively, that each time the program looks and feels different. This points to the different agendas, styles, and preferences that each group, and individual member of each group, will have.

Question to Consider

What modules are you seeing evolve in your initial design work?

TEMPLATES FOR DEVELOPING GROUP COACHING PROGRAMS

Some coaches may find that they are comfortable with using either the end product of a MindMap or the index cards to draw up their group coaching program and begin a session. If you are sitting along the Group Program continuum of running a purer group coaching program, you will focus more on using your coaching skills and likely won't need a detailed outline. If you are wanting to provide some content and are further to the right of the continuum (i.e., towards training), it is likely that you will want to create a more detailed road map of how the session(s) may look.

Templates are a great tool that can be used to quickly design and develop material, either separately or consecutively. You will find other templates to use, such as the Group Coaching Exercise Template in the Appendix. The main template I use for design work is the Group Coaching Design Matrix™.

After completing my brainstorming work around a program, my next step will be to take all these high-level ideas and place them into a matrix.

In general, the matrix I use for group coaching and other group programs includes the following sections:

1. Topic name;
2. Main points of the topic/learning points/content;
3. Activities/coaching questions;
4. Duration; and
5. Materials needed.

The order of these categories can be interchanged according to the way you work best. A blank template is provided for you to use.

Using the information you have come up with from either your index cards or MindMap, use the template to design either of your sessions, or one of the topics you have identified.

It is likely that your template, or matrix, will go through several different drafts, so feel free to make as many copies as you need.

To illustrate how you may want to approach it, here is the core of a coaching session I undertook with a coach to walk them through the Group Coaching Design Matrix™. I will encourage you to follow along yourself with your own program idea.

CLIENT: Jenn, I am getting really stuck with where I go after the MindMap. I have all these great ideas but I am getting stuck and I just don't know what to do next.

JB: OK. Let's break this down. First of all, what is the topic you want to further flesh out?

CLIENT: I know that I want to include a lot of different topics in the program including—values, vision, etc.

JB: OK, which one do you want to look at first?

CLIENT: Let's look at values.

JB: OK, pull out a blank Group Coaching Design Matrix. Keep in mind this is a first draft, so we want to approach this from a brainstorming perspective. I want you to get all of your ideas out—no censoring at this place.

First, under topic name, what do you want to call the topic?

CLIENT: Let's call it "My Values."

JB: OK. Write that down under "Topic name." How much time do you have available for this session?

CLIENT: 75 minutes.

JB: Write that down under "Topic Length." And this is done in person, right?

CLIENT: Yes.

JB: What are the specific things that you would like participants to leave with, or things that clients have identified as being important for them?

CLIENT: I think that it is important for clients to discover what their values are in order to support them in making more effective decisions. Values are like a compass for us in terms of deciding whether it is really aligned with us or not.

JB: Write these down under "Overall goals/objectives of the client." Anything else you want them to take away as a result of this session?

CLIENT: I want to keep the teaching piece really short to be more aligned with group coaching. I'd rather they discovered it for themselves.

JB: Perfect! Let's shift gears a bit. So what did you come up with on your MindMap for exercises? Let's start with that column on the matrix.

CLIENT: Well, there are three different ways I tend to look at the topic of values with a client:

1. I undertake values mining work with a client.
2. I could do a demonstration (demo) coaching with one client at the start of the room and have everyone else watch and observe.
3. I could give clients a values checklist to fill out before, or during, the session.

JB: Let's capture those three separate ideas under the exercises section of the template. Write those down—each on a different line. (Client writes them down.) Now how much time do you think each one would take?

CLIENT: Demo coaching may take 10 minutes followed by people moving into small groups and discussing what they saw, or perhaps asking each other coaching questions. So let's say 30 minutes in total.

In terms of values mining work, I would want to have people mine their values in a group context after they have completed a values checklist, so let's put a checklist followed by values mining.

JB: So, I am hearing that you are going to shift the values mining later. How much time do you think the checklist will take?

CLIENT: Let's give them 12–15 minutes to complete it individually.

JB: OK, write that down in the time frame. How about the values mining exercise? How long will that take?

CLIENT: I'm thinking that there is probably some really good discussion there, so let's say, 20 minutes for sharing and debrief.

JB: Great—write that in accordingly and let's move on. What materials will you need for each of the different approaches? Do you have a checklist already?

CLIENT: Demo coaching—I would want to have some core questions written down on a flip chart, and I think I would want to note these.

Values checklist—I will need to put one of these in their notebook. Luckily I already have one that I can adapt for this group.

Values mining—I would have them write it down in their manual/notebook.

JB: Perfect. I think that you are getting the hang of this. My request is that you complete at least one, if not more, drafts of the Design Matrix for this module before our next call. Will you do that?

CLIENT: Yes, I will. In fact, by our next call I want to have mapped out the first three[1] modules of the series as my program is launching in a few weeks. I think that this will keep me motivated and will give me a start.

JB: Great work! Let's check in around this next call.

To the reader: Now here is your task. Using the Group Coaching Design Matrix™ template on the next page, draft at least one of your modules.

Some General Principles for Design Work

- Allow yourself to freely brainstorm—don't self-censor.
- Use the approach that works best for you—by hand or computer.
- Keep drafts—you may wish to start a file or even a binder with your Mind-Maps and design matrices. Note the date and version on ones you file away. You never know when earlier design ideas will spark new program ideas or be suitable for another client group.
- Version your drafts as Version 1.0, 1.1, 1.2 and date them so you can see the progression.

Additional Considerations during the Design Phase

There are several additional considerations to keep in mind during the design phase. These include:

- Creating a powerful vision for your group coaching work.
- How much do I include? Consider the 80/20 rule.
- The "accordion approach" to design.
- What's the essence I want to create?
- What are my client's needs and preferences?
- How much time will this take?
- Look at the three "Rs" to program development.

Table 5.2: Group Coaching Design Matrix™

Topic name: _____

Topic length: _____

Overall goals or objectives of the topic/what you want the clients to take away from the session:

_____

_____

_____

Duration	Content/Learning Points	Activities/Coaching Questions	Materials Needed

Creating a Powerful Vision for Your Group Coaching Work

Having a clear vision of where you want to go with group coaching in your business or work will often make your design work much clearer as well as more fun. Creating a powerful vision helps us see the bigger picture and is often a motivator when we hit rocky patches.

Take some time to reflect on the following questions: What is your intention for group coaching? What do you want to create? What topics do you, or your clients, want to sink their teeth into?

Here are some other questions to get you **focusing** in on your group coaching vision:

- Who is your audience?
- What type of group coaching program do you want to develop—in person, by phone?
- When will you launch the program?
- When will you offer the program?
- How many clients do you want to serve this year through group coaching?
- How much revenue do you want to create from group coaching?
- Who can you partner with?
- What resources do you already have available?
- What additional resources do you need?
- How will you publicize your program(s)?
- What marketing tools will you use?
- It is two years from now and I have accomplished the following with my group coaching work:
  - I have worked with _____ clients;
  - I have delivered _____ programs.

How Much Do I Include? The 80/20 Rule

A number of coaches often ask me, "How do I know how much content to fit into a group coaching session?" As we discussed in Chapter 1, there is the Continuum of Group Processes of where you sit along the range of group programs—from the traditional "teleclass" model, where the coach does the vast majority of the talking and information delivery, to an organic "dance" and purer group coaching model with the clients, where the clients bring the agenda at the start of the session or program and this shapes your direction.

Regardless of where you sit along the continuum, there is an innate tendency for coaches (as well as trainers and speakers) to want to fit "everything" into their program. This can lead to overload for the participants, as well as a more directive program leaving little space for the participants to:

- Discover new information or insights;
- Integrate what they are learning;
- Discuss with colleagues; and
- Create action plans or identify commitments essential before the next session.

These four activities are all in the group coaching approach.

I often speak about the 80/20 rule when designing programs for groups. The 80/20 rule works like this: Take a look at the overall information you want to cover during an upcoming program or session. As you look at everything you want to cover, carve out 20 percent of it. Put this aside—you may want to put this in another file. This can become the seeds for another new program or topic. You will be left with about 80 percent of the content now.

What happens when you take away 20 percent of the material? Notice what happens. Does it leave more space for personal discovery? Less overload? More space for discussion and sharing?

My request for you is to carve up your upcoming program into the 20 percent you will put aside for another program, and the 80 percent you are going to keep. What happens?

The Accordion Approach to Design

One of the most fascinating things that keeps group coaching really fresh for me is the fact that each time I run a program it looks different—because each group and the people within that group are different!

In creating a road map for where you are going to go prior to the session, it is often useful to keep in mind the idea of a metaphor of an accordion:

- Which pieces or exercises can be expanded if time is moving very quickly and you have lots of time?
- Which pieces can be contracted/shortened or not touched if the discussion has elongated in another session?

Take note of these, especially if you are co-facilitating.

As you become more experienced as a group coach, your pre-session preparation may simply be a design matrix with some notes around what gets "accordioned" out and in.

What Is the Essence of Your Program?

You may be faced with the situation of having to design programs that are very similar for different audiences. Whether it's been for couples' retreats, leadership development programs, or small business workshops, I've often had the design of similar programs on the go. A key question I like to consider is:

What's the essence I want to create in this program? How is it different from other programs?

Here is an example of how essence became important in a couples retreat program called Relationships On Fire I run with coach Sharon Miller.

To help us become clear on what we wanted to create, we asked questions such as:

- What is the energy we want to create?
- What is the ambiance?
- What colors come to mind with the program?
- What are some of the metaphors which would represent the program?
- What is the feel we want to create?

Keep in mind that we had already drafted the program and objectives. By being really clear on the essence we wanted to create, it gave us a new strategic focus and made it really easy to start developing our marketing message for the retreat.

Time, Time ... How Much Time Will This Take?

A question I often get asked is: how much time will it take me to design this program? A standard statistic I throw out is a commonly held instructional design metric—that for every one hour of classroom instruction it may take upwards of forty hours of preparation.[2]

Depending on where you put yourself on the continuum, prep time to get ready for one hour of face-to-face (or voice-to-voice) work will probably not take forty hours; however, do take the following into consideration with your time investment:

- Pre-session discussions with clients—finding out who they are, along with their needs and preferences.
- Marketing the program—strategy development, material design, website/blog/brochure, etc., and promotion.
- Systems development—payment, registration, and bridgeline (refer to Chapter 9).
- Program vision and design work—this can take the bulk of the time depending on how you work.

What else would you include as pre-program time investment?

Don't fall into the trap of needing to be 100 percent prepared (or the place of analysis/paralysis). If you are a coach, you will already have a number of core skills you can use right way with your group. Our best work as coaches occurs when we are fully present and able to listen to what the client needs, and respond by moving on our feet. Practically, this may mean coming to a session with a number of ideas about tools or exercises to select from "in the moment" rather than having everything laid out. As coaches gain more experience, it is likely that your pre-preparation time will be shortened.

The Three "Rs" to Program Development—Reduce, Reuse, and Recycle

Many of us are very familiar with the three "Rs" to environmental action—Reduce, Reuse, and Recycle. The three "Rs" are great principles to apply when developing your next group program—workshop, retreat, or group coaching program.

1. Reduce: Follow the **less is more** principle. Rather than trying to fit everything, including the kitchen sink, into your next group program, apply the 80/20 rule and set at least 20 percent of the content aside. This content can be used as the foundation for a new program or as follow-up to your program. Participants will thank you as they avoid being overwhelmed with information overload, and have a chance to really engage with, and integrate, the material you do provide.

What program content can you reduce or practice the 80/20 rule on?

2. Reuse: What programs are you currently offering? How could you leverage and repackage these program offerings so that they could be delivered to a wider audience?

For example, over the years I have developed a number of different streams of group programs: The Your Balanced Life™ program and the BizSuccess Group Coaching™ program for business owners. I offer these programs in a number of different formats—ninety-day group coaching program by phone, a weekend retreat, a virtual retreat (by phone over a six-hour period over one to two days), short-term speaking engagements, and also corporate workshops (Your Balanced Life). The skeleton and main content for each of these programs is the same, it's just put together with different delivery options and some changes to meet the needs of different groups.

What programs can you reuse to meet the needs of different audiences? How could you deliver some of your current programs differently?

3. Recycle: You have just read about the modular approach to program development, where discrete mini-sessions are developed as separate entities which can then be put together with other modules to create entirely new programs, depending on the needs of the audience.

Think about modular program development like the building blocks of different pieces of LEGO. You may have a one-hour module on developing your vision, a one-hour module on leadership, a one-hour module on providing feedback, and one on values. Depending on the needs of the client or the group you are developing your program for, you can select different LEGO pieces or building blocks to create an entirely different structure. With a few small tweaks to further customize, you've got a new program there!

What modules do you already have on hand? What can you construct from what you have right now?

Generational Preferences

There has been quite a bit of writing about generational preferences for learning. In knowing your client, you will want to consider how your learners' generational affiliation (Veteran, Boomer, Gen Xer, Millennial, etc.) will shape design considerations such as delivery mechanisms (virtual versus in person), how materials are produced (online PDFs, USBs versus hard-copy manuals), and how exercises are facilitated.

Over the years, different generations have been socialized to learn in different ways:

Veterans (pre-1945): Veterans grew up in the world of chalk-and-talk, rote memorization, and extensive classroom lectures.

Baby Boomers (1946–1964): Boomers typically had a lecture-based learning environment, and over the course of their careers engaged in more book learning and most likely structured seminars and lecture-based programs. Within the Boomer generation there often exists a wide range of experiences and preferences in terms of learning approaches.

Additional considerations when working with Boomers include:

- How to leverage and draw in their extensive expertise; and
- How to support them through any technology issues/challenges they perceive (i.e., webinar/teleconferencing logistics or e-learning platforms).

Gen Xer: 1965–1980: Gen Xers grew up with hands-on learning, and learned a lot through play and small group experiences. We had large computers in the classroom as we got older. CDs and distance learning is probably more familiar. Finally becoming the managers of today, Gen Xers are quite familiar with juggling different demands. Despite what's said, many Gen Xers may be technologically savvy, adopting blogs, podcasts, and other social media tools for their learning. Not all of us are as "cynical" as we are perceived to be, although I think it is fair to say we want good value and ways to make our life, work, and family merge together. Gen Xers will appreciate the link back to reality.

Millennials/Gen Y: 1980–1999: Digital natives. Technology has always been a part of their lives and this generation grew up with computers in the classroom from a very early age. Millennials and Gen Ys value collaboration, and are often the pioneers in matching technology with collaboration. Gen Ys will be very comfortable engaging with m-learning strategies such as podcasts, learning on demand, etc. Wikis, blogs, and social media are a natural part of their everyday world of work and communication, and consideration should be taken about their inclusion in group coaching programs specific to this generation. Listen carefully for what members of this group really want and who they are influenced by, as this group is more connected and savvy than most others.

In contrast to Gen Xers who have developed a reputation of being "cynical" as a generation; Gen Ys are seen as being very impatient in wanting to move forward with their careers. Gen Ys/Millennials will benefit from being in the spotlight and having their needs explicitly addressed.

Working with Gen Ys, as well as Gen Xers, as clients will provide coaches the space to undertake some very innovative, and likely groundbreaking, work.

Questions to Consider

What do you know about the generational preferences of your clients?

What impact will this have on your group coaching design and/or delivery?

CHAPTER REVIEW

Before moving forward to the next chapter:

- ☐ Spend at least 15 minutes brainstorming your ideas for your group coaching program. You may choose to:
  - MindMap
  - Use index cards
  - Make a list of your ideas
- ☐ Complete drafts of your own design matrix/ces.
- ☐ Identify your big picture group coaching vision.

CHAPTER 6

POWERFUL DELIVERY OPTIONS: IN PERSON OR VIRTUAL

Group coaching programs can be delivered in person or virtually (by phone or web.) This chapter will focus on a number of important differences between in-person and phone-based programs, as well as key considerations for coaches when deciding what they want to create for their clients and **how** they want to deliver their programs.

The focus in this chapter will be to equip you for work in the virtual environment, particularly by phone. In-person issues are covered in greater depth in further chapters—namely, Chapters 7, 9, and 10. A short self-assessment to check your readiness for hosting and leading a virtual program is also provided.

By this stage you may have a good idea as to whether you want to deliver your program in person or virtually, either by phone and/or web. In general, some of the factors that will influence your delivery method include:

- Location of clients;
- Preference of clients;
- Your personal preferences;
- Your own location;
- Your niche/area of focus; and
- Technologies available to you and your clients.

Questions to consider when deciding whether to go virtual, include:

- Where are my clients?
- What are their preferences?

- What is their comfort level using technology?
- What is my comfort level using technology?
- Which technologies are they most comfortable with?
- What barriers may exist with my clients in terms of services available (i.e., bandwidth, speed, etc.)?
- What materials do I need to adapt?
- How do I need to adapt them?

THE ADVANTAGES AND DISADVANTAGES OF IN-PERSON AND VIRTUAL PROGRAMS

Both delivery methods—in person and virtual—have unique advantages as well as disadvantages. Some of these advantages and disadvantages are listed below:

Table 6.1: Advantages and Disadvantages of In-Person and Virtual Programs

Delivery Mode	Advantages	Disadvantages
In Person	Leverages basic small group facilitation skills Able to see participants and benefit from the visual cues of the group Many clients will have a preference for this. The ICF Global Coaching Survey found that 50% of client respondents preferred face-to-face sessions[1]	Costs (financial/time) involved for participants to participate from around the world Overhead costs for facilitator—venue rental Time involved to travel to venue (for participants and coach) Limited ability of a wider cross-section of clients to participate in the program, depending on their geographic location
By Phone/ Virtual (held by phone or web)	No, or low, overhead cost Allows for a wider cross-section of individuals from diverse geographies to participate People can participate from their home, office, cottage, or other location Advantage of lower travel costs to participate Able to work with groups from diverse backgrounds	Phone-based programs' lack of visual cues can lead to the need for a different facilitation approach More logistics required to break the group into smaller groups May require even more developed facilitation skills given the virtual environment

| | Many coaches already have strong skills in phone-based work | |
| | Greener—reduces the carbon footprint[2] as participants and coach do not need to travel. Materials may also be produced electronically only | |

When we look at coaching in general, the ICF Global Coaching Client Survey found almost an even split between phone (47 percent) and in person (50 percent) work which coaches undertake, although it varies from region to region.[3] When clients were asked which method they prefer, a majority of clients, 60 percent, prefer in person coaching. Approximately 35 percent prefer telephone coaching.

SYNCHRONOUS OR ASYNCHRONOUS?

Learning is characterized as happening either synchronous (at the same time) or asynchronous (at different times).

Synchronous (Real-Time Learning)

In the first instance, you can have people learning in the *same time/same place* or what we know as traditional face-to-face learning.

Two, you may hold learning events which are held in the *same time/different place*. These approaches may include teleconference, web, teleconferencing, or video conferencing. Many group coaching programs leverage either of these approaches. The immediate connection and real-time interaction adds great value for clients.

Commonly referred to as **synchronous online learning**—"Participants in dispersed locations meet online in real time and communicate via text with chat, visuals such as PowerPoint slides and whiteboards, and audio tools that include Voice Over IP and teleconferencing.[4]"

Asynchronous Learning (Self-Paced)

> *"Asynchronous online learning: Self-paced as opposed to real time; participants access the training at their convenience."*[5]

There may be instances in any learning program where people are logging in at *different times and the same place*.

Example:

Organizations often roll out e-learning to their workforce using an asynchronous approach—where all staff can participate in the same e-training on a topic such as security or leadership, but at different times. The materials may be housed on an intranet or other web portal.

Finally, you may have learning events where people are logging in from *different times and different places*—this may include email communication and shared documents. Many online learning platforms operate with this one-way component, linking learners from around the world who can access the information at their time/place and pace.

This different time/different approach is commonly used in training and may be a support component for a group coaching program. Several coach interviews have asynchronous components to their programs—such as my 90 Day BizSuccess e-BizTopics which are delivered to participants, as well as Mary Allen's and Eva Gregory's use of a Yahoo! group to share information and conversation.

This chapter focuses primarily on synchronous (same time) and distributed (different place) learning opportunities—i.e., phone-based group coaching programs, as well as those programs using a teleseminar or webinar approach.

Virtual Programs

There are a range of virtual programs available in the marketplace, including:

- One-month programs
- Ninety-day programs
- Six-month programs
- One-year programs
- Hybrid programs consisting of a mix of one-on-one and group coaching sessions
- Virtual retreats
- Accountability days.

Many coaches are focusing 100 percent of their time on delivering virtual group coaching programs. Others opt to continue to have a mix of in person and virtual programs. Several years ago when my son was born, I decided that I wanted to be home with him as much possible. This led to my own preference for virtual work (one-on-one and group coaching). Even now, about 80 percent of my work with clients is virtual.

With technology changing so rapidly, new approaches to undertake our work are opening up all of the time.

What follows are three different examples of how coaches are delivering group coaching, primarily via virtual channels.

In the Spotlight:
Heidi Michaels, CPCC, Virtual Vision Board
(www.heidimichaels.com)

I offer a variety of workshops, seminars, and webinars. I utilize workshops as an inexpensive way for people to experience coaching. It's also a way for me to gain exposure and bring people into my "funnel." My seminars are a sequential type of workshop; usually I offer four- to five-week sessions and they are at a slightly higher price point. My newest venture is what I call my "Virtual Vision Board" workshop.

Virtual Vision Board: I offer this once each month. I co-host this with my web designer, Misty. I provide the coaching, she provides the technical know-how. Participants take a look at where they are now and where they'd like to be and create the vision of that by creating a vision board. The vision board is created on their own computers using photos clipped from a clipart site we provide.

This program first started as a Vision Board Workshop which was offered to small groups at my office. I then started offering it as a "Girls Night Out" event, which women could participate in, rather than going out. Now it has evolved to the Virtual Vision Board program, where participants work on computer. It's like virtual scrapbooking and I've had participants from all over, including California and New York.

In the Spotlight:
Eva Gregory, CPCC
(www.leadingedgecoaching.com)

Eva Gregory has been a group coach for almost ten years. A majority of her work is done virtually.

Gregory notes that the timing for group coaching couldn't be better specifically with the economy right now. Some of the benefits include:

- It allows you to work with clients who can't afford it. You can create group programs and allow them to work with us at a less expensive rate.

- Group coaching involves the whole power of having a group. Gregory notes the following about the group process:
  - Wisdom of group coaching;
  - Questions of the group will trigger new insights;
  - Observing the coach—witnessing the coach can trigger new insights; and
  - Community that gets created—support not just about them.

Gregory offers a range of programs, including:

- Beyond Six Figures for Coaches Certification Program: Launching and Leading Group Coaching Program;
- Bigger Impact Law of Attraction Certification Program;
- Six-Figure Biz Builder;
- The Prosperity Game; and
- Channel Surfing: Riding the Waves of Inner Guidance.

What have been your successes with group coaching?

I broke through the $100,000 annual revenue mark to make a healthy six-figure income by launching and leading my own group coaching programs called "Leading Edge Living One Year Success Program," which I ran for about six years. The clients in my program created their own great results and many asked for a year two program, so my "Leading Edge Living Year Two Mastery Program" was born.

In fact, I so love the group coaching work that I stopped working with one-on-one clients except on rare occasions. My main focus is on launching and leading my group programs.

What do you see as essential "must-haves" for coaches?

1. Create a client list. Social media is making this much easier. The good news is that it does not take that long to cultivate a list.
2. Acquire the skills for group coaching—get a clear idea of what you want to create with your group coaching work.

Why offer group coaching?

As Eva Gregory and her partner Mary Allen write, the seven reasons to offer group coaching programs are:

1. **Offering group coaching programs establishes you as an expert in your area of focus.**

   It becomes assumed, that if you're leading groups you must have something important to say. *Boosting your credibility* is a wonderful benefit. This means you'll be getting more invitations to speak, do media appearances, and become more visible in your niche.

2. **You'll be *helping more clients*, and as you do, you will exponentially grow your skills as a coach and expert.**

   For any coach who works with a larger number of people, it's the perfect structure to challenge the best from you. We've grown and strengthened our skills and expertise because we've worked with lots of *real* people.

3. **Your confidence will soar as your participants appreciate and acknowledge your brilliance as a coach.**

   There is something about the group setting which encourages lots of feedback. You will get validation beyond belief. We personally love this one. Eva Gregory was voted International Coach of the Year due to all the people she impacted worldwide.

4. **Your one–on–one coaching practice will grow too (if you want it to)!**

   By witnessing you in a group setting, your clients' confidence in you skyrockets. About 25 percent of our group coaching clients hire us for one–on–one work. And some clients will decide they just want one–on–one, as you market your group programs.

5. **Your income will become more stable and *profitable*.**

   Leading groups offers security, especially when you're leading six-month and year-long programs. Clients may come and go, but groups commit to a designated period of time up-front. This gives you additional peace of mind, financially.

   (Continued)

6. **All *seven-figure* coaches run group coaching programs.**

   You've probably heard of these famous coaches: Jack Canfield of *Chicken Soup for the Soul* fame; Marc Allen, founder of *New World Library* and publisher of Eckhart Tolle's *The Power of Now* and *A New Earth*; and Bob Proctor and Joe Vitale featured in *The Secret*. They all offer group coaching programs!

7. **Group coaching offers exponential *value* to clients you simply can't deliver as a solo coach.**

   In addition to having your support, they benefit exponentially through the group interactions in countless ways. We've seen numerous life-long friendships born via group coaching programs. Participants also benefit as they witness you coaching others. *It's a win-win for you and your clients.* And, if you design your programs as we have, your clients will inspire and empower other participants in ways you could never do running a business solo.

(Source: www.sixfiguresforcoaches.com)

As far as Eva's personal bottom line, she went from earning about $60,000–$70,000 per year to almost $250,000 from launching and leading group coaching programs.

 ## In the Spotlight:
Mary Allen, MCC, CPCC, GUG

I have been heavily immersed in group coaching for the last three and a half to four years, and lightly for six years. I modeled Eva Gregory, who was one of my MasterMind partners for ten years. When Eva Gregory launched a year-long program at $99 a month, I thought this sounded great. I had about $30,000 in debt and was engaged to be married. After I came off my book tour for *Power of Inner Choice*, I realized books sales were not going to handle the debt. My tax accountant shared a story about how he waited five years to marry his wife until she got out of debt . . . and that put a fire under me.

How I Did It

I created a marketing letter in December, invited people in January, the first group started in February, the second group in May, the third in August, and the fourth in September. In nine months, I went from being $30,000 in debt to having $20,000 in savings by adding group coaching programs.

Group coaching programs Mary Allen offers include:

- The Success and Inner Peace Boot Camp: A Year-long Life Mastery Group Coaching Program: four calls per month—three with a lesson focus and on the fourth call, all groups roll into the call for an open coaching forum or guest expert call.
- Quantum Inner Peace Mastermind (for graduates of the Success and Inner Peace Boot Camp): Six months—four calls a month as above.
- Beyond Six Figures for Coaches: Six-month certification program training coaches to launch and lead their own group coaching programs. (Three group calls per month, plus ten guest expert calls over six months, plus masterminding among participants.)

All programs are offered virtually. She also offers a weekend workshop for the Quantum Inner Peace Mastermind group.

What attracted me to group coaching is a desire to help more people. I had reached a limit of people I could take on in my one-on practice and I wanted/needed to make more money to handle debt.

I launched four groups within eight months—twelve, twenty, eighteen, and twenty-one—a lot harvested from my e-zine list. I also host free live conference call interviews (Conversations with the Masters). People knew me and wanted something more. Until group coaching, I didn't have anything to offer—and as soon as I did, they jumped at it!

WHEN YOU HAVE DECIDED TO GO VIRTUAL

The role of the virtual facilitator is quite similar to facilitating an in-person group with some additional considerations. Coaches working in virtual environments need to bring the core skills mentioned in Chapter 3, in addition to enhanced skills in:

- Listening—to what *is* said and *not* said;
- Call management;
- Group process; and
- Dealing with difficult issues and people.

Six Critical Success Factors for Virtual Meetings:

1. Planning a viable agenda or series of agendas
2. Effective use of technology
3. Preparing participants and pre-work (have people attend the call, and ensure people are focused—use ground rules)
4. Keeping participants focused and engaged during a virtual meeting
5. Building trust and social capital
6. Maintaining momentum between meetings

Source: Julia Young, 2009[6]

Skills Needed for the Virtual Environment

William Rothwell states: "The reality is that the competencies essential for a good facilitator are pretty much the same regardless of venue. It is true, however, that online and other electronically mediated facilitation may require special competencies in using the technology."[7]

The vast majority of literature about virtual learning places it in the context of *virtual* teams. Although group coaches may not work with teams, many of these principles can be adapted for the group context.

Fran Rees, the author of *Facilitator Excellence,* states: "Facilitators of virtual teams must find ways for team members to give input, see one another's ideas, respond to teammates ideas, and brainstorm effective solutions."[8]

Margaret Bailey and Lara Luetkehans[9] identify core areas which facilitators must consider when working with virtual learning teams, including task/problem, team dynamics and interaction, team member roles, mediated communication, and facilitation. Specifically they encourage facilitators to:

- Help team members feel connected to the group and the facilitator;
- Provide timely and meaningful feedback; and
- Intervene to highlight areas of common ground among conflicting team members.

These core components are just as important in the group coaching context.

Key principles for virtual work you will want to consider are:

- Fostering trust within the group;
- Create space for check-ins;
- Allow participants to get to know each other on the call and outside of it;
- The importance and comfort with silence;
- Minimize group size: Facilitating in a virtual world can be more challenging at first;
- Look at recording options for those who cannot make the call. Be explicit with the group in terms of how you will use the recordings;
- Ask the group "What type of environment do we want to create together?" Create ground rules or ways of working at the start;
- Maintain an environment of confidentiality; and
- Encourage asynchronous communication between sessions—i.e., Yahoo! groups/whiteboard, etc.

Questions to consider when moving an in person program to a virtual setting:

- What are the components I can keep as is?
- What modifications do I need to make?
- Which exercises may be moved to an assignment that participants complete between calls?
- How do I need to change the materials I provide?
- How long will this program take in a virtual setting?

Keeping Your Clients Engaged Virtually

Keeping clients engaged in a virtual environment is very important. You may be competing with e-mail and other immediate distractions. Ways to engage participants in a virtual environment include:

- Start your call with a check-in so everyone is heard;
- Take a break every 7–10 minutes to check in or change pace;
- Vary approach in delivery—ask questions, mini-lecture;
- Ask participants questions—round-robins;
- Complete short exercises by phone (i.e., mind mapping, vision question, drawing);
- Note who is contributing and who is not;

- Check in regularly with how the pulse of the group is going;
- Start on time and end on time;
- Provide a clear direction of where you are going;
- Create ground rules at the start;
- Encourage everyone to be off mute; and
- Look at different roles group members can take (time keeper, scribe, etc.).

Tips for Your Next Phone-Based Program

Whether you are new or experienced when it comes to phone-based group coaching work, here are some key considerations when hosting your next call.

Logistics/Bridgelines

1. **Select a reliable bridgeline service:** Not all bridgeline services are equal. Select a bridgeline that works for you and your clients in terms of location, reliability, and services associated. Does the bridgeline offer a toll free call-in option? At what cost? Does the bridgeline offer call recording services—free or at cost? What is call quality like? What is the maximum number of callers it can host? Do you need to reserve the line or is it available to you 24/7?

2. **Call recording:** I often get asked about recording group coaching calls—How do you do it? and Should I do it? Typically, I digitally record each call for internal group playback only. This added feature is often seen as a great benefit for participants who might not be able to make all the calls and want to be able to listen in at their convenience. I often get asked, "Why not bundle your program into a home study course?" At this point, to maintain the integrity and confidentiality of coaching, I have opted to share recordings only within the individual coaching groups, unless consent has been obtained from participants that I can share their materials. Always have a back-up bridgeline that you can switch to, and alert participants that should there need to be a change, either to call that number or that you will email them with instructions.

3. **Examine your call length:** How long do you really need for your group coaching call? Will an hour be enough? Map out your exercises and

content prior to finalizing your call length and time (see next point). An average of about 60–90 minutes was indicated by the coaches interviewed as their preferred time frame for call length.

4. **Examine your call content:** Less is more. Consider the 80/20 rule to content development. When considering what to include in your next group coaching session, set aside 20 percent of what you thought you would cover and leave this as the seeds for a new program or a new session. Notice what happens when you provide more space for dialogue. Remember that group coaching is more about dialogue and reflection than content and teaching.

Process Tips

1. **Provide an agenda at the start of the call:** Let people know where you are going even if it is a broad-stroke picture. Refer to this throughout the call, as people do not have the same visual cues and can find it disruptive.

2. **Discuss expectations at the start of the call:** This can be done prior to the program through one-on-one calls or as part of a mini-exercise undertaken round-robin (i.e., hopes, fears, and fantasies).

3. **Create ground rules at the start of a series of programs.** While there are some core ground rules you want to include in all programs (refer to Chapter 4), there are additional ground rules to consider for phone-based programs. These can be found in a text box in this chapter.

4. **Recap main points/themes emerging along the way** for reinforcement, summary, and to support non-auditory learners.

5. **Check in with your clients regularly to see how they are doing and if there are any questions:** Lacking the visual cues of face-to-face work, group coaching work by phone requires a different focus on keeping your clients engaged and interactive throughout the session. Check in frequently with your clients. Several ways to do this may be by asking a question and having all participants "pop" with their responses, or it may be asking them to self-evaluate their own engagement levels on a 0–10 scale. Recommendation—check in with clients every 7–10 minutes.

6. These breaks/resting spots every 7 minutes throughout the call allow for space to change the pace and activity type. They also provide opportunities for interaction between group members or for participants to ask questions and to keep people engaged.

Learning Styles

1. Provide visual cues wherever possible: Remember that 60 percent of adult learners are primarily visual. This could mean providing them with the following:
   - A handout/workbook prior to the call, which they can take notes in (and reference is made to throughout the call).
   - Adding a webinar component—webinars have the added advantage that there may be a whiteboard which everyone can see. Do not assume, however, that all callers are able to log in and/or access the technology.
2. Meet the needs of various learning styles throughout your call: Ask yourself: What can I do to meet the needs of:
   - Kinesthetic learners—those learners who learn through activity?
   - Visual learners—those learners who learn by seeing?
   - Auditory learners—those learners who learn by hearing?
   - Given that the channel of phone-based work is primarily auditory, is there anything else you want to put in place to support these learners?

Exercises In the Virtual Environment

1. **Include exercises in your online session** just as you would in person, but now with a **twist.** Exercises may be as simple as undertaking mind mapping, personal logos, or SWOT analysis, but have people engaged and active during the call. Use a variety of exercises—have people not only speak but also write.
2. **Consider what twists or adaptations you need to make** on some of your favorite face-to-face exercises and tools. Many coaches and facilitators are surprised at how some of their favorite activities can be adapted for phone-based work. What changes do you need to make? What pre-work can be undertaken before the call? What new supports/tools need to be developed to have this exercise fly by phone? A number of exercises found in the Appendix include suggestions on how to adapt exercises for the virtual domain.
3. **Consider what pre-work is needed:** Phone-based call time can go by very quickly. What pre-work (readings, assessments, exercises, notes, etc.) will help clients come to the call prepared and ready to engage? Consider what materials participants can benefit from before the call. A major difference with virtual programs is that it may be easier to have clients complete as-

signments pre-call rather than undertake longer exercises on the call. Use the call time for discussion and debrief. For reminders/prompts about debriefing, please refer back to the questions included in Chapter 2.

4. **Keep track of participant engagement:** Notice who is speaking and who is quiet. Is anyone hogging the airtime? How does verbal engagement match what you know of the participant—introverted/extroverted and the way they learn?

5. **Create a virtual table:** One way I like to manage group dynamics in a phone-based program is by inviting participants at the start of a call to check in by sitting down at a virtual table. I ask participants at the start of the call to draw a table in their booklet—square/rectangular/circle— and place me at one location of the table. As people check in, I ask group members to write down the names as they "sit" themselves around the table. This visual map helps us quickly go round the circle with discussion questions and also makes the end-of-call checkouts that much faster. This map/approach can be redone each session.

6. **Minimize muting:** In the context of group coaching, I like to minimize the mute function wherever possible. Encourage participants to call in from a landline in a quiet location. Provide instructions to participants at the start of a program on how to mute in the event that it is needed. There is nothing worse than poor call quality because of background noise or heavy breathing from a participant.

   Given the inter-activity, intimate, and personalized nature of group coaching, I encourage participants not to mute themselves unless absolutely necessary.

Refer to the Appendix for a selection of Exercises for Group Coaching, including some twists for the virtual environment.

Ground Rules for the Virtual Environment

Group rules for the virtual environment are similar to other programs (refer to Chapters 4 and 7—Ground Rules).

Additional instructions and ground rules you will want to include for phone-based programs include:

- Reduce any distractions during the call. Please turn off your Black-Berry, cell phones, email, etc.

- Call in on time (and even a minute or two before the call).
- If you are early and no one is on the line, wait. Bridgelines can get busy at the hour.
- If you have call-waiting on your line, please disable it prior to the call.
- Call in from a quiet location or use your phone's mute button if you are in a noisy environment (TV noise, dogs barking, children crying).
- It is ideal to call using a corded land-based phone. Calling in using a cell phone or VoIP may reduce the telephone quality for the whole call. Please avoid these where possible.
- If you have other phones in your room, turn off all ringers before calling in.
- If you become disconnected, call back immediately.
- Please introduce yourself each time you talk so we all know who it is that's speaking. For example, "Hi, this is ..."
- Be sensitive to the fact that we want to hear from everyone. Practice the skill of bottom-lining and be aware of how much airtime you are using.

I often include these in a Frequently Asked Questions (FAQs) one-pager that I send out prior to the call, or have available for download on my website.

Questions to Consider

Phone-based work can have tremendous impact for both your client and yourself.

What's your learning edge around taking your work to a virtual setting?

What skills do you need to develop?

What things (systems) do you need to put into place?

Ten Essential Elements for Any Phone-Based Program

- Bridgeline (with back-up bridgeline as well!).
- Mute function. Things to look for:
  - Mute function on your bridgeline service so:
    - participants can mute and un-mute themselves (as needed); and you can mute others as needed.

- ○ Mute function on your phone set and/or head set (in case you need to cough or sneeze).
- A timer.
- A phone with well-charged battery.
- A quiet room.
- Participant workbook to meet the needs of visual learners.
- Web-based presentation ability (i.e., WebEx or other).
- Recording ability.
- Flash function on your phone—some recording facilities require that you press flash to start the bridgeline recording.
- Instruction sheet or FAQs to send to participants prior to the call. This is very important to have in place for non-coaches who may not be familiar or comfortable with bridgelines, for example.

Table 6.2: Self-Assessment: Are You Ready to Lead a Virtual Program?

Rate yourself on a scale of 1–10 on the following questions related to virtual facilitation (1 being very low, 10 being expert):											
	1	2	3	4	5	6	7	8	9	10	n/a
I know how to use a teleconference bridgeline											
I have a bridgeline available to host my programs											
I know how to use a virtual platform such as WebEx											
I have used a web-based platform to deliver a group program											
I have a virtual "chat" room or communication group such as Yahoo! groups or other, where participants can meet and share information among the group											
I have a plan in the event of technology breakdown											

(Continued)

Table 6.2 (*Continued*)

	1	2	3	4	5	6	7	8	9	10	n/a
I have ground rules established for the virtual meeting											
I know how to record my calls											
I know how to mute all callers if needed											
I have multiple bridgelines available for breakouts											
I know how to create connections between members of the group											
I have a plan to create connections with participants before the program											
I know how to create a safe and confidential environment on the phone											
I know how to build trust within the virtual group											
I know how to manage conflict in a virtual environment											
I am comfortable with silence											
I know how to check whether silence is a sign of agreement/ disagreement											
I know how to adapt some of my favorite coaching exercises for the phone											
I know how to address other learning styles (i.e., visual/kines-thetic) during a virtual program											
Other											

After completing your assessment, review it, and note your responses to these four points:

- My biggest strengths are:
- The areas I want to improve upon are:

- Action steps I need to undertake are:
- I will be accountable to:

Phone-Based Group Coaching Session Quick Road Map

The following list is a quick road map for core activities to undertake before a phone-based session:

- Establish a bridgeline.
- Determine group size (an average may be four to six for group coaching by phone).
- MindMap and/or development of material/content.
- Meet participants prior to class to start to find out more about their interests and develop a one-on-one relationship. Ask them: "What is their goal for the program? What do they want to take away as a result of their participation?" What are the priority areas for them?
- Meetings can be held by phone.
- Can be done via a questionnaire or web survey (e.g., Survey Monkey).
- Send out module to registered participants prior to the call (ideally one or two days prior to the call at minimum).
- The module may contain:
  - Pre-work exercises
  - Resources/reading lists
- Information you will be covering on the call—this allows you to home in on the information of interest rather than spending the call reviewing the information, or substantive background information around the topic (i.e., leadership) so you can spend the call coaching.
- FAQs (Frequently Asked Questions.

FAQs

From experience, for a 60–75 minute call, a typical breakdown might look like:

- Checking in (which may include updates about work they have done between sessions) and finding out what participants specifically want to take away from the call that week (5–10 minutes)
- Overview of program or session (week one only—30 seconds to 3 minutes)

- Develop ground rules (first session only—5–10 minutes)
- Mini lecture on weekly topic (e.g., values)—also include this in the module (3–5 minutes)
- Exercise related to the week's topic: small group (10–30 minutes)
- Discussion: large group (5 minutes)
- Mini lecture (8–10 minutes)
- Exercise or discussion (10–30 minutes)
- Assignment of work between lessons (3–5 minutes)
- Check Out/Mini evaluation[10] (5 minutes)
- Consider your timing. Initially, most of my programs started out as one hour; however, I found that this was not sufficient time to really discuss the material and delve into the questions participants brought to the call. Therefore, most of my phone-based program lengths have evolved into 75-minute sessions. I am still finding that more often than not, there still is even more information that we could cover and/or topics we can explore. Coaches may find that the one-hour format may often be more convenient—look at what's important for your clients.
- Decide on your program length. This will be determined by what you have come up with in terms of topic ideas.

In Summary: Phone-Based Structure

- Welcome/intro, check-in: 10–20 minutes
- Coaching topic area: 40–50 minutes
- Checkout/evaluation: 5–10 minutes

IDEAS FOR HOW TO PREPARE FOR YOUR FIRST VIRTUAL SESSION

Preparing for your first call can be nerve-racking; however, I usually find that once coaches get over the "first-time" hurdle, they love it! Here are some quick ideas to keep in mind for preparation:

1. Attend other calls as a participant to see different styles in action. Ask yourself:
   What did the facilitator do that I liked?
   What did the facilitator do that had a positive impact on the group?

What did the facilitator do that had a negative impact on the group's experience?
What exercises did they use?
How much time was allotted for discussion?
How did the facilitator address different learning styles?
The one learning point I want to take forward is . . .

2. Test-run the technology
3. Refer to FAQs on the website of the technology you are using for tips on how to mute, record, etc.
4. Have PINs/passwords readily at hand
5. Always have a back-up bridgeline
6. Develop a contingency plan — **expect the unexpected!**
7. Send out a reminder before the program —people do forget!
8. Refer to Table 6.3 to identify possible pitfalls

Table 6.3: Possible Pitfalls in the Phone-Based Environment

Pitfall	What to Do
No one talks	Be directive in asking participants for input. Have clients check in at the start of a call and sit themselves down at the virtual table.
Everyone talks at once	Discuss the process with the group. Have the group go around the virtual table they have created.
Bridgeline does not work	Have a back-up bridgeline. Provide callers with explicit instructions at the start of the program on the process for moving to an alternative bridgeline. For example, I might provide the following instructions to callers by email: "In the event of a massive bridgeline quality problem, I will send out an email if we are going to switch. So, please check email if you are having problems getting on and/or no one is there."
One person dominates the call	Set boundaries/be directive in asking for input from everyone. Ask: "What are some other perspectives?" Remind callers about bottom-lining and hogging airtime.
One speaker goes on and on	Talk about the skill of bottom-lining during your first call. Have the group create a structure/code for bottom-lining.
Silence seems to drag	Silence is good, within moderation. Create a "silence is golden rule" so that people know that after 15 seconds or so when you say this, that you will be moving on, unless someone adds something else
Clients arrive late	During your first session, discuss expectations for start time.

WEB 2.0 AND THE IMPACT ON GROUP COACHING

This chapter would not be complete without some discussion of technology and Web 2.0 tools. Technology continues to rapidly change design and delivery options for clients.

Most Web 2.0 tools are designed to facilitate conversation, foster collaboration, and promote information sharing.

In general, Web 2.0 tools include:

- Social networks—e.g., LinkedIn, Facebook
- Blogs
- Wikis: allows groups to share content, build content collaboratively
- Podcasts
- RSS feeds
- Twitter—social messaging—spread the word
- Wikis
- Video/media sharing—e.g., YouTube

All of these platforms have great potential for group coaching. For example, consider the following:

- How can you spread the word about your programs via social networks such as *LinkedIn* and *Facebook*?
- What role would a blog play in supporting your program? Can you establish a private blog site for participants? How will blogging enhance your visibility, go-to status and SEO (Search Engine Optimization)?
- *Wikis*: Allow groups to share content and build content collaboratively. Several years ago I co-facilitated a learning lab on behalf of ASTD for the 2007 international conference. One of the platforms we used to create and capture the collective wisdom and best practices, before, during, and after the program was via a Wiki.
- What benefit would *YouTube* provide for your current program marketing, implementation, or momentum between sessions?

In addition to these general platforms, specific tools that coaches may enjoy leveraging for their group coaching work include:

- Moodle (www.moodle.org)
- Skype (www.skype.com)
- www.freeconferencecalling.com

- AudioAcrobat (www.audioacrobat.com)
- MaestroConference (htpp://myaccount.maestroconference.com/node)

Question to consider:
What virtual tools to do you want to use?

Chapters 9 and 10 will delve into in person programs in much greater depth, including logistical considerations.

CHAPTER REVIEW

☐ What are your main learning areas in order to be able to offer virtual programs?
☐ What program(s) would you likely offer virtually?
☐ What is your next step in moving forward in this area?
☐ Complete Table 6.2 Self-Assessment: Are You Ready to Lead A Virtual Program?

CHAPTER 7

ESSENTIAL ELEMENTS FOR YOUR GROUP COACHING PROGRAM

Excellence is doing ordinary things extraordinarily well.
—John W. Gardner

This chapter a mix of essential elements coaches/practitioners will want to include in a group coaching program.

Throughout my Group Coaching Essentials™ program, participants indicate that they are eager not to reinvent the wheel with their own programs. Therefore, the second part of this chapter will focus on some of the most important lessons learned from other group coaches undertaking this work with organizations and groups.

This chapter addresses a mixture of core ideas and "must-haves" for this work, such as:

- Typical elements of any group coaching program;
- Essential items—group coaching facilitator kit;
- Essential times—participant materials;
- Creating a powerful takeaway for your group;
- Essential needs assessment questions (corporate and public groups);
- Essential tools—Post-it notes and index cards;
- Twenty plus great group questions;
- Essential books and other resources;
- Essential skills for group coaches; and
- From the field—most important reminders and lessons learned.

The chapter also challenges coaches to **open their toolbox**. This checkpoint will ask coaches to look at what they already have, and what they still need, for a successful program.

Business and program systems and logistical issues that will make your work more effective will be addressed in Chapter 9—Preparing for the Program—Systems and Logistics.

TYPICAL ELEMENTS OF A GROUP COACHING PROGRAM

Many coaches are eager to learn more about what the typical structure of a group coaching program might look like.

In general, there are several components of every group coaching program, including:

- Advance preparation;
- Opening the group coaching program;
- The session itself;
- Closure of the program; and
- Follow-up to the group coaching program.

This section looks at the typical elements of any group coaching program and key activities to undertake at each stage.

Advance Preparation

- Complete a Knowing Your Client: Group Coaching Client Assessment™ template (refer to Chapter 5);
- Reaching agreement with the clients (if corporate or intact groups) *or* pre-call one-on-ones with clients;
- Registration (refer to Chapter 8);
- Designing the program (refer to Chapter 5); and
- Addressing logistical issues (Refer to Chapter 9).

Opening the Group Coaching Program

- Welcome;
- Introductions of coach and participants;

- Overview of the program (if the program is multi-session, confirm details of when sessions are held, and what expectations there may be about assignments and amount of time, etc.);
- Expectations of coach and participants;
- Ground rules (refer to Chapter 4);
- Check-in—ask participants questions along the lines of:
  - What is it that you would like to take away from the call/session today?
  - What are the topics you would like some coaching around?
  - Where are we going?
  - Have participants check in on what steps have you taken since the last call/session?

The Session Itself

- In general, I include one to two activities per hour.
- There may be a "mini-teach" piece (i.e., 5 minutes to set the context of a topic such as values/vision, etc.).
- Focus will be on enhancing insights for the clients and supporting them in taking action around the weekly theme.
- Action planning—looking at how the participants will be taking their learning back to their workplace.

Closing the Program

Closure is a critical part of any program, and is often overlooked. (Refer to the Appendix for closure exercises.) Closure may include a:

- Closure activity
- Session (or course) evaluation.

Post-Group Coaching Program Work

- Follow up on one-on-one issues.
- Reporting if required. (This typically is requested for corporate or government-funded programs. In general, I will only report on the number of sessions undertaken and the dates these were held. Any specific details need to be divulged by the group client. If a meeting is requested, I will suggest that I facilitate a discussion between the client(s) and sponsor

if they are not comfortable in doing so. Often the group comes up with its own list of items they want to share internally with their sponsor and/or peers.)

- Review of evaluation.
- Capture lessons learned.
- Program redesign.

Ask yourself: *What components do you want to build into your next program? Take out your Group Coaching Design Matrix and build these in right now.*

ESSENTIAL ITEMS—GROUP COACHING FACILITATOR KIT

Over time, you will want to pull together a group coaching facilitator kit. Whether it is housed in a Tupperware container, a bag or box, my favorite ten items to include in my group coaching facilitator kit are:

1. My three essential evaluation questions: What worked well? What are you taking away? What should we do differently next time?
2. Markers—the unscented ones (some participants are highly allergic to the standard highly scented markers).
3. Blank index cards.
4. Lots of 4×6 inch Post-it notes.
5. Stickers and colored paper.
6. Tape—masking tape or some of the fun, colored sticky tape you can buy at most dollar stores. I also usually like to have a spare on hand (just in case).
7. Pair of scissors—you never know when you are going to need them.
8. Colored dots: These can be used for a number of purposes, including having group members "vote" for their favorite(s) or indicate their preference. It is a quick, colorful visual way to have all voices and opinions heard/seen within a group or team.
9. Blank name tags (and usually blank name cards): It is very useful to be able to quickly see who is in the group and call them by name.
10. Blank postcards with the program name on it for participants to write a message/reminder on it. I collect these and put them into envelopes and send them out after a program. It's a great way to keep the learning alive after a program.

Question: What else would you put in your group coaching facilitator kit?

ESSENTIAL ITEMS—PARTICIPANT MATERIALS

There are a number of core materials you will want to include in any package for participants, such as:

1. Welcome letter;
2. Learning guide/manual to accompany the program (with ample space to write on/in);
3. Book (or e-book link to sustain the learning once back at home/the office);
4. Notice of group follow-up call or individual coaching session;
5. Invitation/announcements of future programs;
6. Resource list/bibliography for further follow-up;
7. Business card;
8. Postcard (which participants can also use at the end of the program as a "letter to themselves" about their greatest learning which you collect and mail out at a later date to remind them);
9. Personalized pen from your company; or
10. Gift certificate for discount to future programs or services.

These resource kits may be hard copy or electronic, depending on how you are delivering your program.

What materials do you have? What essential materials do you want to create for your welcome kits?

CREATING A POWERFUL TAKEAWAY FOR YOUR GROUP

Keeping in mind that 60 percent of learners have a preference for visual learning, it is important to consider what you will provide as a reference or resource guide for your group. My personal preference is to create a short booklet for coaching groups which I bring to the session (if in person) or send out before (by email if a virtual program). I continue to have people contact me to indicate that they have again picked up the guide for a group coaching program they attended years ago.

Some key considerations for designing a takeaway from your group is:

1. Make it relevant;
2. Make it user-friendly;
3. Ensure that it meets the needs of the client;
4. Ensure that it has enough room for writing in;
5. Delivery mode—virtual or hard copy?
   - Environmental footprint/green business;
   - USB example;
   - Online resource site—membership site—Yahoo! groups;
6. Replicate (How can you re-package it for another group); and
7. Always leave space for learners to capture:
   - Lessons learned; and
   - Next steps.

You will also need to decide on the material format. In a recent corporate program, we decided to go completely virtual and provided participants with a USB that included their participant materials and other resources.

Another option is to use one page of paper and create a short printed booklet format, where you shrink four pages onto that one page of paper. The text may include core elements of the exercises you are going to use, powerful questions with space for participants to write, and/or an action plan section. This shorter booklet format may be appropriate for shorter sessions.

Longer programs usually consist of full-page booklets or toolkits (hard copy or soft copy). For virtual programs, I have a tendency to send out materials weekly as modules, to avoid the pitfall of overwhelming the client and to also have the flexibility to adjust the materials as themes/topics emerge in a previous session.

You may also want to consider how you can provide online materials for your participants. Whether these are included on a whiteboard, as a file in a Yahoo! group, or as a members-only section on your website or separate blog, it can be useful with bigger groups to have one location which houses additional online materials.

Of course, with all of your material, always include your contact information.

ESSENTIAL NEEDS ASSESSMENT QUESTIONS

What Questions Should I Be Asking Before a Program?
As mentioned, needs assessment, or finding out what clients want, is generally recommended to take 15 percent of the time of traditional training design (**Carliner, 2003**). Given an even stronger focus on the client in group coaching,

it is critical to spend time up-front designing the coaching relationship. This may consist of a series of one-on-one discussions, as well as designing the relationship with the entire group.

The following includes a list of questions to ask individual, as well as corporate, clients who are attending your program:

Table 7.1: Pre-Program Questions for Clients

Corporate Clients	Individual/Public Clients
What do you want to get out of your involvement in this program?	What do you want to get out of your involvement in this program?
What are your needs and preferences around:	What topics do you want to explore?
Delivery?	What should I know about you?
Topic areas?	What should I know about your goals?
Learning styles?	What should I know about your learning style?
How do you want your participation to link to your:	How will this link back to your work? Your life? Your relationships?
Performance goals?	What are the most important topics around _____(insert topic name)?
Role (individually and within your team)?	
Developmental needs?	
How will you feed back what you are learning to your:	
Team?	
Supervisor?	
Organization?	
Life?	

ESSENTIAL TOOL: POST-IT NOTES AND INDEX CARDS—A FACILITATOR'S ALLIES

One tool that I will not leave home without is Post-it notes or index cards. They are great tools for a number of uses, including:

1. **For program development**—using a new Post-it or index card, brainstorm all the ideas you have about upcoming programs. Lay them out on a table or floor to start sorting/grouping.

2. **To get quick feedback** from all participants during a program—as an evaluation tool, have participants write out their responses to your evaluation questions (one question/answer per card), and have them post them on the wall.

3. **For business planning or strategic planning sessions**—there is nothing like getting people up and moving to boost engagement, excitement, and ownership of their work! Consider using either tool with large and small group exercises based on activities, priorities, etc.

4. **As a quick poll of the group** regarding what questions are "popping" for the group.

5. **To ensure that all voices of the group are being heard.** It is quite common for groups to be dominated by certain members. As a group coaching facilitator, it is important to ensure that all voices are heard. Having participants write out their questions or responses, and then posting or sharing them, can provide participants who are introverts, more shy, or those who require more time to process questions, the opportunity to participate and "be heard." Using Post-it notes or index cards enables everyone to have their insights seen, giving everyone in the group an equal voice.

6. **To take a "vote" regarding where to go:** Have participants show their support for a discussion item by putting up a Post-it note (different colors can represent different categories).

7. **As a brainstorming tool:** You can bring Post-its/index cards into exercises where participants want/need to brainstorm. For example:
   - Small business owners working on their business vision;
   - Professionals who are in career transition;
   - Stay-at-home moms who are returning to the workforce;
   - Teams working on their quarterly/annual planning; or
   - Couples who are creating their budget or a plan for their year.

The possibilities are endless. How would you like to bring Post-it notes or index cards into your next program?

Twenty-Plus Great Group Questions for Your Next Program

We often say that questions are a coach's best tool. Powerful questions, in particular, are especially useful in helping your clients self-discover knowledge and wisdom.

In the next few days, become consciously aware of the questions you are bringing into your work with clients, whether it's in one-on-one work or with groups or teams. Are your questions:

- Open-ended?
- Leaving the client breathless before they answer, or leading them to pause or say "Wow. That's a great question"?
- Typically fewer than ten words in length? One of my key takeaways from my own coach certification years ago was that powerful questions usually are five or six words long—take a listen to yours!
- Leading a client to really think differently, or deepen their understanding, as a result of the question?

Here are some of my favorite core questions for the group context. They are not all powerful questions, but they do get people thinking and conversations flowing:

Starters/warm-up:

- What's your hope for today's session? What are your fears? What's your fantasy?
- What do you want to take away from today's session?
- What is your intention for the day?
- What will you commit to bringing to the group?
- What role do you want to play in the group?
- On a scale of 0–10, how engaged will you be with the process?
- What risk will you take today?
- What is one action you can take today to stretch your comfort zone?

Check-in Questions:

- Where are you today?
- How are you today?
- On a scale of 1–10 where are you with respect to (*insert item related to theme of program*)?
- What has happened since our last session?
- What have you accomplished?
- What's gotten in the way?
- What's supported you?
- What new choices or decisions have you made?
- What's new that has emerged and has shifted things?

Focus for the Session:

- Where do you want to go today?
- What's your big question related to the topic of XX?
- What do you want to get out of today's session?
- What's the focus you've brought to the session?
- What's the stake you want to hold for the group today around the topic of ___?
- What's the perspective/role you want to hold within the group?

Check-ins along the Way:

- What's been your biggest "aha!" so far?
- What is one thing that you can do in the next hour/day/session that will stretch your comfort zones?
- What will enhance your learning?
- What can we do differently later today/in our next session?
- What will turn up the volume on your learning so far? What has shifted for you since we started?

Taking Action:

- What action can you take to make this happen?
- On a scale of 1–10 how exciting is that for you?
- On a scale of 1–10 how committed are you to it?
- What do you want to commit to?
- What do you need to say yes to? What do you need to say no to?
- What will success look like?

End-of-Session Accountabilities:

- What are you taking away?
- What's going to be your primary focus?
- What might get in the way?
- What's going to support you with this?
- What are you committing to doing/being before our next call/session?

ESSENTIAL BOOKS AND OTHER RESOURCES

Building up your own library of resources is likely to be a key consideration as you grow into this work.

Several coaches were asked: "What are the essential resources you would recommend?" Here are some of their recommendations:

Table 7.2: Essential Books

Rita Weiss	*Million Dollar Consulting* by Alan Weiss (no relation!). "The best book I've read on how to build a thriving practice." *Social Intelligence* by Daniel Goleman. "Great insights into human behavior which can be very useful for a coach."
Marlo Nikkila	*The Big Book of Presentation Games* by John Newstrom and Edward Scannell *101 Ways to Make Training Active* by Mel Silberman and Karen Lawson *Design Your Own Games and Activities* by Sivasailam Thiagarajan *The Complete Games Trainers Play* by Edward Scannell and John Newstrom
Ann Deaton	*The Five Dysfunctions of a Team* by Patrick Lencioni *Fierce Conversations* by Susan Scott

Jenn's Baker's Dozen List of Essential Books

The following are some of my favorite resources that I use in design, facilitation, and coaching work.

Program Design/Exercises:

1. Facilitative Coaching: A Toolkit for Expanding Your Repertoire and Achieving Lasting Results by Dale Schwarz and Anne Davidson (John Wiley & Sons, 2008).
2. Retreats that Work: Everything You Need to Know About Planning and Leading Great Offsites by Merianne Liteman, Sheila Campbell, Jeffrey Liteman (John Wiley & Sons, 2006).
3. 90 World-Class Activities by 90 World-Class Trainers Edited by Elaine Biech (John Wiley & Sons, 2006).
4. Quicksilver: Adventure Games, Initiative Problems, Trust Activities & a Guide to Effective Leadership by Karle Rohnke and Steve Butler (Kendall Hunt Publishing Company, 1995).

Program Design, Training, and Working with Adult Learners:

5. The Trainer's Handbook by Karen Lawson (Jossey-Bass, 1998).
6. ISD From the Ground Up: A No-Nonsense Approach to Instructional Design by Chuck Hodell (ASTD, 2006).

Facilitation Skills:

7. The Facilitator's Guide to Participatory Decision Making by Sam Kaner, Lenny Lind, Duane Berger, Catherine Toldi, Sarah Fisk (New Society Publishers, 1996).
8. Facilitating with Ease!, with CD: Core Skills for Facilitators, Team Leaders and Members, Managers, Consultants, and Trainers by Ingrid Bens (John Wiley & Sons, 2005).

Building Your Business:

9. Get Clients Now!: A 28-Day Marketing Program for Professionals, Cunsultants and Coaches! 2nd edition by C. J. Hayden (Amacom, 2006).
10. Building A Dream: A Canadian Guide to Starting Your Own Business by Walter S Good (McGraw-Hill, 2002).

Coaching:

11. Co-Active Coaching: New Skills For Coaching People Toward Success In Work And, Life, 2nd Edition by Laura Whitworth (Davies-Black Publishing, 2007).
12. Appreciative Coaching: A Positive Process for Change by Sara L. Orem, Jacqueline Binkert, Ann L. Clancy, Sara L. Orem, Jacqueline Binkert, Ann L. Clancy (John Wiley & Sons, 2007).
13. Coach U's Essential Coaching Tools: Your Complete Practice Resource by Coach U, Inc. (John Wiley & Sons, 2005).

ESSENTIAL SKILLS FOR THIS WORK

Some of the core "must-haves" or essential skills identified by coaches interviewed included:

- Skills in group coaching;
- Skills in facilitation; and
- Exercises to leverage your work.

A fourth area that has been identified is a list for building relationships with your market for your group coaching programs. Mary Allen and Eva Gregory found that 93 percent of coaches surveyed only had 0–500 people on their mailing list. Developing a strong "name for yourself" or enhancing your visibility is very important. The topic of marketing is covered in greater depth in Chapter 8: Marketing.

 From the Field:
Most Important Reminders and Lessons Learned

Our work as group coaches is all about collaboration. In writing this book I wanted to provide coaches with a more diverse perspective on this work, and I interviewed twelve coaches who are undertaking, and leading, group coaching work.

Here are the golden nuggets *other* group coaches have shared, in their own words, as some of their most important lessons learned. As you read through these, take note of the ones you would like to incorporate into your work.

Ginger Cockerham, MCC:
Once a group becomes a formed group, they accept ownership of the group and co-create the group's agenda and share the very best of their business acumen, their personal wisdom, and insights, the group then becomes a powerful and transformative environment. The best practice is not to be the teacher or instructor in group coaching, but to be their coach. Some other reminders of approaches to use are:

- To ask "What's on the agenda?"
- Wisdom of groups.
- It's all about the client—provide opportunities for them to discuss. Sitting then listening. Be a part of conversation.
- It's about being a coach—financial recruiters asked how I could teach them recruiting skills. They themselves are the experts at recruiting. As your coach, I can help you follow through and achieve the goals you have not been able to do on your own.

- Have integrity about **who** you are—and not something you are not. You don't have to have experience in an industry to be a great coach for your clients. In group coaching, peers share expertise and resources with each other.
- Coaching versus training.
- Group members bring the agenda—encourage them to grow—coaching/instructor basis.

Rita Weiss:

- Trust the group coaching process.
- Recognize and appreciate the ability of group members to support each other.
- Let go of having to have all of the answers as the coach and allow group members and the group dynamic to accelerate the achievement of results.
- Allow yourself to learn from the group as they learn from you.

Deena Kolbert, CPCC, ORSCC:

- Trust in the group process—it works!
- As a coach, while I am the coach, I am **not** leading the group on my own. I lean into the group—the group forms another entity which we all lean into.
- Building relationships, word-of-mouth, creativity, and in person contact is the best marketing tool I own.
- The group ultimately provides the agenda, even though I have created an outer structure to bring them together in the group process.
- Once the group is formed and a designed alliance is set, the agenda needs to stay fluid and changeable within each session. Groups like structure and knowing that they will each participate.
- Resistance to making change is edge work and not everyone in the group is willing/able to move at the same pace. It takes skill, patience, and time with much support, love, and nuance to help participants over their edge(s), individually and as a group.
- Intensity over time can burn out a group... make time for play to keep the program, as a whole, balanced.

- Continuing education in the broadest sense—building our inner resources is paramount to being alive, conscious, present in the group dynamic.
- We, as coaches, have to be what we want for our clients.
- Allow for unfolding instead of taking a linear approach.
- Lean into all participants fairly; it's surprising who can become leaders, if given the chance.
- Consideration of length of each session and program as a whole—how to run a group in a professional manner without compromising the quality of the work.
- Keeping a meta-view perspective that there is a whole world out there, especially while there is an economic downturn.

Ann Deaton, PhD:

- You don't have to invent the wheel over again. Once you have a good group design, it can be adapted for many different kind of clients.
- There is power in numbers: Throughout the group process, clients can see self in others.
- Group accountability (i.e., women business owners). Action and reporting. If they have to report to me as a one-on-one coach they will typically do it. When reporting back to eight people, it is rare that they don't do what they say they will. With group coaching they are excited, and almost always accomplish, and may even exceed, the original commitment.

Victoria FittsMilgrim, CPCC:

- To trust not just my experience and intuition, but to trust that there is learning happening outside the calls and in the lives of the clients.
- Be ready to share tools/material etc., but also be ready to let it go if something more powerful is happening.
- Feel your market and price accordingly. Have marketing be consistent and clear.
- For me, don't give away a free month that comes at the end of the program. You will not be paid for that month and if a lot of people took this option, it can be harsh on your checkbook. Find another way to give a free offer.

- Do offer some kind of follow-up coaching after the group ends—you may want to poll the group about how they want to raise the participation level.

Mary Allen, MCC:

- The importance of multiple opportunities for participants to enroll in programs. You can't just let people know about your new group coaching program once or twice, most need multiple exposures.
- The power of group coaching is in the interaction. You don't have to fill all the space—it's more powerful when you're drawing on the wisdom of the group and looking for coaching moments.
- Less is more.
- Giving potential participants an opportunity to engage with you through interactive calls, exercises, and emails prior to inviting them to enroll in your program.

Maureen Clarke, ACC

The need to use a description **for** coaching (and ROI for coaching), then educating corporate client groups about the benefits of this type of coaching. I do not spend time mainstream marketing my group coaching programs—I usually end up doing referral work.

Jill MacFadyen, ACC

My biggest lesson was that it is better to not go it alone. I hired my daughter-in-law, an instructional designer, to help polish the slides and participant manual. It really helped to have a second pair of eyes and to have a professional make suggestions.

Lynda Monk, CPCC

Like Bernadette Doyle says—I have to find a "hungry crowd"—it is not enough for people to **need** what I have to offer (i.e., most helping professionals need more self-care, stress management, time to focus on themselves, since they give so much of themselves to others in their work and in their lives, etc.). However, they have to **want** it (and then I have to be positioned for them to find what I have to offer, etc.)—so the marketing is a big piece of the puzzle to successfully implement a group coaching program (in my experience so far).

Creating emotional safety and trust is critical as a best practice within group coaching—co-creating the agenda, confidentiality, working with the wisdom and experience of the participants, etc. is all part of creating this emotional safety.

Suzee Eibling, PCC

Ensure that everyone in the group is included every time the group meets. I do this through circles. Remember that there are three stages. First, check-in: brief where there is a pulse check and you look at what's going on with the group. I often ask for wins or "what is going on?" Second, there is the assessment phase. Third, ensure there is closure.

The Magic Six-Week Rule is another must have—sometimes groups get it on the first session. I usually like the group to take more time. Make it at least six weeks—and you will see magic!

Eva Gregory, CPCC:

1. Do not wait until you feel ready to begin. **Just do it**.
2. Do not wait to market your program until **after** you've developed it—create the general outline and then create your promo copy and see if there is interest.
3. Do not wait until you have the entire program developed from soup to nuts to launch. Have the general outline, set your date, start marketing and signing folks up, and allow them to help you design the program as you go, based on what happens on the calls each week.
4. Block out time on your calendar **weekly** to refine and hone your content for the upcoming calls if you are still in the design phases of a new program.
5. If you love the program, don't wait until one is complete to begin launching the next ones. For a while, I was launching my Leading Edge Living One Year Success program every month, and then eventually every other month, etc.
6. Make sure you are designing the programs to support your lifestyle. For instance, because I was running year-long programs, I needed to factor in time off, so the calls were the first three weeks of each month. The fourth week was either a guest expert or we were "off for good behavior." If I did have a trip that happened within the first three weeks, it was easy to shift the calls around so I **did** lead on the

fourth week to make sure it still was taken care of in the same month, versus tacking on extra weeks of makeup at the end of the course.

7. Include smaller groups of Mastermind Partners to meet weekly outside your program calls. The added support, connection, and momentum of them meeting on my "off" weeks kept the synergy and energy alive.

8. Always be doing something weekly to grow and create relationships with your list so when you **are** ready to launch a program, you have a responsive list.

9. Learn Facebook and Twitter and create a STRATEGY for building relationships with your target market.

10. If you have a small list, joint-venture with others who also have a list of your target market (synergistic not competitive) and for everyone who signs up with you in your program, pay a referral fee.

At this stage of the book I would like to encourage you to Open Your Own Toolkit and take a review of where you are at – what you have and what you still need:

Table 7.3: Checkpoint: Opening Your Toolkit

Ideas I have right now:	
Skills I have:	
What I have in place (list these):	
Systems in place (refer to chapter 9)	
Marketing Materials	
Networking Opportunities	
Communication	
Financial	
Materials/Resources Exercises Ready-Made Content Other Programs Assessments	
Other resources I have available to me right now:	

What do I still need?	
Skills	
Materials	
Systems – Financial, other	
Resources	
Exercises	
Marketing	
Materials to develop	
What questions do I need to ask?	
My goals for the next period are: (Make them SMART-E!: Specific, Measurable, Achievable, Realistic, Time bound and Exciting)	
My next steps are:	
I will be accountable to:	

Look back at the Group Coaching Self-Assessment from Chapter 4 to see how you have progressed.

CHAPTER REVIEW

Undertake a regular review of where you are with your group programs on a regular basis. These questions may serve as useful in taking the pulse of your programs on an ongoing basis.

- ☐ The major steps I have taken since I started reading this book are . . .
- ☐ The major goals that I have completed since I read this book are . . .
- ☐ I am really pleased that I have accomplished _____ this year/ quarter/month/week.
- ☐ The projects I currently have on the go are . . .
- ☐ The opportunities that are facing me/my business/my programs right now are . . .
- ☐ The challenges that are facing me/my business/my programs right now are . . .
- ☐ I want to keep the following on my radar screen for the remainder of the year . . .

- ☐ I want to put more attention on _____ for the next quarter/month.
- ☐ My priorities for the next six months/quarter are . . .
- ☐ I want to be energized/fueled by _____ for the remainder of the year.
- ☐ By _____ (insert date) I will have . . .
- ☐ My next steps are . . .
- ☐ I will be accountable to . . .

CHAPTER 8

MARKETING—ESSENTIAL PRINCIPLES

A successful group coaching program needs participants. For external coaches and group facilitators this may be one of the most challenging aspects in making their group coaching efforts successful. Internal coaches or HR professionals will often need to market their program internally, which may include the advocacy for the approval of budgetary processes as well as senior management approval.

This chapter will provide you with some core information and approaches to marketing. Whether you are an internal or external provider, this section will provide a focus on some core marketing components, such as:

Part 1: Marketing Fundamentals—The Five Ps
Part 2: It's All About You—Niche and Sweet Spot
Part 3: Marketing Practicalities for Group Coaching
Part 4: Developing Your Marketing Message
Part 5: General Marketing Tips and Leverage
Part 6: Marketing Plan and Strategy
Part 7: Marketing for Corporate Group Coaching

PART 1: MARKETING FUNDAMENTALS — THE FIVE Ps

Marketing is often one of the most overlooked components of making a group coaching experience work. Perhaps you are fortunate enough to have been engaged by an intact group, so getting bodies in seats or voices on the phone is not a major issue. However, marketing is often the make it or break it for many coaches. You can have a great program on paper, but this will not translate to reality without participants.

As a former Business Studies Faculty member myself, as well as a former manager who sat at the budgetary decision-making table, I know how challenging marketing can be as an external or internal professional. Having worked with hundreds of entrepreneurs from across industries to launch successful businesses, my aim in this chapter is to start you thinking about and getting into action around the marketing aspect of your group coaching work.

We could write a whole book on this topic; however, my aim here is to leverage your time when it comes to marketing. One of the group coaching programs that I have run since 2006 is the 90 Day BizSuccess Group Coaching™ program which helps business owners create focused attention and action around their own business.

In fact, you've already started undertaking some important foundational work on marketing in Chapter 5 under the heading "Knowing Your Client." You will recall that we have talked about the importance of knowing your client to design a group coaching program. This information is foundational in marketing. Take a moment to pull out your notes about knowing your client to re-acquaint yourself.

Let's first look at the question: **What exactly is marketing**? We often speak about the four (or five) Ps of marketing—product, place, price, promotion, and finally, people.

This marketing mix of five Ps is no different:

- **Product**: What products or services you are offering?
- **Price**: How much will customers pay for the product?
- **Place**: Where and when is your product available to clients?
- **Promotion**: The visibility and image of the product to customers, and
- **People**: The people who will be there to support you—sometimes referred to as your team.

Some marketing models replace "people" with "participation" or the process of actively engaging your prospects through the marketing process. Let's take a look at the five Ps in turn.

1. Product

The base in marketing is what you have to offer. What are the specific services or products you are offering?

For many coaches the product and service offering may include:

- Individual coaching
- Group coaching
- Team coaching
- Workshops, retreats
- Speaking engagements
- CDs/audio programs
- E-books.

Make a list of the specific products and services you are currently offering internally or externally.

Create Your Own Product (and Service) Funnel

Figure 8.1: The Product Funnel

The idea of a product funnel has existed for quite some time within the marketing world. It was made popular in the coaching profession by Andrea J. Lee's book *Multiple Streams of Coaching Income*. A product funnel is a way to look at how to develop multiple streams of income towards your business.

The basic premise behind the product funnel is that clients are first introduced to you with a free item, and then move into the funnel by purchasing the lowest-priced items as they get to know you and what you have to offer. Over time, they will buy more offerings, at increasingly expensive price points as they get to "know, like, and trust you." As you look at the product funnel you will also note that more people will tend to access your resources/products/services at the free stage, and fewer at the highest price points. This may not always be a linear process, and some clients may start working with you directly at the highest price point.

If we apply the product funnel to coaching, at the **free level** we may have items such as:

- Complimentary e-book
- Complimentary teleclass and/or
- White paper.

In the lowest price point category, you may include:

- A one-off teleclass
- For a fee e-book
- Group coaching and/or
- A membership site.

In the medium price point level you may offer:

- Group coaching
- Retreat/workshop
- Home study program and/or
- Audio/CD program.

Finally, in the **highest price point category**, you could offer:

- Group coaching
- Organizational work and/or
- One-on-one coaching.

Ask yourself:

- What are in the different levels of your product funnel?
- Where you do place group coaching in your overall mix? (*You will notice here that group coaching has shown up hypothetically at all three levels of the funnel. Where do you want to position it yourself?*)

2. Pricing Your Group Coaching

How do I price my group coaching program? is another strategic question to consider. Pricing can often be more like an art, rather than a science.

In coming up with a price point for your program, consider the following:

1. What is the current pricing in your market (geographic/niche or other) for a similar program? What is the current pricing for corporations or for the public market?
2. How much are your clients willing to spend on group coaching?
3. What can your clients afford? What are they willing to pay?
4. When do they have the financial resources available to participate?
5. Where does group coaching fit into your overall mix of products and services, or as we say, within your product funnel?
6. Where does it fit in your overall mix of products and services?—high, medium, or low?
7. What do other programs cost in the marketplace? How are these similar to yours? How are these different from yours?
8. What is the market rate for your area for similar programs?
9. How do you want to position yourself in the marketplace—industry price leader, at market rate, or at a lower price point?
10. What is included in the registration cost?
11. What overhead costs do you need to cover (venue, insurance, etc.)?
12. Is there an introductory price the first time you offer your program?
13. Do you want to provide other discounts to registrants?

3. Promotion

When we talk about marketing, we often just think about promotion — how do you let the world know about your product?

There are a number of ways you can promote your services, including:

*   Word of mouth
*   Advertising—newspapers, direct mail, radio, publications, web, blogs
*   Interviews—TV, radio, Internet, newspaper
*   Referrals: alumni/past clients
*   Sales promotions
*   Your website
*   Your blogs
*   Sponsorships—special events, silent auctions
*   Social media—Twitter, LinkedIn, Facebook, MySpace and others
*   Trade shows
*   Podcasts
*   E-zines or newsletters

- Publicity and public relations—pro bono coaching for special events (i.e., door prizes, silent auctions)
- Speaking engagements (paid and unpaid) or
- Via other services and programs you run.

Word of mouth and referral from those who already have benefited from your services are typically the most effective promotional method (and usually at the lowest cost!), often ensuring the **most repeat buyers**.

4. Place

Place refers to where your product or service will be offered. Where can people access your group coaching programs? Virtually, in person, through affiliates? Your placement is a key consideration, one which many group coaches have often given significant thought to. You may also want to consider co-facilitating or offering your program through other venues (i.e., a university, community college, Board of Education, gym, fitness club, etc). For futher information about co-facilation and working through others to let the world know about your programs and services, click over to http://www.groupcoachingessentials.com to access the bonus chapter on co-facilitation.

5. People

People are often included as the fifth component of the Five Ps. "People" includes your team, all those people you partner with to make your program a reality.
Reflect on the following questions:

- Who is positioned to deliver your product or service (direct providers, as well as affiliates, strategic partners, etc.)?
- Who is on your team?
- Who else do you need on your team?
- Who else can help you spread the word about what you have to offer?
- What do they say about you and your product (directly, indirectly, and by reputation)?
- What is your customer service like?
- How do your business and group program systems (refer to Chapter 9) support what your team needs to do?
- What are the action steps you could take to strengthen the fifth P—people?

PART 2: IT'S ALL ABOUT YOU—NICHE AND SWEET SPOT

One thing that I have learned in working with so many entrepreneurs and business owners is that passion, success, hard work, and leverage go hand in hand. I am a firm believer that we should enjoy what we do, whether we work for others or work for ourselves.

Thoughout the 90 Day BizSuccess Group Coaching™ program, I talk about the "sweet spot" of marketing and business development. Inspired by Jim Collins's "Hedgehog Principle" in *Good to Great*, the sweet spot of marketing is based on three questions:

1. What are you good at?
2. What do you love to do?
3. What does your market need?

Exercise:
You will need about 15–20 minutes to fully complete this next exercise, which can help you get focused strategically on marketing approaches and next steps.

Take a few moments and complete your own Marketing Sweet Spot diagram.

Figure 8.2: The Marketing Sweet Spot

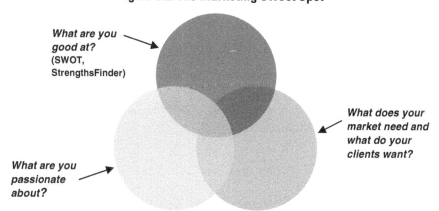

What are you good at? (SWOT, StrengthsFinder)

What does your market need and what do your clients want?

What are you passionate about?

Take about five minutes to work through each of the different circles of the Marketing Sweet Spot Diagram. Consider the three questions that make up the marketing sweet spot:

1. What am I good at? Ask yourself:
What are the things you are really good at when it comes to marketing?
Make a list of all the things you are good at. Perhaps it is speaking, or maybe you love to write. Perhaps you are blessed with technological skills and can edit short films on your computer, which could then be posted to YouTube to help spread the word virally about your programs and other offerings.

2. What do you love to do? Ask yourself:
What are the things you love to do?
This may be speaking, writing, podcasting. Think about what marketing and promotional efforts you love to do. *What issues are you passionate about?*

3. What does your market need? Refer to Chapter 5 and the Group Coaching Client Assessment™—Knowing Your Client. Ask yourself:

- What does your market need? What do they want?
- What are the issues they are concerned about? (commonly referred to as "What is their pain?")
- Where do they congregate, come together, or hang out?
- Where do they look for information?

The way you market your program—the **why, what, when, where,** and **how**—really comes down to *knowing your client*. Marketing a corporate program is going to have a very different approach than a public program. Your client base will inform everything from when, where, and how you offer your program, and how much you charge, to the topics that are covered.

The marketing sweet spot exists when these three circles overlap. Take a look at your sweet spot and ask yourself:

- What is the sweet spot for you?
- What is the overlap for you?
- What is apparent now?
- How can this inform your marketing?

The Low-Hanging Fruit

In marketing, it can be useful to identify the "low-hanging fruit." What is the low-hanging fruit? They are those opportunities that are closer than others to fruition. Perhaps you have some warm leads or an opportunity that is in development. You may also have a waiting list for programs or people who have indicated that they want to participate in a group coaching program.

List five of your low-hanging fruit opportunities here:

1.
2.
3.
4.
5.

One-Percent Rule

Marketing is often overwhelming to coaches and business owners due to what is perceived as a monumental amount of things to do. I often speak about the "One-Percent Rule." Think about one of the goals you have had on your "To-Do List" for a while. Pick one of the bigger goals you have, one that you have not wanted to take action on as it seems *so big*.

What would it look like, or be like, to take a one-percent step towards that goal today? Write this down.

Now think about what would it be like to take small action steps towards that goal on a daily basis? What would the impact be if you took one percent action every day for the span of a month?

Thirty percent change, right? How much easier was it to take the one-percent change every day?

What does the One-Percent Rule look like for your next program?

Take Action and TRACK IT!

Moss doesn't grow on a rolling stone. What's the amount of moss surrounding your business these days? How much action have you been taking in the last few months? What action has been showing measurable results? Are you keeping track?

I am a real proponent for **strategic action** based in solid planning and vision for business owners. However, what often happens is that we get so caught up in the planning and visioning that we don't actually move into the action phase. It may be because we feel we don't have enough information to get into action (for example, we need more education/more networking/more courses, we are not prepared enough, we're scared, we're not good enough). These are often the things we hear from our clients when we look at limiting beliefs.

What *limiting beliefs* are you setting with your business or programs? What actions are you shying away from? What excuses are you making?

On the flipside, sometimes we can't take action because there is so much on our plate. When was the last time you took time to strategically look at what your business priorities are, what's paying off, and what is becoming dead weight?

I would challenge each one of you to take a look at where you have been spending your time and energy, what the results are, and what might not be serving you any more. The "**Not To-Do**" List can often be just as powerful as the "To-Do" List.

Marketing Exercise

Activity:

1. Create a MindMap on marketing ideas for your group coaching programs.
2. Select the top three to five to focus on for the next few months.
3. Create SMART-E goals for each one of these focus areas.
4. Follow the One-Percent Rule—Imagine if you took action to make a one-percent change in action towards any of your goals on a daily basis. What sort of movement forward would you see in a month? Ask yourself on a daily basis: What is the one-percent change/action I can take today?
5. Keep track of what's working and what's not over the short and long term. Remember that many of these marketing activities are like planting seeds and may require ongoing attention/focus as well as time before they sprout.

Your Niche in Group Coaching

There is a lot written in the world of marketing about *niche* and for good reason. Niches can help us stand out in a crowded marketplace. It is one way to differentiate yourself from others.

Wikipedia defines a niche market as follows:

A niche market is the subset of the market on which a specific product is focusing on; therefore the market niche defines the specific product features aimed at satisfying specific market needs, as well as the price range, production quality, and the demographics.

As we look across coaching, there are specific niches dedicated to small business coaching, leadership coaching, coaching for working moms, and career transition coaching. Many marketing gurus recommend that you create a niche for yourself in one area—some of you, like myself, may choose to multi-niche (or specialize) in a couple of specific areas, depending on your areas of expertise, passions, and energy. While multi-niching can be an effective strategy to maintain diversification, the challenges in multi-niching revolve around not getting too diffuse, and maintaining a presence with all areas.

The benefits of having a niche or area of specialization include the following:

- A niche enables you to focus your resources and your attention to specific areas.
- Niches allow you to identify yourself as an expert in certain areas or become a "go-to" person.
- A niche helps you stand out in a busy marketplace.

Consider the following questions about your niche:

> *How would you describe your level of knowledge of this niche? (fair, good, expert)*
>
> *What do you offer to this niche that is unique? What makes you different than everyone else—what different skills, interests, passions do you have?*
>
> *Who else occupies this niche (competitors)? Who is the best in this niche? What do they excel at? Where are the gaps?*
>
> *What are the major needs of this niche?*
>
> *What allows you to stand out in this niche?*
>
> *What do your clients want from this niche?*
>
> *How well do they know you?*
>
> *How does this niche connect with your values? Your vision? Your passions?*
>
> *What are the steps you need to take to more clearly define and communicate your niche?*

PART 3: MARKETING PRACTICALITIES FOR GROUP COACHING

In addition to the big picture there are several marketing practicalities which often get asked about. This section will explore several key questions:

1. Is there a difference between marketing in person and virtual group coaching programs?
2. How long will it take me to market my program?
3. What's the difference between marketing to the corporate sector and to individuals?
4. What marketing materials should I have on hand?

What Is the Difference between Marketing In Person and Virtual Group Coaching Programs?

One of the main benefits in running virtual group programs is that your catchment base is much wider. Your audience base may be national or even global. It is still important to remember that visibility is critical to registrations—the main difference may be that the vehicles are different.

How Long Will It Take Me to Market My Program?

Marketing should not be looked upon as a one-off venture, especially with group coaching programs. Marketing should be a continuous approach to being in dialogue about, and providing value for, what you have to offer.

Mary Allen, MCC, of www.BeyondSixFiguresforCoaches.com indicates that one of her biggest learning points for group coaching is "The importance of multiple opportunities for participants to enroll in programs. You can't just let people know about your new group coaching program once or twice, you need multiple exposures."

Marketers often say that it may take seven to eleven touch-points before someone decides to purchase a product or service. These touch-points may include a number of messages delivered by blog, speaking engagement, word of mouth, e-newsletter, media article in a paper, etc. What are the different touch-points you are creating with your audience?

In addition, as we have already discussed it may take longer to market an in person program than a phone-based program, due to practicalities such as booking a venue.

In determining how long it will take, you need to look at knowing your client, where they are based, what lead time your potential clients will need, etc.

Some best practices with marketing involve:

- Regular on-going communication about your program;
- Promoting (via blog/newsletter/email) and/or posting your program dates as far out as possible in terms of timeframes;
- Ongoing communication right up to deadline dates;
- Add value while promoting your programs (see text box *Marketing Is All About Building Relationships and Adding Value*).

What's The Difference in Marketing to the Corporate Sector?

The last section of this chapter addresses this issue specifically, but key differences in marketing to the corporate sector include:

- Longer lead time and/or sales cycle;
- More comprehensive proposals required;
- Linking components and outcomes of the program back to business/corporate vision, objectives, strategies, and priorities; and
- Confidentiality and reporting.

What Marketing Materials Should I Have on Hand?

There are some key marketing materials which I encourage coaches to develop over time. The key here is, *over time.* You may also wish to modify these according to your own market and program needs. For example, someone running phone-based programs will probably place more emphasis on components related to a web presence than hard-copy brochures.

The following list includes several items you will wish to consider developing over time:

- Email messages;
- E-zine announcements;
- Brochures—include dates, times, a brief description (especially if you offer it regularly throughout the year) and also information on how to register;
- Group coaching program information packages—more information is better!; Consider including the following in a package:
  - Program outline
  - Logistical information
  - Course dates and times
  - Pricing (and payment options)
  - Testimonials

- – Background on yourself and your company; and
- – How to register;
- • Registration package (refer to the heading Registration Kits in Chapter 9); and
- • Group coaching kit for participants—journals, handouts, booklets (refer to Chapter 7)

Remember that quality does not always equal cost. What low-cost, innovative marketing approaches can you undertake for your next group coaching program?

PART 4: DEVELOPING YOUR MARKETING MESSAGE

Whether you are an internal or external coach, you are going to need to create a powerful message about what you have to offer.

Marketing experts often talk about the **FAB** approach.[1] This stands for **features**, **attributes**, and **benefits**.

- • **Features:** What is the program going to look like? How many sessions? In person? By phone?
- • **Attributes:** Are sometimes associated with advantages? What is it like?
- • **Benefits**: What are the benefits? What will the customer gain throughout the program?

To illustrate the FAB principle consider this for a hypothetical business development program similar to the Business Success™ program.

Features: Six-month program which includes two one-hour calls per month, plus a 30-minute individual coaching call with the coach each month.

Attributes: Hands-on, customized business development program grounded in a solid group coaching approach. Each session will focus on a different core area of business success.

Benefits: Dedicated focus to your business. Tangible takeaways include your business vision, a marketing plan for the next year, identification of your core business values, etc.

Reminder, we saw a number of benefits as articulated by other coaches in Chapter 2: Making It Stick!

Consider including the following in your general message:

- Who should attend
- The benefits of your program
- Topics and themes which will be covered
- What the program includes (meals/accommodation/materials/coaching; sessions/manuals; pre- and post-program support)
- Cost, venue/location
- How to register (phone, mail, online)
- Testimonials from past participants.

Technology

Technology often has a profound impact, depending on your client group, niche, and geographic focus.

Technology today has greatly changed the way many of us do business, including how we let others know about our products and services.

Much can be said about leveraging the changing face of marketing your group programs. To do this topic justice, a complete book would be beneficial. Technology is literally changing things on an extremely frequent basis.

Some of the newer marketing vehicles are found under the entire umbrella of social media and social networking.

This includes the communication and networking tools of:

- LinkedIn
- Twitter
- Facebook.

What do you need to know when using these mediums? What approaches do you want to leverage?

General Principles for Describing Your Programs

Use your clients' language: As coaches we often get very hung up on "coach-ese," the language of the coaching world, which not all clients will understand. Utilize the language of your clients. For example, if you are running corporate programs, use the language of their industry and link your program to it.

Know what the benefits really are: Ensure that benefits are meaningful and relevant to your program. (For further benefits from group coaching, please refer to Chapter 2.) The need to be clear about benefits points to the important role evaluation plays in your programs. Evaluating your program as you go and also at the end will provide you with clients' perspectives of what the benefits really are. (Please refer to Chapter 10 for more information about evaluation approaches and questions.)

Gather testimonials from participants: Wherever possible, gather testimonials from participants on:

- The impact the program had on them (short-term and long-term).
- The new insights they gained.
- Any skills they acquired.
- Results they achieved because of their participation in your program.

We are often tempted to evaluate only once, right at the end of a program. Unfortunately, this does not capture medium- and long-term impacts. Consider how you can track this.

Pilot if needed: Sometimes coaches may wish to do a dry run of the program at no or low cost to pilot the program. This may be an opportunity to increase confidence or to see how the program will run. If you are piloting the material, look at how you can leverage this experience.

Persevere: Remember it may take seven to eleven approaches before someone decides to buy. Purchasing coaching services is not often an off the cuff decision. I am always amazed, and reinforced, by people who may have been following the dates on a program for months, or even years.

Website Considerations for Your Group Coaching Programs

If you are looking to run a virtual program, your own website will be a must-have. Some of the pieces you will want to include on your website are:

- Program description page
- Features and benefits

- How is the program delivered?
- What is included?
- How to register
- Phone number and contact email to ask questions
- Online payment link
- Testimonials
- Other upcoming dates
- Link to newsletter or program announcement booklet.

PART 5: GENERAL TIPS AND LEVERAGE

One of the questions I often ask business owners that I coach regarding marketing is "What activities will give you the most leverage and impact?"

This question is quite strategic. Where do you want to be focusing your marketing efforts? What's the priority? You may have a list of twenty things you want to do, but which ones are really important?

Ask yourself, which ones are going to give me the greatest impact? The Pareto Principle states that 80 percent of our results come from 20 percent of our efforts. That is true leverage. What 20 percent of your activities will give you 80 percent of your results? That sweet spot can give you further insight regarding your priorities.

So, instead of asking, "What are the ten things you are going to do this week regarding building your business or marketing?" I will ask, "What are the one or two things you are going to do this week which will give you the most leverage and impact?"

Create Leverage through Other Events

Don't look at marketing your group coaching as a one-off event. You may be very interested to see how there is a cross-fertilization effect between clients who attend your group coaching programs and those who may later become an individual client and vice versa. During events that you are hosting, consider the following:

- Promote your other services—the participants of group coaching already know the value of your worth, so take advantage of sharing with them what other services and products you offer.
- Have organizational materials on hand, such as:

- Brochures/handouts on other programs you offer;
- Bookmarks;
- Registration forms for any retreats/programs/teleseminars you offer; and/or
- Coaching services.
- Have a sample coaching session sign-up sheet.
- Offer a draw for a month of complimentary coaching.

Building Relationships and Adding Value

It's not just about building a list; it is essential to build relationships of trust by providing value over time. Articles, assessments, links to valued resources, daily quotes or an invitation to a live conference call interview are all simple ways to offer value and stay "top of mind" in the eyes of thousands.
—Mary Allen and Eva Gregory[2]

Successful marketing is grounded in a relationship-based approach, and one that adds value to your market. You never know when someone is going to be ready to sign up for your next group coaching program. Sometimes it may take three months or three years before the timing is right, funds are available, and they are ready to take the program.

Marketing is all about building relationships and adding value

A 2006 study by Next Century Media, Inc. found an interesting relationship between consumers and education.

Customers you educate are:

- 29 times more likely to buy products compared to media ads;
- 5 times more likely to buy, compared to direct marketing;
- 93 percent more likely to tell friends and colleagues about their experience; and
- 94 percent more satisfied with their purchase.

Source: Next Century Media, Inc.[3]

Questions:
How are you building relationships with your marketing efforts?
How are you at adding value with your marketing efforts?

Seven Quick Marketing Tips for Group Coaching, Workshops, and Retreats

Take a look at the text box below entitled "Twenty Quick Ideas for Marketing Your Programs." Which ones have you tried? Which ones have worked already? Which ones have planted new seeds? What short-, medium-, and long-term marketing strategies do you want to undertake in spreading the word about your programs?

There are seven quick tips to keep in mind when marketing your next group coaching program, workshop, or retreat. Keep in mind that the philosophy behind this is to market with value and to build relationships with your prospect base.

Tip 1: Persevere with marketing! The Seven Times Rule. It often takes seven to eleven approaches before someone will decide to purchase your product or service. How many approaches have you made?

Tip 2: Develop new products and services for past and current clients. Those who already know you or have experienced your services will "purchase" more easily. These people already have grown to know, like, and trust you. What offerings do you have for people who have already experienced and enjoyed your services?

Tip 3: Ask for referrals: Word-of-mouth referral often yields some of the highest return rates if you offer a solid program or service. Have you asked for your clients/customers to refer or recommend you?

Tip 4: Collect testimonials: Prospective customers want to know what others think about your services. What testimonials (written, audio, and video) do you have from clients/customers?

Tip 5: Develop streams of programs from your current offerings: Be creative! Don't reinvent the wheel. What streams of programs can you develop from your retreat or group coaching program? What programs do you already have that can be developed into a retreat, workshop, or group coaching program? How can a current offering be adapted for a different audience?

Tip 6: Consider an early bird discount: What price reduction do you offer for registrants who sign up early? Is there enough incentive for you to fill seats early to ensure that you have the numbers to proceed with an in-person venue?

Tip 7: Spread the word through your networks: Have you done everything in your power to spread the word about your upcoming program? Have you passed on the information to everyone in your network? Let people know what you have planned consistently. You never know who may find it useful.

Twenty Quick Ideas for Marketing Your Programs

1. Start a blog on issues related to the program topics.
2. Undertake speaking engagements.
3. Know your audience.
4. Join a professional association.
5. Host a podcast.
6. Develop an e-zine (electronic newsletter to be send monthly/weekly/etc.).
7. Write articles on topics you are knowledgeable about, passionate about, or are related to your group program.
8. Develop postcards for your business (www.Vistaprint.com).
9. Partner/collaborate with others on a joint venture.
10. Ask for referrals from past participants, colleagues, and others who know you.
11. Donate a prize for a silent auction.
12. Develop a "white paper" for your industry.
13. Develop a free e-course.
14. Write a book.
15. Review your business vision regularly.
16. Refer to your business plan regularly.
17. Update your business plan, marketing plan, and marketing vision on a regular basis.
18. Build strategic relationships.
19. Offer a complimentary teleseminar program on a regular basis on a topic related to your group program.
20. Send out handwritten notes along with your program notice by mail to those in your network—you may wish to utilize a service such as www.SendOutCards.com.

PART 6: DEVELOPING YOUR MARKETING PLAN

Now that you have some ideas on how you want to spread the word about your programs, take the time to write them out. The following is a format I have used for many years with great success. You will note that there is space for you to **track** the outcome (do this so you can have some baseline information as to what has worked and how), as well as space to note the cost, any deadlines (date), and the name of the initiative and a brief description. Feel free to adapt this for your own use.

Track your results on an ongoing basis, and over time notice what is, and what is not, giving you impact. Which events do you need to consistently undertake or attend?

Table 8.1: Marketing Plan Template

For period:

Name	Description	Cost	Date	Outcome/ response
General — web/print/blog				
Teleclasses/referral				

(Continued)

Table 8.1 (*Continued*)

Name	Description	Cost	Date	Outcome/ response
Memberships				
General PR				
Newsletter articles				
Trade shows				
Speaking engagements				

Other				

PART 7: MARKETING TO ORGANIZATIONS

A number of readers will be undertaking work specifically for corporations—whether you are internal or external service provider, coach, HR professional, or other.

This section includes some brief information specific to marketing to organizations—for profit, nonprofit, and governmental entities.

In undertaking corporate, or organizational work, there are a number of special considerations for marketing, contracting, and in many instances, design. This section will explore a number of core differences briefly including:

- Building relationships;
- Timing;
- Budget;
- Proposal;
- Needs assessment;
- Language used; and
- Positioning—mix of programs and services.

Building relationships: Most organizations want to build solid long-term relationships with their vendors. How are you connected with these organizations?

Timing: When marketing to organizations, you will likely want to consider a longer lead time, as the sales cycle can take longer. As you think about the organizations you are providing services to, find out what lead time they require from:

- A logistical standpoint;
- A budgetary standpoint—What is their fiscal period? When would programs need to be approved or included for upcoming groups?
- A program standpoint—What are the organization's current learning, HR, or developmental priorities? How much lead time do they require to have programs included?

Budget: What is the budget range the organization can afford, in general? Per capita? Should you be considering a volume discount?

Proposals: Most organizations have their own internal requirements for proposals, work selection, and standard contracts. Agreements may range from written approval of proposals to letters of agreement. The organization may have their own standard format, or they may ask you to provide one. Much of this depends on your local context.

With your organizational contact or the sponsor, confirm what is required in a proposal. Basic elements you will want to consider including are:

- Background;
- Objectives;
- Program components—including needs assessment, design, delivery, evaluation, and any other follow-up;
- Proposed work schedule;
- Pricing;
- Similar programs delivered (maintaining confidentiality and non-disclosure as needed);
- Any subcontractors (or other coaches) you will be using—including their bio); and
- References/testimonials

Language used: One of the most important pieces in marketing corporate group coaching is to speak the language of the business, management, and employees. This may require some learning on your part, and most likely some investigation as to what the corporate priorities are, what the culture is like, and what "languaging" they use. Invest in further professional development yourself by attending events in the realm of HR, training, and performance improvement.

Link to business objectives: Part of your initial discussions and/or research with an organization is to discover how a group coaching program would link to the organization's business objectives.

A critical consideration for most organizational group coaching programs will include the link to business objectives. How do your programs support:

- The strategic plan?
- The annual plan?
- The company's competencies (i.e., leadership competencies/management competencies)?
- Any key performance indicators the company has?
- Other corporate initiatives?

Discussion should also include how evaluation will take place, and if there are certain metrics the organization would like measured as a result of the program. You will also want to consider if this is something you can do yourself, or if there are some additional resources you may want to bring in.

Positioning: As a group coach you will also want to consider the mix of programs and services. Do you want to provide one-on-one and group coaching to the same corporation? Will all the work be delivered by yourself or will you bring in other coaches?

Confidentiality and reporting: In maintaining the Ethical Code of Conduct of the ICF, maintaining confidentiality will be a critical consideration for the group coaching work you undertake within an organization. This will be an important component to spell out in the proposal or scoping stage. In general, in order to maintain confidentiality I indicate that any information flowing to the sponsor beyond logistical reporting (i.e., how many sessions undertaken, when, for how long, numbers participating [and not names]) will come from the group itself. If more detailed reporting is required, then I will have the clients generate the report content with me. Very simply, this is usually done through a facilitated discussion, brainstorming, and flip charts.

Needs Assessment

Once you have landed the work, you will want to consider needs assessment. In corporate work, you may not be able to reach out **individually** to undertake Knowing Your Client work (Chapter 5). It is good practice to ask the sponsor what will be possible. My group coaching program needs assessment processes have ranged from:

- Individual 30-minute face-to-face discussions with each staff member one-on-one, where I used four to five standard questions to learn more about them, their role, and what they wanted out of a group coaching program. This helped to identify expectations before the program, and identify themes/topics for the program.
- Individual phone-based one-on-ones: Using a similar format of questions above.
- Web-based surveys using Survey Monkey.
- Email surveys.

Recommended Resources

The following books are ones that I continue to find invaluable resources in support of the organizational work that I do.

For developing proposals:
The Business of Consulting: The Basics and Beyond, Elaine Biech, Pfeiffer, 1998.
Flawless Consulting: A Guide to Getting Your Expertise Used, Peter Block, Pfeiffer, 1999.

Communicating your value:
Quick! Show Me Your Value, Theresa Seagraves, ASTD Press, 2004.

Marketing to businesses:
Selling to Big Companies, Jill Konrath, Kaplan Business, 2005.

CHAPTER REVIEW

Given the amount of material covered in this chapter, you may wish to break it down and focus on it over a seven-week period. Follow the specific questions included in each section.

In general:

☐ What are your priorities for marketing right now?
☐ What is the first step you are going to take with your marketing?
☐ What do you first need to put into place?
☐ What additional resources do you require?
☐ What additional questions do you have?

CHAPTER 9

PREPARING FOR THE PROGRAM—SYSTEMS AND LOGISTICS

*Over-**preparation** is the foe of inspiration.*
—Napoleon Bonaparte

Remember the dynamic tension of preparation and dancing in the moment discussed earlier? Across the profession there continues to be divergent views about pre-session preparation and showing up and coaching in the moment. I do believe that there is something important to be said about preparing the ground for your program—developing systems that will work for you, your business, and your clients, as well as paying attention to logistical issues. In saying this, it is important that you do not over-prepare and lose the space for inspiration and intuition to play a role in your group coaching.

This chapter focuses on systems that practitioners will want to put into place for highly effective group coaching programs, and it also covers logistical issues. Checklists and resources to support the logistical aspect of a group coaching program such as bridgelines, room setup and flipchart essentials are included.

TIP: PREPARATION

Preparation is a coach's best friend. As a coach you have probably already done a huge amount of preparation and you have most likely undertaken countless hours of coach training and work with individual clients. Remember that your core coaching skills remain the foundation for your group coaching work.

I often get asked how much time you need to prepare for a group program. Industry standards in the area of classroom-based training have often used a 40:1 ratio—that is, for every one hour of classroom-based training that is created, forty hours of work goes into the development (including session outlines, participant and facilitator guides, etc.). But does this hold true for group coaching?

As we have seen earlier, one of the main distinctions between group coaching and workshops is the difference in who holds the agenda. Is it the participant/client or facilitator/coach? Who holds the agenda will have a large impact on my preparation time leading up to either a group coaching session or workshop.

In traditional training, the agenda or objectives are typically set by the organization and often participants (in more participatory learning environments), according to the KSAs (knowledge, skills, and abilities) that the program is to achieve or improve. Preparation with training may involve setting the objectives, developing the sessions and evaluation structure, designing the materials, and really keeping the goals/objectives out-front during the entire session.

Group coaching takes a different tack and has a softer focus. Recall that group coaching looks to the client to set the balance between content, structure, and space. In keeping aligned with the coaching profession, the coach/facilitator is there to hold the client's agenda (the client in this case being the individual members of the group).

What this usually means for my preparation is a focus on getting to know the participants as much as possible prior to the group coaching session. For the more extended programs I run (one-month to ninety-day programs), I meet with each participant by phone to find out more about their expectations about the program, what they want to achieve and take away. This then gives me an idea of the client's agenda, which we can dance with, within the context of the program.

I often get asked: What's the balance between structure and the client's agenda in group coaching? From personal experience, I tend to structure my programs along thematic lines (i.e., work-life balance, business success, leadership, organization issues), finding that this gives the group more traction and a common purpose. There is still plenty of room for going in many different directions. While each week has a different theme, there is still flexibility in meeting the clients' agendas as we move through the session. Again, it's a softer focus and less reliance on a hard "schedule."

As a group coaching facilitator, it's always a fine balance and dance between the structure and meeting the needs and agendas of the clients in the "here and now" of the session. It's about being unattached to the actual timeline of the session, while creating a framework for the clients to explore and move forward with their own agendas. You will find as a coach that each session is going to turn out differently.

WHY SYSTEMS?

Systems are streamlined processes which will allow you to replicate core pieces of your business. Systems also help to institutionalize knowledge and allow others to take on activities as your own work expands. Once in place, systems should be updated on a regular basis (quarterly or annually).

As a group coach, it is important to look at systems on two levels:

1. Systems for group coaching programs.
2. Systems for business in general.

Business systems can support you to leverage your time and resources, while supporting your growth, productivity, and efficiency. Systems for group coaching will make your program work that much more streamlined and easier to have multiple groups on the go at any one time.

In general, there are certain areas where business systems may provide support for you in the short and long term, including:

- Sales and marketing
- Clients
- Invoicing;
- Registration systems,
- Telephone—bridgeline and long-distance packages.

Principle: Keep It Simple— Systems for Your Group Programs

Keeping it simple for your group programs may involve automating or systematizing different components of your group programs. Core systems you will want to have in place will include:

1. An easy way to accept registrations.
2. A list of your upcoming programs that you can quickly refer to (all in one place).
3. Credit card processing facilities/online merchant (so you aren't waiting for the check that is in the mail).

4. A list of possible venues (including contacts, pricing, requirements) for your group programs.
5. A selection of bridgelines you can use.
6. Recording facilities (if needed).
7. Course materials and/or modules completed that can be modified and combined for different programs.
8. Promotional material that can be adapted for new program announcements (e.g., postcards, website, blog, brochure, or media kit).
9. A system to track course registration and payment information.
10. A system to get the word out quickly to potential participants about your upcoming programs (e-newsletter, facilities to post your information electronically, a mailing list).
11. A program/course overview or information package.
12. Online shopping cart.

These are several systems you may want to consider developing for your group coaching programs as they evolve. The great thing about many of these tools is that once developed, they can be reused every time you run the program or leveraged when you add new ones.

Some changes in recent years include a shift in systems such as:

- **Changes in communication vehicles:** Clients continue to become increasingly savvy. Email is no longer the only way to communicate with clients. I find that focusing in on referrals as well as blogging, e-zines, and postcards helps to spread the word about my programs.
- **Payment systems:** Clients often want to choose from a variety of online and offline options. Would it be beneficial to set up credit card merchant services such as Visa, AMEX, or MasterCard by phone in addition to online payment processing such as PayPal? Is there another shopping cart which may be useful for you? It is interesting how many clients want to pay offline, due to online payment experiences.
- **Recording calls** has become a much more popular must-have for participants (preferably with an online listening option or the ability to download the calls as an MP3).

Ask yourself:

1. What systems do you currently have in place that really work for your group coaching?

2. What **one** new system would really make a difference with your upcoming programs?
3. What new systems would you add to the list?

Build a Solid Foundation: Core Business Systems

Whether you've been in business for six weeks or six years it is often very useful to reflect on the systems we have in general, and how these work for our business.

Core business systems each business should have on hand include:

Sales and marketing:
- Marketing materials
- Fact sheets
- Website
- Blog or other online presence (i.e., Twitter, Facebook, LinkedIn)
- Systems to keep in touch with your client base/list — phone, email, newsletters, cards
- Networking
- Building your platform
- Proposal templates
- FAQs.

Financial:
- Budgets
- Bank accounts
- Merchant account (AMEX, Visa, MasterCard, or other)
- Invoicing system
- Shopping cart
- Affiliate system.

Communication: How will you maintain communication with clients?
- Phone packages
- Mobile/toll free numbers
- Internet
- Newsletter
- Blogs.

Systems for your group programs:
- Registrations (more to come in this chapter)
- Venues

- Insurance
- Bridgelines

Program and product delivery.

On a general business level...

1. What are your best systems for your business?
2. What systems do you still want to put in place for your work?
3. On a business level—what one new business system would help you focus and get more results?

Registration Systems

The ability to process registrations seamlessly can support you in running multiple programs at any one time.

Considerations for developing your registration system include:

- **Make it easy!** How can participants register? How can they reach you if they have questions? Be clear in your instructions—website, phone, email contacts.
- **Develop forms** to track inquiries, payments received, confirmations, pre-calls, and one-on-one meetings.
- **Provide payment options**—What payment options do you provide? PayPal, shopping carts, personal/business check, currencies.
- **Deadline dates:** Be explicit with any deadlines. These may include:
  - Align with deadlines for venue/food; and
  - Deadline dates for any pre-program discounts (i.e., early-bird pricing).
- **Cancellation policy:**
  - How do you address program cancellations?
  - For public programs:
  - Can people apply their registration to a future program?
  - Is there an administrative charge for changes?
  - For corporate programs:
    - What is your policy on cancellation of face to face and/or phone based sessions?
    - How explicit is this in your proposals or contracts?

- **Refund policy**: What is your refund policy?
- **Follow-up:** Always follow up after the registration has been made.

Registration Kit—The Basics

You may wish to send the following to participants prior to the start of the program. You may send this out electronically, have it posted on a website, or cover this verbally with participants.

Typical kit components may include:

- Detailed description of the program (or at a minimum, the weekly themes which may emerge);
- Detailed descriptions on how to get to the venue or the bridgeline;
- What's included in the registration pricing (meals, materials, and/or coaching services);
- What people should bring to, or prepare for, the session;
- What to expect—detailed text on what the program is about. If appropriate, draft an agenda. If the program is delivered over several sessions, what type of work can they expect in return;
- Pre-work: Any instructions needed prior to the start of a program. For example, readings to be undertaken, materials to be printed, audios to be downloaded;
- Policies and procedures—e.g., refunds/cancelation; and
- FAQs.

LOGISTICS

Many coaches have questions about the basic logistics of running group coaching programs such as bridgeline services. This section also includes information on tips on flip charts and PowerPoint. In addition, you will find information about selecting venues and bridgelines. This chapter ends with a checklist of things to consider for your program.

Selecting a Venue

Selecting the right venue for your group program—whether it is a workshop, retreat, or group coaching program—can be a time-consuming and challenging process for those who are not logistically savvy. Here are some things to consider when selecting your next venue:

1. **Ease of accessibility for your participants. Consider the needs of your participants:**
   - Is there parking?
   - Is parking free or at a cost?
   - What modes of transport will participants be able to take to get there?
   - Is the facility accessible for all "ability" levels (i.e., can it accommodate walkers, wheelchairs, if needed?)?
   - Attach a map or link to a map so participants know where the location is and can look after their own travel requirements.

2. **The environment:**
   - What is the feel of the venue?
   - Does it match the environment you want to create?
   - Is there sufficient space for you to undertake the exercises you want to do?
   - What changes, if any, will need to be made to the room layout for your program (i.e., is the change you need possible or is the furniture fixed in place?)?
   - Are there additional rooms available if you need breakout sessions?
   - What is their policy regarding participants using other parts of the facility—any areas out of bounds?

3. **Room booking charges:**
   - How much will it cost to retain the space?
   - Are deposits refundable? What is their payment policy?
   - What is their cancelation policy?
   - If numbers change closer to the launch of the program, what impact will this have on pricing?

4. **Insurance:** Many facilities require that you hold sufficient liability insurance. What are the facility requirements? What insurance do you need to put in place?

5. **Meals:**
   - What dietary requirements do your participants have? Food allergies?
   - Can your needs be met by the facility? In your budget?
   - What are their offerings/special packages?
   - What are the exact times for breaks and other meals?
   - When and where will meals be served?

- What is the venue's policy on ordering or providing lunch?
- Will there be sufficient time with your schedule to have all participants eat leisurely through the lunch period?
- What if numbers change before the program? Can meal amounts be modified? Up to what date?
- Interestingly, meals can take a lot of time for a program. Buffet can often be the safest bet, don't order off the menu unless they can take pre-orders and guarantee when it will be ready!

6. **Equipment rental:** Often venues will provide certain pieces of equipment (flip charts, markers) at cost or sometimes free. Clarify what is included in the room rental and what might need to be rented at an additional cost. Also inquire what their policy is regarding bringing your equipment in from your organization—is this allowed?

These are some of the nitty-gritty issues you may want to consider as you select your next venue. Are there other things to consider when selecting your group program venues?

Room Setup: In Person

There are many ways a room can be set up for group coaching. Sometimes you have a choice on how it is displayed, sometimes you will not. Think about how participants will learn best during your program, as well as what will be most comfortable and convenient for the exercises you have planned. You will also want to consider the group size you are working with. Here are some possible layouts.

Figure 9.1: Room Layout 1—Small Groups (five to eight per table) seated at round tables

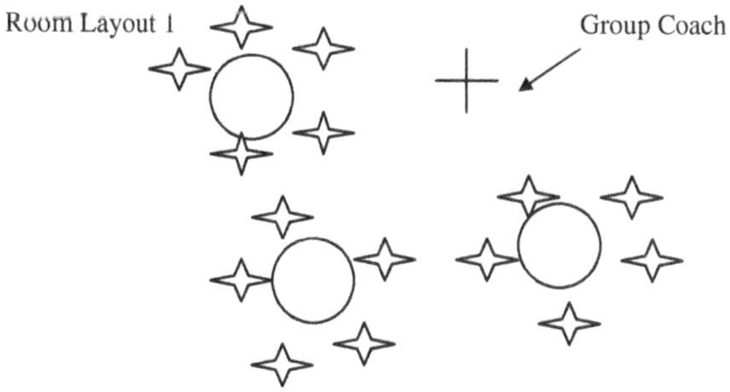

Good for:	Drawbacks:	How to facilitate:
Creating a supportive learning environment Ensuring participants are able to write and sit comfortably Creating connections between smaller groups within a large group setting Ensuring a platform for small group discussion, review, etc.	May inhibit participants from meeting others around the room. Suggestion: have participants change tables during program Requires a lot of space Need to ensure all participants can view flip charts/speakers, etc.	Use small group discussions at tables when appropriate Build in checkpoints to share small group learning with the larger group Ensure questions for discussion are posted on a flip chart for everyone to see

Figure 9.2: Room Layout 2 — "U" Shape (note the U can be made with chairs or table layout—preferred format)

Room Layout 2 (Note the chairs should go around the outside of the U if you can imagine the facilitator at top. I have put xes in.)

(Group Coach)

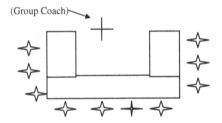

With table (as Above) or Chairs only (below)

Chairs in a U Shape Design can also be used for this configuration which makes the room movable, and allows you to redesign the room as needed for different exercises.

Good for:	Drawbacks:	Facilitation type:
Movable chairs allow you to quickly re-design the room Promotes smaller group discussion	Depending on room size, may make it difficult for participants to break into smaller groups for discussion and small group work	Create a mix of larger and small group discussions

Ensures all participants can see the front of the room	Not all locations are visible to all participants—make sure everyone can be seen and heard	Don't get stuck in the rut of having everyone stay in the same place—mix it up!

Chairs in a U-shape design can also be used for this configuration which makes the room movable, and allows you to redesign the room as needed for different exercises.

Figure 9.3: Room Layout 3—Traditional Classroom

Room Layout 3 – Traditional Classroom (Note all of these squares are seats)

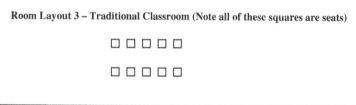

Good for:	Drawbacks:	Facilitation tips:
Large group plenary sessions where room size is limited	Very challenging for group coaching work Association with "classroom days" Does not promote interaction among participants Does not facilitate an "active" approach to learning Participants in back may get "lost" as they feel they can't be seen or heard	Provide each client with a workbook which contains flip chart questions, room for writing To create client involvement, have them turn to their neighbor to speak Provide coaching questions for dyads/triads to discuss

When considering your room layout, ask yourself:

- How many participants do you expect for your program?
- What presentation methods will you use throughout the program?
- What will the room layout look like?
- What modifications do you need to make to the layout?
- Will your exercises/activities require any changes to the room layout during the course of the program?

PowerPoint Essentials

There may be some instances, although not many with group coaching, when you will need or want to use PowerPoint. PowerPoint does have the added advantage of working well for the visual learning style. It is also an important vehicle if you are leading larger group presentations.

To make your presentation most effective, you will want to keep in mind the following points:

- Keep it simple—do not try to include all information on the slide;
- Only six lines per page;
- Make sure graphics serve to reinforce message;
- Don't go overboard with animation—if you do, ensure you are well prepared; and
- Headings should vary in point size between 40 and 44 points. Body text is between 20 and 36 points. Captions 24–32 points[1].

If you find the slides are too busy, ask yourself: What should be included in a guide instead? Great resources for PowerPoint include: Garr Reynolds's *Presentation Zen* (book and blog) at www.presentationzen.com.

Flipchart Essentials

Many coaches will find that flipcharts are an essential part of group coaching work. When using flipcharts, keep in mind these finer technical points:

- Use three or four different colors maximum on each flip chart;
- Red and green can be great reinforcing points, but keep in mind that some participants can be color blind;
- Post flipcharts around the room, rather than letting them get buried on the pad;
- Number flipcharts to remember the order they were written in;
- Ask participants to help you with posting flip charts as they are written. Rotate this role;
- There may be certain flipcharts you want to bring back session after session—for example, ground rules. Make a note of these and ensure you pack them up separately; and
- Avoid writing in all capital letters—this is harder for the eye to read.

ESSENTIAL GO-TO SERVICE PROVIDERS

Every coach will have their own favorite service providers. Here are some of my essential must-haves for any program:

1. **www.TrainersWarehouse.com:** They have a huge range of training supplies which are great for anyone who is doing work face-to-face.
2. **Post-it notes:** These make my list every year as an essential must-have. Refer to Chapter 7 for all the ways you can use them.
3. **www.Vistaprint.com:** On-demand printing across a range of products. In the past I've ordered their T-shirts, business cards, postcards, and also rack cards. It's been a great investment and "leave behind" at speaking events, workshops, etc.
4. **www.PlanetTeleclass.com:** Another great resource to get the word out about your next teleclass.
5. **www.FreeConferenceCalling.com:** My favorite bridgeline and recording service.
6. **Staples Inc.:** Never fails with last-minute printing needs.
7. **Social media and social networking:** A new approach to marketing. Facebook, Twitter, and my blog continue to be new ways of reaching out to others.
8. **www.PDF995.com:** Helps you create PDF files.
9. **www.SendOutCards.com:** As people are once again preferring the impact of a handwritten card, this site provides an opportunity to build relationships and be in connection with others.
10. **www.MindJet.com:** I continue to see the extraordinary impact of mind mapping for individuals, teams, and business owners in everything from program design and article writing to team communication issues. The MindJet tool is fantastic!

Bridgeline Facilities

Whether you are leading a fully virtual program or want to add a phone-based group follow-up call at the end, keep the following in mind:

- How many people will you have in the program?
- Where will they be calling in from?
- Do you want to be able to access your bridgeline service at any time?
- Do you want to record calls?

- Do you have a budget?
- Will you need any additional breakout rooms (virtual)?

Also consider the questions posed in Chapter 6—Powerful Delivery Options.

BRIDGELINE SERVICES
FOR PHONE-BASED PROGRAMS

The following service providers offer bridgeline services to the general public. Services do vary amongst providers, so make sure to undertake your own research.

MaestroConference: (http://maestroconference.com/) This service, launched in 2009, provides a range of services to facilitate small group breakouts even in a large call. This is a fee-based service; however, it does offer a number of unique services.

www.freeconference.com: Free bridgeline rentals. They have both a reservation-less service for free (which sometimes can encounter accessing problems when brigelines are full), as well as a free web-scheduled program (for up to 100 callers). With the web-scheduled programs you can reserve space for a specific date and time and a bridgeline will be assigned to you.

www.mrconference.com: Also provides free bridgeline rentals. Many of the bridgelines do not have chimes enabling you to know whether participants are entering or exiting the teleconference. Note that you can enable or disable this function with FreeConference.com.

www.budgetconferencing.com: A bridgeline rental company with bridgelines available in many of the major urban centers. There is some cost to this service.

www.freeaudioconferencing.com: I added a back-up bridgeline service through this company as they provide quite a range of options (at additional cost), including MP3 recording and downloading capability. You are assigned your own bridgeline with a dedicated access code that can be used twenty-four hours a day, four days a week. Basic bridgeline rental is free of charge.

www.freeconferencecall.com: Provides a free bridgeline account as well as free audiopodium/playback facility (until you record over it). Your account is valid for a 120-day period, after which you have the option to renew (again at no cost). It is a ninety-six caller automated 24/7 reservation-less conference call account.

Most telephone companies will also provide bridgeline/conference calling services at a cost.

GROUP COACHING PROGRAM CONSIDERATIONS

We learn by trial and error, and here are items you will want to make sure you have "packed" and ready for your program. Here are some of the items on my checklist that have been tried and tested throughout the years:

Participant materials:

When running in-person programs:

1. Make sure you have sufficient copies of materials for all participants plus one extra.
2. Include a copy of the handout/participant material for yourself.
3. Your own design notes.
4. Materials required for any exercises.

For virtual programs:

Consider the following with phone/virtural programs:

1. PDF capability for materials.
2. File size.
3. How will you bundle your materials? How and when are they distributed?
4. Do any forms need to be typeable?
5. Acquire consent to send out materials to the group having all email addresses visible. Has everyone given permission for their email address to be shared with the group?

Computer and LCD Projector:

1. Necessary power cords.
2. Mouse/pointer as needed.
3. All passwords.
4. Battery
5. Materials on USB/Flash drives.

Miscellaneous Program Kit:

1. Glue sticks, flip chart paper, masking tape, Blu-Tack, index cards of varying sizes
2. Post-it notes
3. Markers—for flip charts and participants to use
4. Pens, pencils, stickers
5. Old magazines (for collage work—if applicable)
6. Participant name tags or name cards
7. Prizes for participants
8. Clock/watch to keep the time
9. Chime/bell

Some of these materials may be provided by the venue—check with them, as well as what additional charges they may levy.

Question to Consider

Are there any other items you might add to your travelling training kit?

Group Coaching Program Checklist

Here is a short checklist that you may wish to use, or adapt for your next program:

Group Coaching Program Checklist

Pre-Registration:

☐ Registration forms developed

☐ Registration forms available online

☐ Registration forms available electronically

☐ Registration cut-off date established:
   List date: _____

☐ Early bird or other special pricing established

_____

_____

☐ Registration meetings/client meetings determined

Marketing:

- ☐ Identified marketing sources
- ☐ List marketing sources: _____

  _____

  _____

  _____

  _____

- ☐ Target marketing dates
- ☐ Communication #1 out
- ☐ Communication #2 out
- ☐ Marketing materials created (check all that apply):
  - ☐ Online information
  - ☐ Brochure
  - ☐ One-pager
  - ☐ E-zine
  - ☐ Blog post
  - ☐ Social media announcement
  - ☐ Other:
  - ☐ Other:

Program Material:

- ☐ Program material developed
- ☐ Program outline developed (for marketing and participants)
- ☐ Participant's materials/manuals/handouts developed
- ☐ Program material sent to all participants

Bridgeline (For Telephone-based Programs):

- ☐ Bridgeline reserved
- ☐ Bridgeline information sent out to all participants, along with information about course start dates
- ☐ Recording ability

For In-Person Programs:

- ☐ Venue identified
- ☐ Meals ordered

- ☐ Participant food allergies noted
- ☐ Insurance coverage
- ☐ Cancellation policies discussed
- ☐ Payment policies discussed
- ☐ Meeting room layout discussed
- ☐ Visit undertaken (if appropriate)
- ☐ Participant materials copied (plus a couple of extra) and packed
- ☐ Flipchart material available
- ☐ Extra markers
- ☐ Name tags for participants
- ☐ Other materials needed: (list)
- ☐ _____
- ☐ _____
- ☐ _____
- ☐ _____
- ☐ _____
- ☐ _____
- ☐ _____
- ☐ _____
- ☐ _____

Other Notes:

_____

_____

CHAPTER REVIEW

- ☐ What systems do you want to put into place for your group coaching work?
- ☐ What systems do you want to put into place for your business?
- ☐ What preparation do you want to undertake for your next program?
- ☐ What logistical issues can you address right now?
- ☐ What's your next step as it relates to systems and logistics?

CHAPTER 10

IMPLEMENTING YOUR PROGRAM

The focus of this chapter will focus on the following implementation tips:

- Creating a positive learning environment;
- Voices from the Field—Golden Nuggets;
- Key tips for success (and pitfalls to avoid);
- Dealing with difficult participants;
- Common new group coach challenges—and how to mitigate;
- Why group coaching fails;
- Voices from the Field—challenges and stretch points; and
- Evaluation and follow-up.

Other key implementation tips were covered in Chapter 9 (the systems and logistics for programs) as well as in Chapter 6 (for virtual programs).

CREATING A POWERFUL POSITIVE LEARNING ENVIRONMENT

The environment you create for your group programs can have an incredible impact on the group's experience.

Take a moment and think about your most powerful learning experience. What did the facilitator do? What was the environment like? How did you feel as a learner? What was most profound about the experience?

Now take a moment and think about one of the most negative or disastrous learning experiences you have had—how did the environment play into this?

What Is the Environment You Want to Create for Your Programs?

There are a number of key foundational pieces that successful programs include. From a learner's perspective, there must be trust, safety, and confidentiality. How do you create this?

Practicalities—The Room and Location Setup

The actual location of a program will have a powerful impact on a participant's experience. As you think about creating your learning environment, consider the following:

If you are holding your program indoors:

- What is the room setup like?
- How does the room setup match your program's objectives and the environment you want to create?
- Can the tables, chairs, and furniture be moved as your program progresses to allow for small/large group work or individual work?
- Is there natural lighting? Even having one window available can make a difference.
- What is the room temperature like? How is it controlled?
- Is there sufficient room for the number of participants?
- Is there space to lay out resources, books, and information about your upcoming programs?
- If you are offering food at breaks, water or other beverages, where will these be located?

If you are holding your program outdoors:

- How can you make use of the entire surroundings? Perhaps you can run exercises in different areas?
- What is your back-up plan in case of poor weather?
- Where is shade available? Sunlight available? (Having run programs in the tropics for many years, I am quite sensitive to finding the shady areas!)
- What will the balance be between indoor and outdoor work?
- Are there any special communication mechanisms you need to establish to ensure that everyone can remain in contact?
- Are all of your watches synched?

If you are holding your program on the phone:

- What do you want to create in the virtual environment?
- How will you prepare to be ready for the start of the call?
- What instructions do you want to provide for your participants regarding pre-call preparations?
- What instructions have you provided about muting, starting, and ending on time?

These are just a few considerations when looking at running your next group program. Take some time to envision what the environment will be like for your participants—what is the space you wish to create?

Make additional notes here:

_____

_____

_____

_____

_____

 ## Voices from the Field: Key Tips and Golden Nuggets to Share

Here are some other coaches' "golden nuggets" or tips to share:

Rita Weiss:
- Trust the group coaching process.
- Recognize and appreciate the ability of group members to support each other.
- Let go of having to have all of the answers as the coach, and allow group members and the group dynamic to accelerate the achievement of results.
- Allow yourself to learn from the group as they learn from you.

Lynda Monk, CPCC:
Trust the wisdom of the participants—be a true coach—don't take charge of the process, but rather guide it, nurture it, inspire it, cherish it—and watch the magic take place!

Heidi Michaels, CPCC:
Just be you... group coaching is nothing more than individual coaching. Remember the KISS (Keep It Simple Smarty) motto and that less is better.

Ginger Cockerham, MCC:
Trust the coaching process.

Jill MacFadyen, ACC:
Follow your niche.

Maureen Clark, ACC:
Take off the trainer hat and put on your coach as facilitator hat—dance in the moment with your groups.

Marlo Nikkila:
Less is more. There is always so much to say. Break it down so it is in absorbable pieces.

Deena Kolbert, CPCC, ORSCC:
Listen carefully, there's plenty of learning in every situation for everyone, including coaches.

Ann Deaton, PhD:
Be comfortable being transparent and participating in the exercises yourself when it makes sense to do so—e.g., uneven dyads, complex concepts, creation of safety.

Victoria FittsMilgrim, CPCC:
Design as many ways as possible for the group to interact, listen to each other, and connect even outside of the scheduled calls (Yahoo! group, buddy system that rotates) all fosters more trust and openness among participants. This, in turn, makes the calls more lively and open, as people feel safe to be transparent. They can remove their masks.

Mary Allen, MCC:

Leading group coaching allowed me to step up and grow beyond my skills of a one-on-one coach. I am a stronger, sharper coach because of group coaching. I feel more like an expert and have an expanded visibility in the marketplace.

Eva Gregory, CPCC:

If you want to lead group coaching programs, don't try to reinvent the wheel. Be willing to invest in yourself and get the training and education on how to do it from those who've successfully done it themselves and worked out the kinks for you—and then **get into action.**

Don't wait until you feel ready to launch group programs. I had done some very short programs with a partner and **loved, loved, loved** them. I kept saying, I sooo love group coaching programs, I really want to be doing my own group coaching programs, and didn't do anything about it until my life partner lost his three-year contract without warning and I became the sole breadwinner. It was one of the best things that could have happened!

JUST. DO. IT.

TRICKY ISSUES

As with any coaching, tricky issues can emerge. This section covers tricky issues such as dealing with difficult participants and dealing with conflict. This section also covers common implementation challenges, and refers to the *2009 Group Executive Coaching Survey* from Air Institute. We will also hear from coaches undertaking this work in the field as to what their challenges and stretch points are.

Dealing with Difficult Participants

How often do you come across difficult participants in programs that you run?

Difficult participants can come in all shapes and sizes:

- the bossy talker who likes to take over the group process;
- the cynical silencer who sits with their arms folded and doesn't say a word throughout the entire program;

- the corporate employee who states at the start of the session that they are sick and tired of another "useless waste of time"; and
- the "know it all" who has an answer to everything and knows more about the material than you do as coach or facilitator.

For many coaches new to group coaching, dealing with difficult participants can be a tricky issue.

Here are a few suggestions to consider implementing to avoid some of the difficult participant traps:

1. **When feasible, meet with participants prior to the start of a program.** This is part of every process for me with group and team coaching programs, but may not always happen if I am running a workshop or facilitation session.

    Sometimes "difficult participants" emerge if they feel that their voice is not being heard, or their needs are not being met. I typically spend 10–15 minutes with each participant before the start of a program (by phone) and find out about why they have signed up for a program, what they want to take away from the program and how the program fits into their larger picture of their life and work.

    This approach may appear time consuming, but it provides the opportunity to connect with each participant to ensure that their needs are actually being met and that the program is the proper fit for their needs. This up-front work allows for a more tailored program and for some discussion on expectations even before we are together. These pre-program calls also identify clients who may not be suitable for group coaching.

2. **Have the group develop "Ways of Working," "terms of engagement," or "ground rules" at the start of every engagement** (during the first session if it is a multi-session program). By having the group take ownership of their own process from the start, this can allow for peer influence, as well as a reference point for future sessions. When difficult issues emerge, you will be able to point difficult participants back to what the group has agreed to abide by.

3. **Address any concerns individually with participants as soon as possible.** This is one of those diplomatic skills you will develop over time. Your personality and style will play a key role in how it plays out. If I notice behavior that is disruptive to the group process, I will speak to the participant one-on-one at the first break about what I am noticing. Sometimes they are not aware of the impact their behavior is having on the group.

"Awareness allows for choice"—by pointing out what you are observing, the participant will be able to choose how to modify their behavior.

If the impact a participant's behavior is having on the group is quite extreme, it may be a good idea to create an unscheduled break to address the issue right away.

4.   **Get the difficult participant involved.** Sometimes participants crave the spotlight, and if they don't get it, they will try to hijack the group process to get more attention. Several years ago during a two-week training program, a participant continuously challenged the process (which was designed by the organization), but the situation turned itself around when I got her to undertake the flip charting for the brainstorming sessions we held on a daily basis. All of a sudden, the group's greatest critic had became the greatest advocate for the process. A real turning point!

Could your difficult participant help with flip charting? Distributing materials?

5.   **Put it back to the group: How can we make this a really good use of our time?** Once in a while you will come across groups that are highly cynical and feel that the process is a huge waste of their time (especially when it is a corporate mandate). I faced a situation like this not long ago, and when I asked the group "How can we make this a really good use of our time?" we were able to cover both the corporate mandated material, as well as address some of their concerns. I won't say that it was an easy process, but everyone did stay the full time! Remind participants that with group coaching it is about their agenda. What do they want to discuss? What is meaningful and relevant in the moment?

6.   **As a coach—come from a place of curiosity:** As I've pointed out time and time again throughout this book, one of the main differences with group coaching is that we do not need to assume the role of expert. Be curious in inquiring about the behavior you are noticing.

When Conflict Emerges

Another million-dollar question is: *What to do when conflict emerges within the group you are working with?*

As we saw earlier in the stages of group development, conflict is a normal part of the process of group formation. It typically shows up in what is called the "storming" stage. As the individual group members start to feel out their roles within the group, conflict is inevitable.

Conflict can emerge when:

- there is lack of clarity of roles within the group;
- there is lack of clarity, or uncertainty, about where the program is going;
- there is insecurity;
- there is fear; and/or
- expectations are not being met.

Conflict can be as subtle as the withdrawal of a participant (a participant shuts down) or as extreme as verbal conflict emerging between two participants. Not all conflict is unhealthy or negative. In fact, creativity has its roots in creative conflict.

So what do you do when faced with conflict in a group?

Typically, when conflict emerges in one of the groups I am working with, I point to what I am observing, indicating that conflict is the sign of a healthy team/ group. Often, acknowledgement and normalizing that conflict is part of a healthy group process and is enough to normalize the situation.

If the conflict is disruptive for the group process, I will speak privately with the pair/individual at a break (at the usual time or a "spontaneous break" if things are spiraling downward). During this one-on-one discussion I will indicate what I am observing and what I am seeing in terms of the impact on the group. Using a powerful question such as "What do you want to create in this environment?" shifts the responsibility for outcomes towards the participant. Again, awareness leads to choice.

Two factors can go a long way in mitigating conflict—building trust within the group and having clients take ownership and responsibility for their outcomes.

Common Implementation Challenges

A decade ago, Swanson and Falkman[1] identified twelve issues as the most common training delivery problems for new facilitators. These twelve pitfalls are also relevant to the group coaching context. Swanson and Falkman: 12 issues are listed, as well as possible solutions in the group coaching context, in the following chart:

Table 10.1: Common Implementation Challenges

Issue	Solutions
Fear	Be well prepared Prepare mentally or run a pilot Know what the fear represents and what limiting beliefs you are holding Acknowledge and use self-talk
Credibility	Pre-calls allow you to share your background and personal expertise Focus on the skills the group brings
Personal experience	Coaching is about our experience and how we perceive the world Foster an environment where all participants are encouraged to share their personal experience Practice the skill of self-management and share personal experience with the issues/topics, as relevant
Difficult learners	Use small groups Have the "difficult participant" take on roles—i.e., flipcharting If behavior persists, have a one-on-one conversation with them
Participation	Use open-ended questions Use powerful questions Structure activities to draw on resources of the group—small group exercises, dyads/pairs, case studies, role plays
Timing— too little	Prioritize activities, practice presenting material Use the Accordion Approach Implement the 80/20 rule of content development Work with a mentor coach/facilitator Decide on what is a "must-have" and what is a "nice-to-have"
Adjusting Instruction	Determine the needs of the group early on. Start sessions with round about asking "What is it that you want to take out of today's session?" Ask for feedback Re-design at breaks and throughout the program Co-design with participants—make changes as needed Listen to what clients want and be unattached to your own outcomes Come to the session with several possible exercises/options for the theme/topic you are coaching around—see what needs and priorities emerge from the group
Questions— answering and asking	Remember, as a coach, you do not need to be an expert Write out key questions people may have in advance and provide these as a FAQs sheet Put the question back to the group—draw on the group's knowledge Follow up on questions you couldn't answer

Feedback	Ask for feedback throughout the program Don't leave feedback for the last day—refer to evaluation methods later in the chapter
Media, materials, and facilities	Visit the venue beforehand, if at all possible Practice with a dry run with friends/colleagues Have backup just in case—extra material Try all materials Refer to group coaching checklists Don't assume—make sure you review with the host/location what materials you need
Opening and closing techniques	Have a file of ideas Greet clients when they enter Review program to give an overview of what participants can expect Create the environment and set ground rules—you may want to suggest some Provide participants with closure Thank participants Clearly indicate follow-up activities

 ## In the Spotlight: Marlo Nikkila

One of the main "stretches" I have seen from new group coaches is letting go of the actual outcome of the session. Here is what group coach Marlo Nikkila told me about a huge shift she undertook with her facilitation approach earlier this year:

My group coaching program really shifted last week.

Before, I was offering notes for the call that people could fill in as we talked. On the third session, I felt discouraged and realized it was because I hadn't gotten through all the material I thought would be important for people to benefit from. Suddenly, it clicked. It had ultimately become more about me and what I thought they needed.

So, I followed your format in providing everything before the call and letting them read and process it. Then I reserved the call to answer their questions and really do the coaching thing, rather than being in the teaching mode.

I was a little concerned about sending them so much info before the call, so I asked them at the end of the call what their opinion was for the new format. They **loved** it. They loved having the info beforehand and felt they got a lot more out of the call to deepen their understanding and apply to them specifically. Plus, they had the resources to go back and re-read the material.

I realize this is not an aha! for you since you have done it this way, but for me it was amazing. What it has also done is speed up the home study guide, because what I write to them is now part of the guide itself.

In the Spotlight:
Heidi Michaels, Certified Life Coach

Here is what Heidi Michaels said back in 2007 after leading her first series of group coaching sessions:

My learning: I understand much better what details to pay attention to and what not to. Pay attention to having things settled and ready to go, have a map of what you want to accomplish, but let go of getting to the exact destination. It's like being on a sightseeing tour—you are there to see something wonderful but at the same time, there might be a beautiful bird that just landed, the sky is blue, or it starts to rain... so you take time to notice it and take it all in. Open the awareness to what turns up.

What are the some of the challenges you think you might face? Write them down here:

_____

_____

_____

_____

Other challenges I might face include:

_____

_____

_____

_____

Why Group Coaching Fails

The Air Group Executive Coaching Survey identified the following reasons for the group coaching process to derail. The top nine reasons identified were:

1. Unwillingness on the part of the client to be coached
2. Mistrust
3. Ineffective coach
4. Monopolizing
5. No management buy-in
6. Commitment (individual)
7. Negative person
8. Leading not coaching (coach)
9. Poor time management

Both the lack of coach experience and the coach leading rather than coaching, were two failure factors on the part of coaches. The survey notes, "These observations point to the importance of having a skilled, experienced coach facilitating the group coaching process."[2]

Additional Group Coaching Pitfalls and How to Mitigate Them

For many coaches starting to do group work, a major question is: *"What are the pitfalls I should be aware of?"* In addition to what has already been covered, the following are some additional pitfalls to consider:

- The room you have booked is not set up as you had hoped.
- Materials that you prepared cannot be printed, due to printer malfunction, ink running out.
- Participants get lost on the way to the venue.
- Bridgeline malfunctions.
- You get laryngitis.

In fact, with all of these issues, we could look at them as something going wrong; however, in fact, they can be great learning moments. The other good piece of news is that for many of these pitfalls, you can mitigate the risk (lessen the likeli-hood) by putting a few systems in place.

Room Set-up and Arrival

A best practice for any in person program is to arrive at the room that you have booked at least half an hour or more before the earliest participant may show up. This may mean one hour to an hour and a half before participants are due to arrive.

Even with the most explicit directions it is quite common that you arrive and the location is not set up as you would have liked. Find out who is in charge of the area and work with them to support you in getting the room in order.

Materials Production

Always have a spare cartridge on hand or even a spare printer. Give yourself enough time. Whether you are producing your own materials or having someone else print them, ensure that they will be ready on time.

Venue Directions

Another best practice is to be explicit with directions so participants don't get lost on the way to the venue. If you are hosting your program in a hotel or other public venue, provide a URL from the venue itself (and ensure that this URL link works).

Laryngitis

Losing your voice can happen from time to time and has less of an impact on face-to-face programs, but tremendous impact for phone-based programs. For phone-based programs, you will want to have a backup—either postpone or provide a recording. For face-to-face programs you may need to use a lot more nonverbal skills than before. It's a great opportunity for participants to take on leading roles (if it is a multi-session group). Provide the group with more questions and give them more time to work in small groups and present back their findings to the larger group.

Bridgeline Malfunctions

Always have a back-up bridgeline **and** a plan that is communicated to participants about what they should do if the bridgeline malfunctions (i.e., you will send out an email or will automatically switch to another line). For large group programs, always do a test! The quality of your bridgeline says a lot about you and your business.

More Tricky Issues
Additional tricky issues can include:

- A few participants take over the conversation
- Participants don't understand what you are saying
- Energy levels are low
- Someone challenges you
- There is a breach in confidentiality
- A participant leaves

What other tricky issues have you encountered? How did you deal with them? What questions do you have?

 ## Voices from the Field: Challenges and Stretch Points

The following challenges and stretch points were identified by coaches undertaking this work with their own clients. Coaches were asked: **What have been your challenges with group coaching?**

Mary Allen, MCC

Challenges and stretch points:

1. Being able to coach in front of all people—stepping up as leader—you are not just in front of one person, but many.
2. Focus most on those that are interacting (i.e., Yahoo! groups). Need to remember to include those who are quieter/just listening on online forums—easier not to support these people.
3. Marketing—applications: How many contacts do you have on your database?:
   a. 93% of coaches surveyed had 0–500 contacts in database.
   b. If you don't have people to market to, it is very difficult to fill groups.

4. Retention—another challenge can be keeping everyone engaged for an entire year. There seems to be a natural drop-off period at three to four months, depending on the group.

Lynda Monk, CPCC:
Marketing and getting registrations. Also, many people I have spoken with are hesitant to participate in a group (fear, not sure what to expect, etc.) and they want one-on-one personal coaching instead (which I am finding a bit of a challenge since my ultimate goal as a coach is to eventually only offer group coaching programs).

Heidi Michaels, CPCC:
Finding a time that works for everyone! Getting people to come. Making sure everyone is stimulated and getting what they need.

Jill MacFadyen, ACC:
The first challenge was the amount of time to write the programs and then it has been a challenge to market them. Now that I am happy with the writing, I will be comfortable putting a notice on my website and planning a webinar.

Coaches working in the corporate sector noted the following challenges:

Ginger Cockerham, MCC:
Initially, getting companies and organizations to understand and value that groups can be coached effectively and more affordably virtually. I do all my groups virtually.

Maureen Clarke, ACC:

- Managing time zones.
- Engaging all members in the group—gaining trust and participation with some more hesitant group members.
- Sometimes, technology challenge.
- Time commitment—number of hours allocated by sponsoring client for group coaching engagement(s).

Rita Weiss:
In many groups, there are one or two people who automatically resist change. Initially, I would try to persuade them regarding the value of leadership development and team collaboration. Sometimes this worked—other times, it caused them to resist even more. I have found that a better approach is to allow them to come to the recognition of the value at their own pace. Often, when they see their peers embracing new ideas and behaviors, the peer pressure of not getting on board creates the required shift in attitude and behavior. I let the power of the group influence the resistant few instead of trying to force the result.

EVALUATION

Evaluation is an often overlooked component of any group program. How do you evaluate your workshop, retreat, or group coaching program?

Evaluation plays a key role in any group program, and can provide the following information:

1. What did the participants like about the program?
2. What did participants learn from the program?
3. What changes may need to be made before the program is run again?
4. What is the value or benefits of the program?

Why do you want to evaluate?

Evaluation can serve a number of purposes, including:

1. Feedback on how well your approach, content/themes, and/or pacing are meeting the needs of the group;
2. Feedback on the length of the course;
3. Feedback on the impact of the program; and
4. Testimonials—very useful for marketing.

Feedback will provide you with useful information on:

- How the program is going in general.

- Follow-up needs—What participants need as a follow-up. What specific steps the client/organization/you will take to track learning and follow up on action plans developed during the workshop.
- Changes needed to the program if it will be offered again. *From experience, make notes about these soon after the program as they are easy to forget!*

What do you want to evaluate?

There are several areas you will want to get feedback on, including:

- Materials
- Venue (room size, arrangement)
- Ease of facilitation
- Cost of the program
- Assignments/work between sessions
- Themes
- Technology used—i.e., bridgelines, whiteboards, webinar platforms

If you are not yet familiar with the work of Donald Kirkpatrick, often called the "Grandfather of Evaluation," I would suggest you check out his book *Evaluating Training Programs*. This is a seminal work in the area of workplace learning and development. His four levels to evaluation are:

1. **Reaction:** What were participants' reactions to the program? Did they like it?
2. **Learning:** What did participants learn from the program? Often measured pre- and post-program.
3. **Behavior:** How did participants' "on the job" behavior change due to the training?
4. **Results:** What business results were obtained due to the changes in participants' behavior on the job?

Many of you will also be familiar with a fifth level of evaluation—**ROI (return on investment)**. This topic deserves a chapter in and of itself. One resource on measuring the ROI of coaching is *Coaching That Counts* by Dianna Anderson and Merrill Anderson. Jack J. Phillips and Patti Phillips have also published a number of books on ROI in the training and performance fields.

Table 10.2: The Four Levels of Evaluation

Level	What	How
Level 1— Reaction *What do clients like about the program?*	*Measures participants' attitudes towards the program, including perceived value and general satisfaction with a variety of aspects of the program* There may be a low correlation with actual learning or subsequent application of learning	*Through questionnaires, smile sheets, round robins, get immediate feedback on:* Usefulness of the material Timeliness of the information Quality of handouts/materials Quality of the venue Mood of the group Group coach/facilitator Participant behaviors
Level 2— Learning *What did clients learn from the program?*	*Measures skill and knowledge acquisition from the program*	*The following methods can be used during the course of a program to measure the participant's skills and knowledge acquired:* Testing what participants have learned through demonstrations, role plays, case studies, simulations, and games, tests Self-assessment—have participants identify what they have learned Facilitator assessments Interviews with participants
Level 3— Application *How have clients applied the learning/insights from the program?*	*Measures the application of skills and knowledge back on the job or in real life*	*After the program has been completed (i.e., six weeks, three months) obtain self-report (and supervisor assessment where appropriate)* Through: Questionnaires—email/online Follow-up group calls Focus group one-on-one phone calls *Note that this will likely add time to your program, so adjust pricing/charges accordingly.

Level 4—Results	Assesses the impact of	In collaboration with organizational
What are the results from the program?	*learning on organizational results, such as:* Reduced costs Reduced turnover Greater number of place-ments/projects approved Increased revenue	partner, develop a comprehensive evaluation framework/process
	On an individual level, clients can also measure their results. If it is a work-life balance program, metrics may include: Reduced absenteeism Reduced expenditure on health care costs	
	Time management metrics may include productivity, etc.	

How to Evaluate

As part of your design, determine what you want to evaluate. You may want to include a mix of qualitative (words) and quantitative (number-based) feedback in your evaluations. By tracking your evaluation results over the course of programs, you can get a better feel as to what is working for the majority of your clients, and where refinement may be needed. Recognize that when serving a wider range of clients, not all clients may find their needs being completely met. Use this constructive feedback to make valuable changes to your programs.

How to Roll Out the Evaluations

In person: If you are running an in person program, ensure that you schedule time for people to complete the survey during the program. Build time into the schedule specifically for this purpose. In today's busy world, experience shows that participants do not often stay behind, so wherever possible, get feedback in the moment while it is fresh.

Phone based: For phone-based programs, send an evaluation prior to the last call by email. You may choose to include an evaluation form in a word processing software, or a web-based survey such as Survey Monkey.

The Simplest Approach

At a minimum, whether I am running a full-blown group program or even offering a one-hour speech, I ask participants three questions:

1. What worked well?
2. What did you take away?
3. What should we do differently next time?

This provides quick Level 1 information that can be noted quickly and tracked as needed.

Best Practice

Follow-Up after a Session

As we saw in Chapter 2: Making It Stick! The Business and Learning Case for Coaching, a key strength of group coaching is helping participants make the link between their insights from the program and transferring these key learnings and commitments to their work and life.

A best practice for group coaching programs—whether virtual or in person—is to schedule a follow-up group call with your group to check in on accountabilities and to see how the "rubber has hit the road" since the last session. You may choose to schedule this call two, four, or even six weeks later to see how they are integrating the learning. This helps you start to look at Level 3 evaluation measures.

If you choose to offer this follow-up call, ensure that you include it in your program description and/or pricing.

CHAPTER REVIEW

- ☐ What are the key steps you want to take in creating a positive learning environment?
- ☐ Which golden nuggets/key tips from the field do you want to remember for your work?
- ☐ What will be your biggest challenges or stretch points as a group coach? What skills and resources can you call upon to help you grow?
- ☐ What will your evaluation process look like?

WHAT'S NEXT? TRENDS IN GROUP COACHING

*I think we're all just scratching the surface of what's truly possible with group
coaching programs. There is so much everyone can learn by participating in a
group coaching program—about being authentic, sharing openly, listening,
pushing their edges as a leader, accountability, and realizing goals.
As our industry grows, I see group coaching impacting millions.*
—Mary Allen, CPCC, MCC

This book would not be complete without asking the powerful question **What's
next?** I hope that you will engage with this inquiry from the perspective of what's
next for our profession, as well as what's next for you, individually, as a group
coach.

I have no doubt that group coaching will continue to grow. Guy Kawasaki, the
former Apple Chief Creator, talks about how innovation happens through arcs,
where practices jump the current curve. Just as Mary Allen has stated, we are just
scratching the surface when it comes to group coaching.

Throughout the interviews for this book, I asked other coaches what they saw
as some of the next trends. Rita Weiss is noticing that a lot more clients are asking for on-site work. One of Mary Allen's next areas to foray into is the world of
integrating video with group coaching.

Ginger Cockerham, MCC, is seeing a number of trends. First, she is seeing
that the cross-cultural groups are helping all of us learn about and appreciate
other cultures.

Most significantly, she stated to me that "Thomas Leonard remarked years ago
that coaching would go around the world and change the way people interact and

communicate forever. As group coaching becomes an integral part of companies, organizations, and people worldwide, his vision is coming true."

WHERE TO NEXT?

I do believe that we are moving past the early adopter phase of group coaching in terms of client knowledge of group coaching. Looking back at the uptake on the part of coaches since early 2006 when I started training coaches globally in this area, it is amazing to see how far we have come. Coaches around the world are now adding group coaching as a new modality for their work. Likewise, professionals from related disciplines (OD, HR, training) are also very eager to look at how they can adapt more of a coaching approach to their group work. I have no doubt that coaches will continue to acquire coach training in the area—both basic and advanced training.

One area where continued expansion will take place is looking at and leveraging how technology can be used to work for, and enhance, group coaching. New changes this year have included Maestro Conferencing, an innovative service which allows for smaller breakout "virtual rooms" during larger calls. Changes like this expede the logistical side of things for group coaching.

This is one of the first books on group coaching to be published, and I have no doubt that others will follow. As this work continues to ripple out globally, coaches and other professionals will continue to be hungry for information to support their work with groups.

So:

What's your next step?

What would be the biggest and boldest step for you in moving forward with this work?

APPENDIX

EXERCISES FOR GROUP COACHING

Group coaching allows you to tap into your creative side when designing exercises and activities to use with your group clients.

Exercises are the cornerstone of group coaching, as well as workshops or retreats. Exercises provide a framework for clients to:

- Explore major themes and topics;
- Expand or deepen their learning;
- Reflect on their experience, knowledge, and feelings;
- Make connections with what they already know; and
- Make it stick! Exercises should also provide the reflection space for participants to make a connection between what they are learning and their "real-life" or work

Exercises can set the tone for a program and also play an important role in energizing a group or providing closure.

This appendix provides you with more information on exercises for group coaching, how to use them, and questions to ask. It also highlights group coaches' favorite exercises from the field, and provides a reference list of other sources you may wish to look into for building "your back pocket" of exercises and resources.

In starting off, reflect on what exercises you have available at your disposal. If you are a coach, what exercises do you currently use with your individual clients that could be translated into the group context?

Make a list of exercises you already have in your coaching toolkit.

As you reflect on these, my guess is that you can come up with a list of at least ten to fifteen that could be modified for the group context.

EXERCISES: THE BACKBONE OF ANY PROGRAM

Exercises really form the backbone of any group coaching or team coaching program.

When considering your next choice of exercise, consider the following questions:

1. What is the theme you are currently working around? (i.e., balance, leadership, change, career, time management)
2. What stage of development is the group in? (Refer to the heading Group Process in Chapter 3.)
3. What does the group need at this stage? (closure, celebration, energizing, check point)
4. What is the message/learning you want to create as a result of the exercise?
5. What's the tempo that will work for the group?
6. How will this exercise support different learning styles?
7. How will the exercise complement other exercises—in terms of theme/ learning styles?
8. What risks are associated with this exercise?
9. When would this exercise be most suited in terms of placement—i.e., icebreaker, closure, etc.?
10. What else does this exercise need as a complement?
11. What questions should follow or be part of this exercise to allow the group to learn the most from it?

Write down three to five follow-up questions for an exercise.

Challenge: If you are preparing for a new program, use these questions to help you take your exercise choice to the next level.

If you don't have a new program on the books but are looking to create the foundation for a new one of your own, pick a theme (i.e., leadership, career transition, work-life balance) and spend 30–60 minutes gathering/researching exercises you could include.

INDIVIDUAL COACHING TOOLS TO BRING INTO THE GROUP COACHING ENVIRONMENT

As a coach, there are a number of one-on-one tools which can be brought into the group coaching environment, including:

Coaching Tool	Use and Description
Wheel of Life	Allows participants to assess where they are at in different areas of their life or work. This provides a snapshot of where people are at, at any given time.
	How to use in a group setting:
	Often used as a foundational exercise (pre-work) or in a first session, this exercise can be repeated during the course of longer group coaching programs. Repeating the exercise will allow participants to see what changes and growth they are undertaking, and how far they are moving.
	Slices of the wheel can also be left blank for participants to fill in.
	Twist it:
	This tool can be used for many different groups you are coaching. Consider making the following adaptations to the labels of the wedges for different client groups:
	Managers—replace with management/leadership competencies
	Business owners—replace with core business skill areas
	Career development—replace with skill areas related to their profession or core job search areas (i.e., resumé/interviewing, etc.)
Metaphors	Metaphors can be used throughout a group coaching program especially in relation to the theme of the program.
	A metaphor is defined in the Merriam-Webster dictionary as "a figure of speech in which a word or phrase literally denoting one kind of object or idea is used in place of another to suggest a likeness or analogy between them (as in *drowning in money*)."
	Examples:
	Metaphors can be brought into almost all of the work you do. Very simply, you may ask group members to come up with a metaphor describing what it is like to be in the group.

(Continued)

An example of how you can use metaphors is to listen for them. For example, a group of business owners who were participating in one of my group coaching programs were discussing the question: What is it like to be a new business owner? A common theme of ignition, like a firecracker, emerged in their answers. Over time, the group labeled themselves the "Sparkers."

Another approach may be to link inquiries with metaphors, for example, "What is it like to be the captain of your ship?"

One of my favorite exercises is an exercise called personal logos, which often leads to unearthing some significant metaphors for participants. The personal logos exercise follows later in this appendix.

Values Clarification
Values work is a core piece of the work we do as coaches. It can be very powerful in individual and organizational settings. Your approach to working with values may differ according to your style, as well as the clients' needs and preferences.

How it can be used:
There are a number of ways I have used values work—two of which are included under the exercise descriptions.

In summary, you may choose to work with values by:

- Providing participants with a checklist of values to help them identify their values (in your session or as between-sessions work);
- Providing laser coaching in the moment with a volunteer at the front of the room;
- Having participants pair up or discuss their insights in smaller groups.

Values may become a whole module/session, or more, of your work.

Perspective Work
Perspective work is a core approach to many coaching models, such as Balance Coaching in the Co-Active Model. The recognition of the power of choice in our work and life is a powerful component of group coaching programs.

Ask participants: *What is the perspective you are standing in?* or *What is the perspective that you are holding on this issue?*

After they have explored that perspective, ask them to select another perspective to stand in on their issue.

Ask clients to consider: *What is the connection between perspectives, choice, and your issue?*

Visualizations   Visualizations can be used for phone and in person group coaching programs.

They can be successful with organizational groups (managers envisioning what they want for their work), for groups in career transition, with new business owners as well as in work-life balance programs.

Examples:

Business owners: Several years ago I was engaged as a coach to develop and deliver the first two weeks of a nine-month program for female entrepreneurs under a government-funded program.

Part of my stake as a coach is that business owners need to focus on business practicalities, as well as uncovering what makes them unique as a business owner. Developing a powerful vision for their businesses and what they wanted to create as business owners was also an important consideration.

Despite being hesitant about bringing visualization to this group of entrepreneurs, I thought that I would try it—and the women loved it. Some of the key learning points for me from this process were:

1. As facilitators we can create our own limitations by saying "That would never work." *Where are you limiting yourself?*

2. Different learning styles exist in each group. Visualization exercises may not be a preference for all learners; however, it can be a powerful tool for many.

(Continued)

More detail about how to use guided meditation is included in the text box with information from Lynda Monk, CPCC.

Key message: You are only as limited to this as you wish in terms of bringing in different styles of exercises. *What biases do you hold as a facilitator?*

Future Self/ Higher Being	Bring future self/higher being exercises and visualizations into exercises, inquiries, requests, etc.
Powerful Questions	Powerful questions are the basis for most group work. Prior to starting a course you will want to develop a list of powerful questions specific to the topic, or use your intuition throughout the course.

Refer to **Twenty-Plus Great Group Questions for Your Next Program** in Chapter 7 for further information.

Homework/ Assignments Between Sessions	As previously indicated, homework or assignments between sessions serve to deepen participants' learning.

Some examples of types of assignments you may want to assign between sessions include:

- Inquiry
- Challenge
- Journaling
- Undertaking an individual assignment—for example, a collage of your vision, complete a self-assessment, undertake a values checklist.

Inquiry	An inquiry is a large question, left for clients to consider between sessions. An inquiry typically is a question that requires deeper thought and may have several outcomes.

There may be particular themes that emerge in a group coaching session either from the group or individuals within the group, during the course of a session.

Examples of inquiries could be:

- What does success look like?
- What does it mean to excel?
- What does balance look like?
- What does it mean to surrender?

- What does it mean to be a leader?
- What is the challenge for me?

Challenges

A challenge is a request designed to have clients move to the outer limits of what they feel is possible. Challenges are much bigger than a request and will typically take a client's breath away. The end result is that clients will generally stretch further from where they were originally, and may even take on more of a task than what was requested.

Again, challenges may be specific to a group or individuals within a group, depending on the themes that emerge during a session.

In issuing challenges, remember that a challenge for one may not be a challenge for all.

Example:
I was working recently with a group of coaches on developing their own group coaching work and the topic was marketing—a sticking point for many. As a takeaway assignment, I challenged the coaches to take five actions related to marketing over the next week.

It was interesting to see the different responses from different members of the group. There was a range from "OK" from those who found it within reach to the typical gasp and "No way!" from those who really found it to be a challenge.

With challenges, give clients the option to say yes, no, or make a counteroffer.

In fact, within this group of five coaches, two opted to take the challenge on as it stood, one increased it to ten steps, and two others reduced it to three steps.

Other Tools

Mind Mapping

As described in Chapter 5, Mind Mapping is a powerful tool for planning and design work within group programs.

Mind mapping is also a powerful tool to use with clients for getting "unstuck" on issues, as well as to support them

(Continued)

in exploring other options, brainstorming, goal setting, and planning.

Example:
During the check-in for a group coaching program for business owners, a theme surfaced from several members of the group who were stuck or overwhelmed with what tasks and activities they had to do.

While we were on the phone, I asked the group to MindMap everything that they had on their mind for three minutes. After three minutes I asked them:

- What was that like?
- How do you feel right now?
- What issues came up for you?

Responses included:

- It was liberating.
- I feel much more focused.
- It was really good to see everything down on paper. It seems much more manageable.
- I realized that most of these issues are stemming from my disorganization. I need to create the time to get organized, something I have been talking about over the last two sessions, but haven't done. I am committing to clearing out my office.

Index Cards   Index cards also are a powerful tool for planning and design of group program work, as well as providing a structure for clients to explore issues, plan, and move forward.

Please refer to the instructions included in Chapter 5 for how to use index cards. Similar to this example, have participants vision around an issue—and use one card per piece of information, or idea.

SWOT Analysis   Usually used in organizational settings, the SWOT can be brought into personal development and to explore change issues for individuals, organizations, and teams.

When to use it:

- Groups of individuals in career transition
- New business owners wanting to get a better understanding of the business environment they operate within
- New groups forming around a certain cause
- Organizational committees

Instructions: A sample SWOT exercise with detailed instructions can be found later in this chapter.

Journaling | Journaling can be used during a group coaching session or in between sessions. You can provide a framework for your participants through inquiries, or it can be left up to your clients. I often give each in person group coaching client their own journal to take away from the program.

Further details about how you may wish to bring journaling into your program is included later in this appendix.

Personal Logos | This exercise is included later in this appendix. It is one of my favorites for both in-person and telephone-based programs.

I use this exercise regularly with clients, with groups who know each other, teams, as well as groups that don't have any connections. It is a wonderful exercise to use at the start of a program.

Guided Walk | Bringing in the natural world to your group coaching programs is always an option. Where venues permit, I often have group coaching clients take a guided walk of the grounds. Sometimes this is done in silence, sometimes with journals, and sometimes with an inquiry in mind. It is a great opportunity for people to become more present or enable them to become more still.

Consider how you may be able to incorporate the natural world into your programs.

Closure | Closure is a critical component of a group coaching program and often overlooked.

How can you make closure special and celebratory?

This appendix provides you with a number of closing activities you may wish to undertake.

In the Spotlight:
Guided Meditation and Group Coaching Lynda
Monk, CPCC www.creativewellnessworks.com

Guided meditation provides a fast, simple, and effective way of uniting your inner source of wisdom and well-being. Powerful visualization, progressive relaxation, and reflection techniques help you achieve increased feelings of calm, peace, balance, and profound relaxation.

Considerations for using guided meditations within your group coaching program:

1. Know why you are using them—guided meditations should be selected on purpose, meaning, know why you are selecting a certain meditation—what purpose do you want it to serve within your group coaching program? What benefits would you like it to have?
2. Introduce the meditations, briefly explaining what they are and why you are suggesting using them.
3. Let participants know, like all tools and exercises introduced within group coaching, they are optional—the participants ultimately choose whether or not they would like to experience the benefits of guided meditation. They are in control.
4. Only introduce guided meditations you are familiar with and that you have, in fact, experienced yourself. The best way to speak authentically about the value of guided meditations and about the overall experience of using them is to have experience with them as the group coach. This allows you to speak briefly about what your clients can expect in using them too, while also acknowledging that *each person will have their own unique experience as a result of the exact same meditation.*

How to use them:

1. Make the guided meditation available to the group coaching participants/clients—have them purchase the meditation you would like

them to use (there are six available at www.creativewellnessworks.com/guidedmeditations) or create your own guided meditations customized for your program/group.

2. Ask participants to listen to the meditation before the group coaching call (assign it as homework between weekly group coaching sessions and/or send it in advance of the group coaching session with directions for use).

3. Suggest to clients that they listen to the meditation in a quiet place, where distractions are less likely, and to simply sit comfortably, eyes closed, and enjoy the meditation. It is important to not multi-task while listening to the meditation (or operate a motor vehicle!).

4. Let participants know there is no right or wrong way to experience a guided meditation, perhaps saying something like: "Your body and mind will take from the meditation exactly what you most need in the moment. Some people drift, almost fall asleep, see images, access intuitive information, and gain clarity—it matters only to stay open and trust the process itself. You do not have to do anything special other than to simply listen to the meditation and give your mind and body permission to relax."

Example of How I Used the Wise Guide Meditation

I sent the link for this 9:47 minute guided meditation to the Spirited Self-Care group coaching clients a week prior to our call together. I asked them to listen to the meditation and to then complete a dialogue writing exercise (for 10 minutes), which involves writing a conversation between yourself and your wise guide. We then shared our dialogue writings within the group coaching call, followed by a group discussion aimed to deepen the learning and forward the action for the group coaching clients. I posed the following reflective questions to the group: What did the participants learn from this exercise? What stands out for them? What new action would they like to take based on the learning from this reflective exercise?

As a group coach, you can have a lot of fun and bring tremendous creativity to your group coaching programs through the use of guided meditations. Enjoy experimenting with this powerful tool for personal growth, transformation, and wellness within your own life and within your coaching work.

Source: Lynda Monk, CPCC, www.creativewellnessworks.com

BEST PRACTICES IN EXERCISES

When incorporating exercises into your group coaching program, consider some of the following:

- Ensure that your exercises are linked to the overall purpose of the session;
- Continue to leverage your core coaching competencies with exercises. Skills you will want to bring into each exercise are:
  - powerful questions;
  - challenges and requests;
  - coming from a place of curiosity; and
  - holding the client's agenda.
- Remember that one of the powerful benefits of group coaching is to tap into the collective wisdom of the group. In order for this to happen, you need to create the space for the group to speak and be in dialogue with one another. It is important that you leave sufficient time for the group to discuss or debrief the exercises. A rule of thumb I was taught early in my career is to include the following mix of exercise/debrief: 2:1 or 1:1. So, if an exercise runs for 15 minutes, make sure and budget to spend at least 7 minutes on discussion and reflection around it (2:1 ratio);
- Create variation with your programs: As a coach you will have your own bias towards exercises. Keep it fresh and move between individual exercises, group exercises, and small group exercises (triads or dyads); and
- Allow sufficient time at the end of a program for closure and celebration.

The Power of the Debrief

Exercises are the backbone to any group facilitation program. Are you getting the maximum impact out of them?

My roots in group work are from the experiential education field which is grounded in interactive exercises. I tend to bring a number of tools forward within my current work from the field of experiential education.

In experiential education, the debrief process after the exercise is just as important as the exercise itself. The debrief stage focuses on creating a framework for participants to identify and lock in their learning. Often a 1:1 or 2:1 ratio will be used for activity:debrief. The gift of the debrief process is to provide participants with space to **reflect on** and **learn from** what they have just experienced.

As we saw in Chapter 3, typical debriefs are divided into three parts— **What? So what? Now what?**

For example, when debriefing you might lead discussions with a selection of questions such as:

What?	So What?	Now What?
What was that exercise like?	So what did you learn? So what are your new insights? So why is this important?	Now knowing what you know, how can you take this forward in your work/life?
What did you notice/ observe?		Now what's the next step?
What was the most challenging thing about that activity?		Now what do you need to do?
What was the easiest?		Now what do you need to learn?

Consider the following:

In your own programs, how do you create the space for participants to identify their learning and new insights from activities?

How do you create structures to take this forward?

Assessments

Assessments can be a great tool for coaches undertaking group coaching, as well as individual and team coaching work.

Guidelines for Exercises and Assessment

Respect copyright and licensing. When you purchase a book there may be instances where you can purchase the license to those exercises (i.e., up to 100 uses per year). Check the exact copyright for each book, and if further clarification is needed, contact the publisher and/or the author.

Listen to what your clients are asking for in terms of assessments. Many assessments come in and out of favor. Which ones should you invest in? Which ones might be useful for the work you are doing?

Some of the popular assessments (and by no means is comprehensive) include:

- MAPP
- DiSC
- StrengthsFinder
- Leadership Practices Inventory
- Leadership Circle
- Team Diagnostic™ Assessment (to identify the strengths of a team system)

You may choose to assign assessments as pre-work before a program or as significant work between sessions. Ensure that you provide sufficient time for clients to process the outcomes of the assessment and answer any questions they may have.

MAIN COMPONENTS OF EXERCISES

There are at least four types of exercises you will want to look at adding to your repertoire and back pocket. These include:

1. Warm-up and introductory icebreakers.
2. Exercises you can use throughout sessions—these may often be thematically related to your program.
3. Exercises between sessions.
4. Closure exercises.

1. Warm-Up Exercises/Icebreakers

Creating a safe space for participants, as well as a high-impact kick-off at the start of the program is important. As research indicates, people typically tend to remember the start and end of events and processes. As it relates to exercises, this means that your selection of warm-up and closure exercises is important.

Warm-up exercises:

- Allow people to get to know each other;
- Set the tone of a program;

- Reduce any concerns clients may have; and
- Provide an overview of the program and where it is going.

Warm-ups may also be needed at the start of new sessions or when topics change.

Activity:
Make a list of warm-up exercises you currently have at your disposal.

2. Exercises You Can Use throughout Sessions

As mentioned previously, make sure that exercises you bring into sessions are reflective of what clients want and need. Start your programs or sessions by asking what are the themes/areas clients wish to explore.

Many of your core individual coaching exercises are ones you can bring into your group coaching sessions with a slight variation.

You may consider using some of these foundational exercises as part of your modules:

- Vision
- Values
- Visualizations
- Wheel of Life
- Tolerations

Remember the impact of the accordion approach to design we discussed in Chapter 5? Keep in mind what exercises are a must have and which are a nice to have should you run out of time, or need to elongate the program.

A series of exercises you may wish to choose from follow at the end of this appendix. Also refer to the list you made at the start of this appendix.

3. Exercises between Sessions

What work have you assigned between sessions to help participants deepen their learning or expand their understanding?

In coaching we often say that the real work happens between coaching sessions, when the client starts to explore and apply to their lives and work what we have discussed in our sessions.

What exercises are you providing between sessions to help deepen their learning or expand their awareness?

What exercises can you create to support them in taking action and making change?

Depending on your program topics and themes, you may want to consider using a number of different exercises between sessions. Possibilities include:

1. Journaling.
2. Inquiries—provide clients with a large question to reflect on.
3. Requests.
4. Challenges.
5. Making a collage.
6. Creating a figurine.

4. Closure Exercises

Closure is an important part of any group program and is often the first thing that is cut out when programs are running a little long. Closure exercises should be undertaken at the end of each session as well as at the end of a program.

Effective closure activities can serve many purposes, including creating:

1. A **framework** for participants to identify:
   - What they have learned from the program;
   - What they will take away in terms of learning, for example, new perspectives/insights, etc.; and
   - How they will apply their new learning into their daily life at work or home.
2. A forum for participants to create an **action plan** to reinforce the learning that they have undertaken during the course of the program. How will the participants be "bringing the learning home" to their real lives?
3. An opportunity to **reflect** upon the learning journey in the context of the program.

4. An opportunity to celebrate accomplishments.
5. An opportunity to give thanks.

Examples of Closure Exercises

What type of closure activities do you use in your programs? Is this the first thing that gets cut off when time is running short?
Here a couple of ideas for your next program:

1. **Develop an action plan** handout (or at the end of a participants note-book/manual) which allows participants to make commitments as to specific actions they are going to undertake.
2. **Learning partners:** Have participants pair up with another/or two other participants to discuss their major learning throughout the program.
   Provide each group with two or three structured questions they can discuss during the check-in, such as:
   • My biggest learning so far has been:
   • I am integrating my learning/insights by:
   • Some of the opportunities that are facing me right now are:
   • _____ may stop me from integrating this learning.
   • The one thing I am committing to doing as a result of the program is:

   Allocate sufficient time for each pair during your program to meet and get to know each other, and design how and when they will reconnect.
   Have learning partners contact each other by email/phone/in person a few weeks after the program to discuss how their learning has affected their work/life.
   Have each group contact you, or the rest of the group, with a summary of the results.
3. **Closure circle:** In a circle (virtual or physical), have each participant share with the group the one most important learning point for them and how they are going to integrate this in their daily life and work.
4. **Nature walk and closure:** To add a creative twist, allow participants 5–10 minutes to undertake a silent walk in the surrounding environment (if venue permits), and have them select a piece of nature which they bring back into the program (i.e., stone/flower/leaf). Participants can close with a discussion of what they have chosen in the closure circle format. A neat thing about it is that participants can take this object home with them as a reminder of their learning and commitments.
5. **Set a time for a group follow-up call:** As discussed in Chapter 4, hold-ing a group follow-up call two, four, or six weeks after your last group

coaching call is a best practice. This follow-up call can provide you with the opportunity to reconnect and discuss:

- What's been useful about the program?
- What action steps have you taken?
- How you are integrating the learning?
- What challenges are emerging?
- What opportunities are emerging?

   This information can also prove useful in marketing your group coaching programs (refer to Chapter 8).

6. **Build closure into each and every session:** Even if you are really pressed for time, it is important to have a brief check-out at the end of each session.

   The "quick and dirty" closure I use when time is running short and I may only have a few minutes to close off on a session is to go around in a circle and have each person provide one word to describe:

- What is the one thing you are taking away as a result of the session?
- What's the one word that describes how you feel?

Essential Tools for Exercises–Sticky Notes and Index Cards

Coaches and trainers often ask what inexpensive items can be used within programs. One of the cheapest items you can add to your toolbox is index cards. There are five ways you can use index cards (and also index card-sized Post-its) in your own group coaching or training programs.

1. **For course design**: Index cards are a great tool to use when designing a course. Set aside 10 minutes to brainstorm on an upcoming program you are offering. Using one card per idea, write down everything that comes to mind. You may want to include topic ideas, exercises, venue, pricing, etc. After you have exhausted all your ideas, lay them out on the floor or on a large table. What connections do you see there? How can these be grouped?

2. **As an icebreaker**: One of my favorite icebreaker activities for corporate and personal sessions is to use a large size index card and have participants fold these over creating a name tent for the session (if we are using tables and chairs as part of the set-up).

   Alternatively, you can have them use these as a name tag. I will often ask them to write down their name and also develop their own personal crest or logo. When we go around for introductions, participants introduce themselves by name and logo. This exercise can also be done in pairs for more detailed dialogue. The logo/crest is a great theme to return to throughout the program.

3. **For evaluation**: In addition to a formal evaluation at the end of every program I run, I seek feedback from participants throughout the length of program (i.e., at the end of a weekly session). Three questions I tend to usually ask are: What worked well? What can we do differently next time? and What are you taking away?

    Index cards (as well as Post-its) can work well for this exercise: Distribute three blank index cards to each participant and have these three questions written up on a piece of flipchart paper. Get participants to write down their answer to each question, and when they are all done (usually 3–5 minutes) have each participant post their cards under the respective question. This can be done individually—so you have everyone come up, read their card, and post it, or it can be done as a group. This will give you a very quick, and visual, overview of what's working, what's landing, and what change may be needed. Participants also tend to find this more participatory and interactive.

4. **To mine expectations**: If you don't have the chance to connect with participants prior to the start of the program, distribute index cards to each individual as part of the kickoff of the program, and have them write down what they want to take away from the program, any hopes they have for the program, and any fears. You can have participants share these as part of their introductions, in small groups, or by posting them individually on a wall.

5. **For deciding where to go**: Sometimes programs will have a very loose structure, and often the methodology on which your programs is based encourages participant-driven agendas. Again, index cards serve a wonderful function for this At the start of a session, distribute two or three index cards per person and have them write down the topics they would like to have covered, or questions answered as a result of their participation. As an exercise, have them post these individually on a blank wall, grouping similar topics. This is another wonderful visual exercise to undertake with a group, ensuring that all voices are heard and represented.

Question: *How can you use index cards or sticky notes in your next program?*

SAMPLE EXERCISES

The following is a short collection of several sample exercises that you can use with your group coaching clients. This appendix includes the following exercises:

- Claiming your brand: personal logos
- My vision
- My values
- My values from a virtual retreat format
- SWOT
- Journaling
- Closure roundabout
- The power of practice

Throughout this section of the appendix, you will also see information on adapting exercises for the virtual environment.

Many of these exercises focus on creating a powerful individual experience within the group context. Several of these can also be adapted to focus more significantly on the group process itself, such as vision, values, personal logos, and the SWOT.

Claiming Your Brand: Personal Logos

Group size:	4 to 20
Purpose:	To enable groups who already know each other to learn more about the personal values that make up the individual team members or nametags
Preparation time:	5 minutes
Facilitation time:	15–30 minutes
Materials needed:	Colored markers or pens (at least one per person)
	Colored card (to make a name placard) or name tags
Preparation:	Collect materials needed

Instructions:

This activity is well suited to groups who know each other and may have had the same coach or facilitator. It does require some level of trust in the group. It could be used midstream in a group coaching program.

The facilitator introduces the concept of personal brands or corporate logos/brands/mottos, which identify them to the outside world. An example I use to set this exercise up is asking the group what comes to mind when I say the word "Nike." Typical responses include: the swoosh logo or "Just do it!" (motto).

Ask the group to design their own name placard or name tag for the program (which will sit on the table or be posted on a wall). Their name placard/tag should include:

- Their name—how they would like to be called or referred to during the program
- Their own personal logo or crest
- A motto (optional)

Indicate to participants that they will be asked to introduce themselves to the group at the end of the exercise and will be asked to share and explain their logo to the group.

You may also want to pose the instructions as: Draw a logo that represents who you are as a _____ (insert role—i.e., business owner, manager, etc.).

Give participants approximately 3–5 minutes to develop their name cards. Ask participants to introduce themselves using their logo. Give them 2–3 minutes each (or as time allows). Prompt them with questions such as:

- What came up for you?
- What's new about this?
- What does "x" represent?
- Where does this logo show up in other areas of your life/work?

For larger groups, participants can share their names with the full group and their logo and motto with smaller groups.

Additional Questions for Debrief:

What values does your logo represent? There is an opportunity to drill down/introduce the concept of individual and organizational values with this exercise.

Ask the Group:

- What did you notice from this exercise?
- What themes do you notice that are present?

- What similarities exist?
- What connections exist within the group?
- Based on this exercise, what else do we need to talk about as a group?

How to Facilitate in a Virtual Environment:

Provide similar instructions for a phone-/web-based environment. This time, have people write down their personal logo on a piece of paper in their workbook (if you are providing one).

After 2–3 minutes, go around the virtual circle and ask people to introduce themselves and provide a description of what they have drawn (if you do not have visual cues—i.e., phone only).

Rather than including this at a first session virtually, you may wish to include it as an exercise to launch an additional session.

Additional Adaptations

This exercise can be very valuable in introducing topics including values (personal) or personal branding, marketing, etc. It can also be used in a team coaching environment with the question adapted to: "Draw the logo which represents who you are within this team."

Hopes, Fears, and Fantasies

Group size:	5 to 30
Purpose:	To create a safe learning environment for participants at the start of a program, also providing the facilitator with information about participant's hopes, fears, and fantasies—expectations—for the program or module
Preparation time:	5 minutes
Facilitation time:	15–30 minutes
Facilitation level:	Intermediate
Materials:	Flipchart (enough for each group or member) Markers

Instructions:

The purpose of this exercise is to draw out from participants the following about the upcoming group program, or larger initiatives facing them (i.e., a new program to be implemented):

Hopes: What do you wish for? For example, to acquire specific learning/skills, etc.

Fears: What are you anxious, fearful of having happen during the training program or with the new initiative?

Fantasies: What is the really extraordinary thing that you are hoping will happen during the course of the program!

This exercise can be undertaken in either a small or large group context.

If the overall group size is large (i.e., twelve plus), divide the group into smaller groups of three or four. Each group will share their own hopes, fears, and fantasies. Give each group approximately 10 minutes to come up with their own list of hopes, fears, and fantasies for the program, and then ask them to share it with the larger group.

If you are working with a group up to twelve people, you may choose to do this as one intact group, and as a facilitator, you can write up their responses onto three separate flipcharts (Hopes, Fears, Fantasies).

This exercise is a wonderful way to find commonalities among the participants in terms of their hopes and fears, while the fantasy part brings in a bit of fun!

This exercise provides an engaging way to look at participants' expectations of the program (their hopes) and as a facilitator to discuss which expectations will be/will not be met. Likewise, this activity will provide the facilitator with an idea of any concerns/fears participants may be bringing to the program, and provides an opportunity to dispel unrealistic fears.

To Facilitate in a Virtual Environment:

Pose the questions, have each person write their hopes, fears, and fantasies down individually. After 1–2 minutes, invite them to share their responses one at a time. This can also be offered as a pre-course exercise which is shared before you meet by email or electronic bulletin board.

My Vision

Time:	One hour
Purpose:	A stand-alone session to support individuals, teams, or organizations in developing their vision
Number of participants:	If done individually, can be used in both small and large groups
Materials:	Handout in participant's manual or blank piece of cardboard
Facilitation experience:	Intermediate

Instructions:

This exercise can be used as a stand-alone session lasting 30 minutes to one hour, depending on the extent of dialogue and the size of the group.

Ensure that you provide each participant with a blank sheet of paper or cardboard. This can be included as part of a participant's manual.

Introduce the exercise as part of creating an individual, team, or organizational vision. Explain the importance of a common vision for team building or the importance of an individual vision for success in life and work. You may want to develop a mini-lecture on visioning, drawing on reference material from other sources.

Provide 10–15 minutes for each person to create their own vision. This can be a drawn picture, with or without a series of words. To stimulate thinking about their personal vision, you may want to provide participants with the following questions:

- What would your ideal work/life/environment/team look like?
- What do you want to surround yourself with?
- In five years (or other timeframe), what do you want your life/team/organization to look like?
- What are those things you need in your life to make you fulfilled? To achieve your highest potential?
- What values do you want represented in your vision?

At the end of the vision creation process, allow time for participants to share their drawings with other group members. If it is a large group, have participants share in dyads or small groups. If you are using this exercise as part of a team-building activity, endeavor to have enough team members to share their pictures individually, as this is an important part of creating a common vision.

After the drawings have been shared, ask participants to note on their drawing one to three concrete action steps or commitments they will need to make in order to move towards their vision in the short term. Have time for each member/team to share this with the group.

Add a twist:

Rather than drawing, have each participant create a collage from magazines/print material you have on hand. Collages typically take more time to develop, so adjust your timing accordingly. Also note what additional materials you will need to have on hand.

If you are using this as part of a wider organizational/departmental team-building process, have groups create their own team/group drawings rather than focusing on the individual level. This can be a powerful process for organizations, and the drawings can be taken back to the office and used in future programs. It is an interesting exercise to incorporate over the longer term to see how vision changes and is achieved.

My Values—Approach #1

Group size:	Up to 20 to 30 participants
Facilitation level required:	Advanced
Purpose:	To support participants in exploring their personal values. This can be used as a stand-alone session or module
Preparation time:	10 minutes
Facilitation time:	45 minutes to one hour
Materials needed:	Values sheet
	Flipchart, markers
Preparation:	One values sheet per participant, pens

Instructions:

This activity helps participants explore their personal values, which can, in turn, lead to greater life and work fulfillment and satisfaction.

The concept of personal values is introduced, along with an example of some of the values the facilitator lives by. Some research on this topic may be required by facilitators who are not familiar with values work.

The facilitator can ask for a volunteer from the audience with whom they will demonstrate the exploration of values.

On a flipchart, the facilitator will want to have questions to help participants explore their values, such as:

- What makes you really mad?
- Who are your heroes?
- What is one of your most powerful life experiences?
- What is a song that represents your life?

The facilitator should listen for any values that come up throughout the discussion (5 minutes) and will want to pick out one or two key values that are coming up. The facilitator will then ask the participant to expand on what they mean by their key value—to provide additional insight/information into that particular value. The outcome is a list of four or five key words that further embellish the core values of the participant.

Give the group 5–7 minutes to identify their core values on the next sheet. After this, have the group, in dyads or triads, complete their own values using the questions provided, as well as expanding on them.

As an additional learning point, have each member identify one or two things they could do to move themselves more into alignment over the next week. This can be linked to learning partners work (refer to the heading Closure Exercises above).

Session Breakdown:

1. What are values? Why are they important? (5 minutes)
2. Demonstration with one volunteer participant (10 minutes)
3. Introduction of the exercise to the group (2 minutes)
4. Individual brainstorming of values (7 minutes)
5. Identification of core values and action steps in pairs—15 minutes per person (30 minutes)
6. Debrief of the activity (10 minutes)
   Debrief questions you may want to consider asking include:
   - What did you find interesting or surprising about your key values?
   - How do your values support you in living full, rich productive lives?
   - How will you be honoring your values this week?

My Core Values (Worksheet)

1. Value:

   Word String:

   Actions:

2. Value:

   Word String:

   Actions:

---

3. Value:

   Word String:

   Actions:

4. Value:

   Word String:

   Actions:

5. Value:

   Word String:

   Actions:

My Values—Approach #2

Group size: Unlimited
Facilitation level: Basic
Purpose: To support participants in exploring their values
Preparation time: 15 minutes
Materials Needed: Values checklist in a PDF or Word format or in the participant's guide

Instructions:

This approach works well for a virtual format or as pre-work before a call.

Provide participants with a copy of the following values checklist and related questions. **Have them complete a checklist prior to the session, or have them work through this online or offline for approximately 20 minutes.**

Provide time for the members of the group to:

- Discuss what their most important value is.
- How are they honoring their important values?
- How are they *not* honoring their values?

- What is the impact of this?
- What changes do they want to make? What are they committing to changing (this week/month/quarter)?

Table A1.1: Sample Values Exercise

(This exercise is taken from a Virtual Retreat Format and is completed offline for 20–30 minutes: Individual Values Work)

How important are these values to you? Reflect on the following values and rank them as of high, medium, or low importance.

Value	High	Medium	Low
Achievement			
Advancement			
Adventure			
Balance			
Competition			
Creativity			
Fairness			
Fame			
Family			
Financial freedom			
Friendship			
Generosity			
Health			
Independence			
Influence			
Integrity			
Learning			
Loyalty			
Nature			
Order			
Stability			
Variety			
Other:			
Other:			

What are your top five values?

    1.
    2.
    3.
    4.
    5.

How are these values reflected in your life?

How are these values reflected in your work?

What can you do to more fully honor these values?

What one value will you focus more on honoring in the next month? What will you do to achieve this?

SWOT

Group Size: One plus
Facilitation level: Any
Preparation time: Minimal—just need a blank SWOT template (A1.2)
Facilitation time: 10–120 minutes
Materials needed: Blank SWOT template (included in this appendix)

A SWOT analysis is a very useful tool for individuals, teams, and organizations. It is a tool that you can use to help you recognize, create, and plan for work and life. Few of us actually dedicate time to looking at our own SWOT (strengths, weaknesses, opportunities, and threats).

This exercise can be used for people moving through:

- Career transition
- Team development
- Leadership development
- Business development

Determine which level you are working on—the individual, team, or organizational level, distribute a SWOT template for completion.

Walk participants through the SWOT explaining: "There is great value in undertaking the time to explore the internal and external environment we operate within, as we move forward with (insert topic—e.g., career transition)."

Strengths and weaknesses are those things internal to us as individuals, teams, or organizations. For example, a strength may be verbal communication skills, clarity regarding values, or teamwork. Weaknesses may include organization skills or communication between departments. Adapt these for the context you are operating within.

Opportunities and threats are those things external to individuals, teams, and organizations. For a business person, opportunities may represent possible new business contacts, legislation changes in your favor, or new certifications. In career transition, it may mean government funding opening up for retraining, a new employer setting up shop. Threats may include: economic factors; government taxes; specific competitors; or other external forces that may pose a "threat to your business or self." Again, adapt these for your context.

How to use this:

Ask clients to complete the SWOT template regarding (Table A1.2) the issue at hand (e.g., career transition, business development, leadership development).

As follow-up, have them discuss what is included in each of their different quadrants and what skills and resources they can draw on to move them forward.

This exercise can also be followed by a vision or an action planning activity where clients are reminded to reflect back on what they are learning.

Coaching Questions:

- What might get in the way for you with this goal?
- What can you leverage throughout this process?
- What areas do you want to focus on?
- Who would you bring onto your "team" to boost your strengths?

Journaling

Group size:	Any
Time required:	Variable
Purpose:	To provide clients with an opportunity to reflect on an issue (e.g., business planning, annual planning)
When you could use this:	During a session In-between session,

Instructions:

Provide clients with a core question to reflect on. Encourage participants to write in their journal uncensored for a period of time.

Questions may take the form of inquiries or a general question, such as:

- What have I learned? What am I learning?
- What's most important?
- What changes do I want to make?

Table: A1.2: SWOT Template

Strengths	**Weaknesses**
What are my greatest assets, gifts, and strengths?	What weaknesses do I have that need to be addressed?
Opportunities	**Threats/Obstacles**
What resources, people, or situations can help me move forward?	What situations, if left unattended, would derail my plans?

- What's next?
- What is choice?
- What is valuable?
- What is the cost of . . . ?
- What is the cost of not . . . ?
- Why would I?
- Why wouldn't I . . . ?
- I want to create . . . ?
- I want to focus on . . .?

Adaptations for the Virtual Environment

Build time into a phone-based session for people to capture initial thoughts in their journal while connected. This may include answers to some of the questions above, or specific action steps they will take away.

Don't always wait until people have signed off the call for them to write. There is something special and community enhancing by writing while remaining part of the group on the phone.

Table A1.3: The Power of Practice Worksheet

The Power of Practice—Marlo Nikkila, Organize Together

Purpose:

To see how practice makes a big difference in their life and how important it is to take time to place things in order.

Time:

10 minutes

Materials needed:

- One handout of crazy numbers per person
- One handout of circle with numbers per person

(Continued)

Grouping:

This is an activity for individuals to do, either in person or via the phone.

Procedure:

Ask each participant to find the crazy number sheet and turn it upside down. When you say "Go," each participant turns it over and locates the numbers 1–40 with their finger. After 30 seconds, ask them to stop and document what number they reached. Do this process again three to five times.

After you have a chance to discuss the questions below, give them the final page upside down and say "Go," and let them tell you when they are done.

Discussion questions:

- How did it feel to do this?
- How does this apply to organizing your paper? Your life?
- How were you talking to yourself as you were doing this?
- How did this activity reflect how you feel about practicing something?
- How will you approach getting organized?
- What is your take away from this activity?

After the circle worksheet:

- How did it feel to trace these numbers?
- What is the biggest difference?
- What is your take away from this activity?

Key points:

1. The crazy numbers may represent our lives of being crazy busy, not knowing where things are, losing track, and feeling frazzled.
2. When we take time to place things in order, life becomes easy and it will feel like we have more time and energy (if the numbers represent hours in our day, notice there are 27 on the circle to express this).
3. The circle or "O" represents the importance of being "organized."

Mission:

Be mindful of how you approach learning something new and the messages you say to yourself.

Options:

You can wait to provide the circle handout until after the session, the next session, or even weeks down the road to reinforce the activity.

Crazy Number Sheet

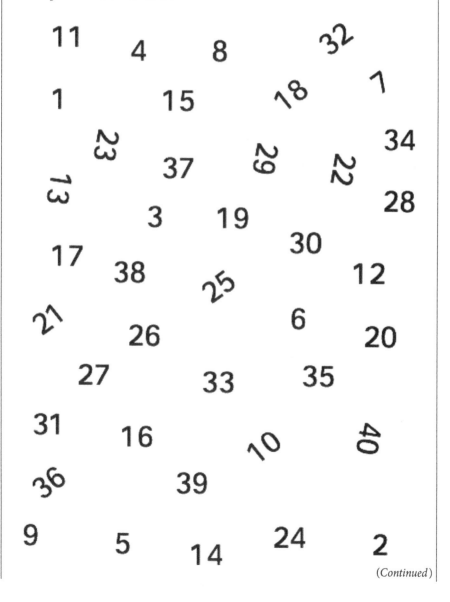

(*Continued*)

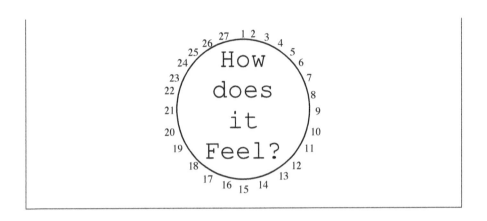

Closure Roundabout

Group size: Fewer than 30
Time required: 5–15 minutes (depending on the size of the group)
Purpose: To provide a quick oral closure for the end of the day, or end of a program
Materials needed: None

Instructions:

This exercise is a quick closure activity, which provides each participant with the opportunity to share verbally with the group how they have found the day or the program.

Participants are invited to share a few brief words with the rest of the team. This can be structured with questions, such as:

> *I would invite each one of you to say one word as to how you are feeling as a result of today's session.*
> *I would invite each one of you to share one important new insight you are taking away as a result of today's session.*
> *What is the one action step you are going to undertake as a result of today's session?*
> *I would invite each one of you to share one celebration as a result of this program.*

The questions are endless—create your own for maximum impact!

To make facilitation easier, you may want to have everyone sitting/standing in a circle, and have a volunteer start, either going clockwise or counterclockwise from there.

Adaptations for the Virtual Environment

Have people check out according to where they are sitting around the virtual table.

**From the Field:
Other Perspectives on Exercises**

What are your favorite exercises which you use with group coaching clients?

Rita Weiss:
I use the DISC assessment to identify preferred leadership and communication styles. Once people have identified their styles and understand the other styles, I break them into groups by style and have them present to the other groups:

- Characteristics of my style
- How to influence my style—what works, what turns me off
- How I prefer to work with others

Victoria FittsMilgrim, CPCC:
I like to use the future self-visualization followed by introductions and sharing by the participants around who they are becoming. In a section about gremlins, I like to have each member of the group role-play their gremlin in a specific situation they're facing.

Another exercise I use involves butcher paper. As we go on a walk, I stop the group at a particular part of a path. Standing in a circle, I ask participants to pull out their paper, pull out their markers and draw their body life size. After everyone has drawn their body shape, they work in pairs and have a partner lie down on the paper. It's really amazing to see that, in general, the bodies that are drawn are much smaller than real life. This then becomes a real metaphor and is very empowering. I often ask questions such as: Where else are you seeing yourself as small? Where are you being small? As a takeaway, participants leave with the paper and the inquiries.

Heidi Michaels, CPCC:
The Wheel of Life—it's an instant and easy impact. It gets things rolling. I also used a wheel I made for sports coaching. I did a wheel that represented the different aspects of mental training. (For a group of baseball players and another group of softball players.)

Jill MacFadyen, CPCC:
My niche is job search. After explaining the technique and giving examples of answering behavioral interview questions, I have participants practice. I usually have a volunteer answer one of the list of prepared questions. I have the other attendees listen carefully and then I ask: "What do we know about this person or what do we like about her because of her answer?" I always find something that makes the person look good and that person just glows. It also reduces fear in the others. It sets them up for success. Pushing self in acknowledging—the exercise provides an opportunity for each member to be acknowledged and then in acknowledging others. I also really like using future self-visualizations and use peak experience to teach resumés.

Maureen Clarke, Blueprint Group:

Creating Community

Objective: To create a learning community and to envision our ideal work-life balance/ideal leader/ideal working mother (dependent upon the group). To gain an understanding of work-life balance and the personal and corporate dilemma from the big picture; learn about challenges and definitions of these roles

Learning: Complete course activity/reading and engage in group discussion initiated by group facilitator.

Example

As we come together as a group, it is important to recognize that we are creating a community—a community of learners learning. In a learning community, learners together value the strengths of all participants and respect interests, abilities, languages, and backgrounds. Through the creation of our learning community in the XYZ course, we will all shift at times between expert, listener, and supporter, learning from one another. As our community develops, we will learn to trust and celebrate one another, creating a safe place to be who we need to be as we create new pathways towards our desired lives in which we are experiencing balance.

A series of reflection questions are asked and members come to the group and begin sharing their responses.

Deena Kolbert, CPCC, ORSCC:
Drawing group paper constellation of "what the group is presently" as they experience it during the first meeting. Then I have them draw a second constellation of what they "would like to see happen to the group." They send it to me and I keep them. Towards the end of the group experience, I repeat the exercise and have them send it to me again. I put both copies together, make copies, and then send out to everyone so we can go over what they are/were experiencing when they see each other's constellations.

Ann Deaton, PhD:
Compelling offer and powerful no practice. Another exercise I like to use is the Journey Line, or similar life path and sharing exercise.

Ginger Cockerham, MCC:
The **gifts I see in you** is a great exercise I use after a group has been together about six months. It is a powerful affirmation of the personal strengths and value each member brings to the group.

Mary Allen, MCC:
Visualizations: inviting participants into an experience of inner peace.

Eva Gregory, CPCC:
What If-Up Game and The Focus Track. The What If-Up Game gets you out of your current reality of what's possible and opens the doors for more. The Focus Track gets them up out of their seats so they are physically moving and experiencing what is happening.

Table A1.4: A Template to Develop Your Own Exercises

Group size:	
Time required:	
Purpose:	
Materials needed:	
Preparation:	
Instructions	
Add a twist … Make it virtual *(Note considerations for virtual environment)*	

Endnotes

Chapter 1

1. KPMG. "International Coach Federation Global Coaching Study, Executive Summary." Rev. 2008. KPMG, 2007, p. 2.
2. Ibid. p. 6.
3. ASTD, "State of the Industry Report 2008," Alexandria: ASTD Press, 2008.
4. Air Institute. "Group Executive Coaching: 2008 Global Survey." Air Institute, 2009, p. 10.
5. Ibid., p. 13.
6. Ibid., p. 3.
7. Saks, Robert R., and Haccoun, Robert R. *Managing Performance Through Training and Development*. Toronto: Thomson Nelson, 2004. p. 5.
8. Bentley, Trevor. *Facilitation—Providing Opportunities for Learning*. McGraw-Hill Companies, 1995, as quoted in Donald V. McCain and Deborah D. Tobey, *Facilitation Skills Training*, ASTD Press, 2007, p. ix.
9. Heron (1989), as referenced in Joanne Knight and Warren Scott, *Co-Facilitation: A Practical Guide to Using Partnerships in Facilitation*, Kogan Page Ltd., 1997, p. 8.
10. Spinks, T. and Clements, P. (1993) as referenced in Knight and Scott, *Co-Facilitation: A Practical Guide to Using Partnerships in Facilitation*, p. 8.
11. Bens, Ingrid. *Facilitating with Ease! A Step-by-Step Guidebook with Customizable Worksheets on CD-Rom*. Jossey-Bass, 2000, p. 28.
12. Bens (2000)
13. Rothwell, William J. *Adult Learning Basics*. Alexandria: ASTD Press, 2008, p. 121–122.

14. International Coach Federation. "ICF Global Coaching Client Study, Executive Summary." International Coach Federation, April 2009.

Chapter 2

1. Bolt, Jim. "Coaching: The Fad that Won't Go Away," *Fast Company*, July 8, 2008. www.fastcompany.com/resources/learning/bolt/041006.html (accessed July 28, 2009).
2. Cockerham, Ginger, and Mitsch, D. J. "Expansion: Scaling the Benefits of Coaching for Groups and Teams," *Choice—The Magazine for Professional Coaches* 6 (2009): no. 4:29–32.
3. Broad, Mary L. "Beyond Transfer of Training: Engaging Systems to Support Performance." CSTD Annual Conference. November 8, 2006.
4. McGovern, Joy, Lindemann, Michael, Vergara, Monica, Murphy, Stacey, Barker, Linda, and Warrenfeltz, Rodney. "Maximizing the Impact of Executive Coaching: Behavioral Change, Organizational Outcomes, and Return on Investment." *The Manchester Review: A Journal for People and Organizations in Transition*. 6 (2001) Reprint. no. 1:1.
5. International Coach Federation. "ICF Global Coaching Client Study, Executive Summary." International Coach Federation, April 2009.
6. McGovern, Joy, et al. "Maximizing the Impact of Executive Coaching: Behavioral Change, Organizational Outcomes, and Return on Investment."
7. Ibid.
8. Carliner, Saul. *Training Design Basics*. Alexandria: ASTD Press, 2003, p. 46.
9. Clarke, Maureen. "Welcoming Wellness." *Benefits Canada*. February 2009. www.benefitscanada.com, p. 49.
10. Biech, Elaine. *Thriving Through Change: A Leader's Practical Guide to Change Mastery*. Alexandria: ASTD Press, 2007, p. 9–10.
11. Turner, F. Ph.D. *CEO Refresher*. (2001) Quoted on: http://www.certifiedcoachesfederation.com/testimonials.html (accessed on September 8, 2009).
12. From Turner, F, PhD. CEO Refresher, 2001 as anotated http://www.coaches-learning-center.com/clc_Resources.htm.
13. Broad, Mary L. "Beyond Transfer of Training: Engaging Systems to Support Performance." CSTD Annual Conference. November 8, 2006.

14. Vidakovik, Jim. *Trainers in Motion: Creating a Participant-Centered Learning Environment.* AMACOM, 2000, p. 25.

Chapter 3

1. Joplin, Lauren. "On Defining Experiential Education." *The Theory of Experiential Education.* 3rd ed. Warren, Karen, Sakots, Mitchell, and Hunt Jr., Jasper S., eds. Association for Experiential Education, 1995.
2. Adult education models can also be represented as a four-stage model (ERGA: experience, reflection, generalization—seeing how it fits into wider contexts, often known as the aha! moment—and application).
3. Tuckman, Bruce, and Jensen, Mary Ann C. "Stages of Small-Group Development Revisited." *Group & Organization Management.* 2 (1977) no. 4:419–427.
4. Russell, Lou. "Accelerated Learning," in Sanders, Ethan J., and Thiaga-rajan "Thiagi," Sivasailam, *Performance Intervention Maps: 36 Strategies for Solving Your Organization's Problems.* Alexandria: ASTD Press, 2001, pp. 5–16.
5. Cranton, Patricia. *Planning Instruction for Adult Learners.* 2nd ed. Toronto: Wall and Emerson Inc., 2000, p. 10.
6. Ibid., p. 10.

Chapter 4

1. Air Institute. "Group Executive Coaching: 2008 Global Survey." Air Institute, 2009.

Chapter 5

1. Carliner, Saul. *Training Design Basics.* Alexandria: ASTD Press, 2003, p. 33.
2. It is interesting how many coaches will opt to more fully outline one to three of the sessions and leave space for "building it as you go." I myself have built a number of programs this way, as has coach Eva Gregory, CPCC, whom we will meet in one of the "In the Spotlight" sections.
3. Carliner, Saul. *Training Design Basics.* Alexandria: ASTD Press, 2003, p. 28.

Chapter 6

1. International Coach Federation. "ICF Global Coaching Client Study, Executive Summary." International Coach Federation, April 2009.
2. Carbon footprint: www.CarbonFootprint.com defines carbon footprint as "a measure of the impact our activities have on the environment, and in particular climate change. It relates to the amount of greenhouse gases produced in our day-to-day lives through burning fossil fuels for electricity, heating, and transportation, etc.

   "The carbon footprint is a measurement of all greenhouse gases we individually produce and has units of tonnes (or kg) of carbon dioxide equivalent."
3. International Coach Federation. "ICF Global Coaching Client Study, Executive Summary." International Coach Federation, April 2009, p. vii.
4. Hugget and Corbett. *Simple, Effective Online Training*, p. 3.
5. Ibid., p. 3.
6. Young, Julia. *Six Critical Success Factors for Running a Successful Virtual Meeting*. From Facilitate.com. www.facilitate.com (2009).
7. Rothwell, William J. *Adult Learning Basics*. Alexandria: ASTD Press, 2008, pp. 123, 125.
8. Rees, Fran. *The Facilitator Excellence Handbook: Helping People Work Creatively and Productively Together*. Pfeiffer, 1998, p. 342.
9. Bailey, Margaret and Leutkehans, Lara. "Ten Great Tips for Facilitating Virtual Learning Teams: Distance Learning, 98." Annual Conference on Distance Teaching and Learning. Madison, WI. August 5–7, 1998.
10. Questions I tend to use at the end of a session include: What worked well? What are you taking away? What should we do differently next time? I leave approximately 5 minutes at the end of every call to allow participants to check out, identify any commitments for the week, and answer each of these questions. I like to hear from each participant at the end of the call and, therefore, I adjust this time frame accordingly.

Chapter 8

1. Straker, David. "Features and Benefits." http://changingminds.org/disciplines/sales/articles/features_benefits.htm.
2. Allan, Mary and Gregory, Eva. "L Comes Before M." *Choice—The Magazine for Professional Coaches* 7 (2009): no. 2:19.

3. Next Century Media, Inc. "Consumer Education Produces High ROI." (2006) from Albers, Judy. "When Marketing Merges with Learning, Customers Profit." *T and D Magazine*, June 2009, pp. 72–74.

Chapter 9

1. Carliner, Saul. *Training Design Basics*. Alexandria: ASTD Press, 2003, p. 147.

Chapter 10

1. Swanson, R. A., and Falkman, S. K. (1997). "Training Delivery Problems and Solutions: Identification of Novice Trainer Problems and Expert Trainer Solutions." *Human Resource Development Quarterly 8* (1997), pp. 305–314.
2. Air Institute. "Group Executive Coaching: 2008 Global Survey." Air Institute, 2009, pp. 34.

Recommended Resources

Chapter 1

ASTD, "State of the Industry Report 2008," Alexandria: ASTD Press, 2008.

Cockerham, Ginger, and Mitsch, D. J. "Expansion: Scaling the Benefits of Coaching for Groups and Teams," *Choice—The Magazine for Professional Coaches* 6 (2009): no. 4:29–32.

Chapter 3

Organizations with additional resources:

www.astd.org: ASTD has a wide variety of resources, programs, and an online store that may be of interest to coaches who are looking for new exercises, professional development (including facilitation training), and other resources. ASTD operates local chapters across the U.S.

www.cstd.org: Canadian Society for Training and Development.

www.iaf.org : The International Association of Facilitators: Offers a wide range of resources and supports to unregistered and registered members.

www.aee.org: The Association of Experiential Educators.

Chapter 5

Needs Assessment:

Gupta, Kavita. *A Practical Guide to Needs Assessments.* Baltimore: Jossey-Bass Pfeiffer, 1999.

Marston, Cam. *Generational Insights. www.marstoncomm.com/www.generationa linsights.com.*

Tobey, Deborah. *Needs Assessment Basics.* Virginia: ASTD Press, 2005.

MindMap Software: www.mindjet.com

Chapter 8

Fairley, Stephen G., and Chris E. Stout. Getting *Started in Personal and Executive Coaching.* New Jersey: Wiley and Sons, 2004.

Hayden, C.J. *Get Clients Now!* (2nd Edition). New York: AMACOM, 2007 (http://www.getclientsnow.com).

Lee, Andrea J. *Multiple Streams of Coaching Income.* Saint Peters: MP Press, 2005.

Konrath, Jill. *Selling to Big Companies.* Chicago: Dearborn Trade Publishing, 2006.

Appendix

Belf, Teri-E, and Ward, Charlotte. *Simply Live It Up: Brief Solutions.* Bethesda: Purposeful Press, 1997.

Gawan, Shakti. *Creative Visualization.* San Francisco: New World Library, 1978.

Holder, Jackee. *Soul Purpose: Self-Affirming Rituals, Mediations and Creative Exercsise to Revive Your Spirit.* London: Piatkus, 1999.

Louden, Jennifer. *The Woman's Retreat Book.* San Francisco: HarperCollins, 1997.

Schwarz, Dale, and Davidson, Anne. *Facilitative Coaching: A Toolkit for Expanding Your Repertoire and Achieving Lasting Results.* Pfeiffer - Wiley, 2009.

Zeus, Perry, and Skiffington, Suzanne. *The Coaching at Work Toolkit: A Complete Guide to Techniques and Practices.* Australia: McGraw-Hill, 2003.

The web is also a great source to adapt exercises for your group coaching programs. ASTD (www.astd.org) also has a range of pre-made exercise books that could always be incorporated into some of your group coaching programs.

Online Exercise Resources:

www.wilderdom.com: Wilderdom.com is a copyleft project from an Australian professor, James Neill. Visit the section on small group exercises and you can add a coaching twist to many of these classic experiential exercises. It is a fantastic resource base of group exercises (copyleft!).

Personal Resources From Jenn:

www.readytorollout.com: Recognizing that content and exercises take a long time, I have partnered with Deborah Grayson-Reigel and we provide ready-to-roll materials for teleclasses/speaking engagements and the like. Workbooks include: Networking Essentials, Managing Up, Personal Productivity and Time Management, Change Management, Should I Stay or Should I Go? (Career).

Engaging Exercises for Teams and Groups: Back in 2005, I published a manual that includes twenty-five exercises. It is still available in e-format.

Visit my **Group Coaching Ins and Outs blog** (http://groupcoaching.blogspot. com) and click on the tag called Exercises for more info/posts on exercises. There is a plethora of posts on everything from designing to implementing group programs, dating back to 2005.

Program Licenses: Coaches may be interested in delivering either the Your Balanced Life or 90 Day BizSuccess programs. Program Licenses are available for coaches to deliver these programs in a group coaching format, or retreat.

Facebook: http://www.facebook.com/effectivegroupcoaching

Bibliography/References

Chapter 1

Air Institute. "Group Executive Coaching: 2008 Global Survey." Air Institute, 2009. www.theairinstitute.com.

ASTD, "State of the Industry Report 2008," Alexandria: ASTD Press, 2008.

Cockerham, Ginger, and Mitsch, D. J. "Expansion: Scaling the Benefits of Coaching for Groups and Teams," *Choice—The Magazine for Professional Coaches* 6 (2009): no. 4:29–32.

International Coach Federation. "ICF Global Coaching Client Study, Executive Summary." International Coach Federation, April 2009. www.coachfederation.org.

Chapter 2

Biech, Elaine. *Thriving Through Change: A Leader's Practical Guide to Change Mastery.* Alexandria: ASTD Press, 2007.

Bolt, Jim. "Coaching: The Fad That Won't Go Away," *Fast Company*, July 8, 2008. www.fastcompany.com/resources/learning/bolt/041006.html (accessed July 28, 2009).

Broad, Mary L. "Beyond Transfer of Training: Engaging Systems to Support Performance." CSTD Annual Conference. November 8, 2006.

Carliner, Saul. *Training Design Basics.* Alexandria: ASTD Press, 2003.

McGovern, Joy, Lindemann, Michael, Vergara, Monica, Murphy, Stacey, Barker, Linda, and Warrenfeltz, Rodney. "Maximizing the Impact of Executive Coaching:

Behavioral Change, Organizational Outcomes, and Return on Investment." *The Manchester Review: A Journal for People and Organizations in Transition.* 6 (2001) Reprint. no. 1:1–9.

Vidakovik, Jim. Trainers in Motion: Creating a Participant-Centered Learning Environment. AMACOM, 2000.

Chapter 3

Bens, Ingrid. *Facilitating with Ease! A Step-by-Step Guidebook with Customizable Worksheets on CD-Rom.* Jossey-Bass, 2000.

Britton, Jennifer. *Train-The-Trainer Manual for UNV Program Officers.* Bridgetown, 2004.

Britton, Jennifer. *Training Essentials for Coaches.* Toronto, 2004.

Cranton, Patricia. *Planning Instruction for Adult Learners.* 2nd ed. Toronto: Wall and Emerson Inc., 2000.

Tuckman, Bruce W. "Forming, Storming, Norming and Performing in Groups." www.Infed.org. http://www.infed.org/thinkers/tuckman.htm (last accessed July 31, 2009).

Joplin, Lauren. "On Defining Experiential Education." *The Theory of Experiential Education.* 3rd ed. Warren, Karen, Sakots, Mitchell, and Hunt Jr., Jasper S., eds. Association for Experiential Education, 1995

Knowles, Malcolm. *The Adult Learner.* Houston: Gulf Publishing, 1990.

Kolb, D. A. *Experiential Learning.* Englewood Cliffs: Prentice Hall, 1984.

Russell Lou. "Accelerated Learning," Sanders, Ethan J., and Thiagarajan "Thiagi," Sivasailam. *Performance Intervention Maps: 36 Strategies for Solving Your Organization's Problems.* Alexandria: ASTD Press, 2001, pp. 5–16.

Tuckman, Bruce, and Jensen, Mary Ann C. "Stages of Small-Group Development Revisited." *Group & Organization Management.* 2 (1977) no. 4:419–427.

Chapter 4

Air Institute. "Group Executive Coaching: 2008 Global Survey." Air Institute, 2009. www.theairinstitute.com.

Carliner, Saul. *Training Design Basics*. Alexandria: ASTD Press, 2003.

International Coach Federation. "ICF Professional Coaching Core Competencies," http://www.coachfederation.org/research-education/icf-credentials/core-competencies/.

International Association of Facilitators. "Facilitator Competencies," http://www.iaf-world.org/i4a/pages/Index.cfm?pageid=3331.

Chapter 5

Britton, Jennifer. "Work Life Quality: What? So What? Now What?", Presentation to the 4th Work-Life Conference, Toronto, March 26, 2009.

Carliner, Saul. *Training Design Basics*. Alexandria: ASTD Press, 2003.

Lawson, Karen. *The Trainer's Handbook*. 2nd ed. San Francisco: Pfeiffer, 2006.

Rothwell, William J. *Adult Learning Basics*. Alexandria: ASTD Press, 2008.

Chapter 6

Bailey, Margaret, and Leutkehans, Lara. "Ten Great Tips for Facilitating Virtual Learning Teams: Distance Learning 98." Annual Conference on Distance Teaching and Learning. Madison, WI. August 5–7, 1998.

Brusino, Justin. *Great Presentations*. ASTD Infoline Issue 0809, Alexandria: ASTD Press, September 2008.

Hugget, Cindy, and Corbett, Wendy Gates. *Simple, Effective Online Training*. ASTD Infoline Issue 0801. Alexandria: ASTD Press, 2008.

International Coach Federation. "ICF Global Coaching Client Study, Executive Summary." International Coach Federation, April 2009. www.coachfederation.org.

Wilson, Shauna. *Successful Online Meetings*. ASTD Infoline Issue 0902, Alexandria: ASTD Press, February 2009.

Young, Julia. Six Critical Success Factors for Running a Successful Virtual Meeting. From Facilitate.com. www.facilitate.com, 2009.

Chapter 8

Albers, Judy. "When Marketing Merges with Learning, Customers Profit," *T and D Magazine* July 2009:72–74.

Allan, Mary, and Gregory, Eva. "L Comes Before M." *Choice—The Magazine for Professional Coaches* 7 (2009): no. 2:19.

Collins, Jim. *Good to Great: Why Some Companies Make the Leap . . . and Others Don't.* HarperBusiness, 2001.

Good, Walter. *Building a Dream: A Canadian Guide to Starting Your Own Business.* 6th ed. Toronto: McGraw-Hill Ryerson, 2005.

Lee, Andrea J. *Multiple Streams of Coaching Income.* Missouri: Femme Osage, 2004.

Levinson, Jay Conrad, and McLaughlin, Michael W. *Guerillas Marketing for Consultants.* John Wiley and Sons, 2005.

Levinson, Jay Conrad, and Lautsenslager, Al. *Guerilla Marketing in 30 Days.* Entrepreneur Press, 2005.

Chapter 9

Carliner, Saul. *Training Design Basics.* Alexandria: ASTD Press, 2003.

Lawson, Karen. *The Trainer's Handbook.* 2nd ed. San Francisco: Pfeiffer, 2006.

Chapter 10

Kirpatrick, Donald. *Evaluating Training Programs.* San Francisco: Berrett-Koehler, 1998.

Swanson, R. A. and Falkman, S.K. "Training delivery problems and solutions: Identification of novice trainer problems and expert trainer solutions," *Human Resource Development Quarterly* 8 (1997) pp. 305–314.

INDEX

Pages numbers in *italics* indicate charts, templates or exercises.

About the Author

Jennifer Britton is the founder of Potentials Realized, a Canadian based performance improvement company. Jennifer works with groups, teams and organizations in the areas of leadership, teamwork, and business success. She works with clients globally across the governmental, corporate and non-profit sectors from financial services, to education and health care. She also offers a range of group coaching programs and retreats for the general public.

Jennifer fuses together her rich experience as a former global program manager with the UN, experiential educator, coach and workshop leader. She has delivered group programs in over eighteen countries in the last 20 years. Since early 2006, her Group Coaching Essentials™ program has supported hundreds of coaches in the creation and implementation of their own group coaching programs.

Accredited as a PCC with the International Coach Federation, Jennifer was originally trained and certified by the Coaches Training Institute as a CPCC. She has also completed advanced coach training in the areas of ORSC, and Shadow Coaching. Jennifer is also a Certified Performance Technologist (CPT) and Certified Human Resource Professional (CHRP). She holds a Masters of Environmental Studies (MES) and a Bachelor of Science in Psychology (McGill University).

To contact Jennifer:

Email: info@potentialsrealized.com
Phone: (416) 996-TEAM (8326)
Web: www.potentialsrealized.com and www.groupcoachingessentials.com
Blog: http://groupcoaching.blogspot.com

Or follow her online at http://twitter.com/jennbritton and
http://www.facebook.com/effectivegroupcoaching